CORE BIBLICAL STUDIES

THE DEAD SEA SCROLLS

THE DEAD SEA SCROLLS

PETER W. FLINT

Abingdon Press
Nashville

To the two youngest people in my life
Jakob Flint Dennis and Olivia Flint

Library of Congress Cataloging-in-Publication Data

Flint, Peter W., author.
   The Dead Sea Scrolls / Peter Flint.
      pages cm — (Core Biblical Studies series)
Summary: The discovery of the Scrolls in the Judean Desert—Archaeology of the Qumran site: the caves, buildings, and cemeteries—Dating the scrolls found at Qumran—The Bible before the scrolls—The Biblical scrolls—The Dead Sea scrolls and contents of the Scriptures used at Qumran—The Nonbiblical scrolls—The movement associated with Qumran and its place in early Judaism—Religious thought and practice reflected in the Qumran scrolls.
   Includes bibliographical references and index.
   ISBN 978-0-687-49449-1 (book - pbk. / trade pbk. : alk. paper)   1. Dead Sea scrolls.   2. Dead Sea scrolls—Relation to the Old Testament.   3. Judaism—History—Post-exilic period, 586 B.C.-210 A.D.   4. Qumran community.   5. Bible. O.T.—Criticism, interpretation, etc.
I. Title.
   BM487.F574 2013
         296.1'55—dc23
                                                                                             2012044021

13 14 15 16 17 18 19 20 21 22—10 9 8 7 6 5 4 3 2 1
MANUFACTURED IN THE UNITED STATES OF AMERICA

Contents

Online Supplement

www.abingdonacademic.com/dsscrolls

In Depth and Further Study:
Detailed Outline of Contents
Discussion Questions for Each Chapter

Images, Study Tools, Online Links:
Photographs of the Dead Sea Scrolls
Study Tools and Electronic Resources
Links and Websites

Complete Indexes:
Index of Biblical Passages
Index of Apocrypha and *Pseudepigrapha*
Index of Dead Sea Scrolls and Related Texts
Index of Other Ancient Writings
Index of Modern Authors (as in Printed Book)
Subject Index

Abbreviations, Definitions, and Key Words

(?)	There is some doubt on identity of a verse or reading.
[ ]	bracketed portion not extant, was originally written (e.g., Da[vid])
10:2a, 10:2b	first part, second part of verse 2 in chapter 10
2:23	chapter and verse (biblical, apocryphal, pseudepigraphical texts)
2:4–5	Dead Sea Scrolls: second extant column, lines 4–5
2.5	Dead Sea Scrolls: fragment 2, line 5
23 ii.7–9	fragment 23, column 2, lines 7–9 (e.g., 4Q405 23 ii.7–9)
20 ii.21–22.8	fragment 20, column 2, line 21 to fragment 22, line 8
1Q, 2Q, etc.	Cave 1 at Qumran, Cave 2, Cave 4, etc.
4QNum^b	Second Numbers scroll from Cave 1 at Qumran
5/6Hev	Caves 5 and 6 at Nahal Hever
A	Codex Alexandrinus (a Greek manuscript)
acrostic	Each verse begins with a successive letter of the Hebrew alphabet.
Adonay	"Lord," a name for God
Ain Feshkha	site near Qumran
Antiquities	Josephus, *Jewish Antiquities*
Apocalypses	writings in which a heavenly being reveals history and end times events

Apocrypha . . . . "hidden or secret writings" = Deuterocanonicals in Catholic Bibles. Books not found in Protestant Bibles.

Apostrophe. . . . . poem addressed to absent person or place (Apos. to Zion, Apos. to Judah)

archaeometrist . . . . one who measures aspects of ancient remains

Archaic Period . . . . date for early script (about 250–50 B.C.E. = Proto-Jewish Period)

Armageddon . . . . location of the final battle (Rev. 16:16)

ASOR . . . . American School of Oriental Research

Astronomical Book . . . . *1 Enoch*, chapters 72–82

b. . . . . *Babylonian Talmud*

B . . . . Codex Vaticanus (Greek manuscript)

B.C.E. . . . . Before the Common Era, equivalent to B.C.

Baba Batra. . . . . section of the *Babylonian Talmud*

Babylonian Talmud. . . . compilation of Rabbinic laws and writings

Babylonian Text . . . . one of the three biblical text-types (Frank Moore Cross)

BAR . . . . *Biblical Archaeology Review*

Bar Kokhba revolt . . . . . against Rome, also called the Second Jewish Revolt (132–135)

Bedouin . . . . Arabian ethnic group living mainly in the desert

Berakhot. . . . . Hebrew for "blessings"

BHQ. . . . . *Biblia Hebraica Quinta* (edition of Hebrew Bible)

BHS . . . . *Biblia Hebraica Stuttgartensia* (edition of Hebrew Bible)

Book of the Twelve . . . . the twelve Minor Prophets

C.E. . . . . Common Era, equivalent to A.D.

Callirhoe . . . . hot springs near eastern shore of the Dead Sea

camps . . . . where the movement's members lived in the *Damascus Document*

canon . . . . closed list of books accepted by a community as authoritative

catena . . . . connected chain of (scriptural) verses or words

CD . . . . abbreviation for the *Damascus Document* found in Cairo

classical writers . . . . Greek and Roman authors such as Pliny, Philo, and Josephus

codex (plural codices) . . book made up of sheets of leather (parchment or vellum)

col(s). . . . . column(s)

colophon . . . . contains details of production

covenant . . . . binding agreement or contract (esp. between God and humans)

Covenant of Grace . . . . . term for the Covenant in the *Rule of the Community* (1QS 1:7)

D . . . . abbreviation for the *Damascus Document*

determinism (fate) . . . . . belief that God has mapped out the course of history in advance

Deuterocanonicals . . . . . used by Catholics for the Apocrypha

Dio Chrysostom . . . . . . Greek orator, historian, and philosopher (about 40–120)

DSS . . . . Dead Sea Scrolls

early Judaism . . . . Jewish history and groups in the Second Temple period

Ecclesiasticus . . . . another name for Sirach (= the Wisdom of Jesus Ben Sira)

École Biblique . . . . French Archaeological School in Jerusalem

Egyptian Text . . . . one of the three biblical text-types (Frank Moore Cross)

Ein Gedi . . . . city and oasis on western shore of the Dead Sea, near Qumran

eschatological banquet . . end times or messianic banquet

eschatology . . . . study of the last things or end times

Ethiopic Enoch . . . . complete book of *1 Enoch* in Ethiopic

exegesis . . . . biblical interpretation

exile . . . . after Nebuchadnezzar destroyed Jerusalem (587/6 B.C.E.)

First Jewish Revolt . . . . . against Rome, 66–73 C.E.

First Temple Period . . . . when Solomon's Temple stood (about 966–587/6 B.C.E.)

Florilegium . . . . collection of excerpts from Scripture, name of a scroll (4Q174)

frg. . . . . fragment

genizah . . . . storeroom for old and damaged manuscripts

Groningen Hypothesis . . includes split in Essene movement, apocalyptic roots of Qumran community

Halakhic Letter . . . . name for *Some of the Works of the Law* (*MMT*)

Harmonistic . . . . another word for Pre-Samaritan (Emanuel Tov)

Hasmonean period . . . . when Judea was ruled by Hasmonean high priests or kings (about 150–30 B.C.E.)

Hellenism . . . . spreading Greek culture and language, sometimes by force

Herodian period . . . . . . when various Herods ruled (30 B.C.E.–70 C.E.)

Hev/Se . . . . Nahal Hever or Wadi Seiyal

Hippolytus . . . . Roman author (about 170–236)

Hodayot . . . . *Thanksgiving Hymns*

intercalate . . . . insert the starting points of priestly cycles

interpolations . . . . insertions

intrusive burials . . . . much later burials in the Qumran cemeteries

Josephus . . . . Flavius Josephus, Jewish and Roman author (37–about 100)

Jubilee . . . . forty-ninth or fiftieth year at end of seven cycles of Sabbatical Years

Judean War . . . . another name for the *Jewish War* by Josephus

Julius Solinus . . . . Roman historian and grammarian (early third century)

kaige-Theodotion . . . . . . revision of the Septuagint (mid-first century B.C.E.)

Karaites . . . . medieval Jewish group

Kethubim . . . . Hebrew for "Writings," the third division of the Jewish Bible

Khirbet Qumran . . . . . . ruin of Qumran

liturgical . . . . concerning worship, usually public but also personal

Local Texts theory . . . . . the three biblical text-types according to Frank Moore Cross

luminaries . . . . heavenly bodies that give light, the sun and the moon

lunar calendar . . . . calendar of 354 days (calculated by the moon)

LXX . . . . Septuagint, literally, by *the Seventy* (translators)

m. Yadayim . . . . Mishnah, tractate *Yadayim*

Maccabean Revolt . . . . . led by the Maccabees (167–64 B.C.E.)

Machaerus . . . . fortress east of the Dead Sea, built by Alexander Jannaeus

Manual of Discipline . . . earlier name for the *Rule of the Community*

Mar . . . . Syrian word for "archbishop"

Masada . . . . site in Judea where several scrolls were found

Mas. . . . . abbreviation for Masada

Mas1b . . . . Masada, scroll 1b = Leviticus (MasLev[b])

Masorah . . . . markings and marginal notes to the MT

Masoretes . . . . group of Jewish scholars from the eighth century onward

Megillat Ta'anit . . . . rabbinic text enumerating 35 eventful days

Metropolitan . . . . archbishop

Midrash . . . . interpretation of Scripture, or a text that does so

miqveh (pl. *miqva'ot*). . . or *miqvah*, pool or bath for ritual washing

Mishmarot . . . . texts detailing Watches or Priestly Courses (4Q320–29)

Mishnah . . . . compilation of rabbinic laws and writings

Motsa clay . . . . red terra rosa clay

Mount Ebal . . . . site of Joshua's altar, near Shechem (modern Nablus)

Mount Gerizim . . . . near Shechem (modern Nablus), sacred to the Samaritans

ms(s) . . . . manuscript(s)

MMT . . . . abbreviation for *Some of the Works of the Law*

MT . . . . Masoretic Text, text of the Hebrew Bible produced by the Masoretes

Murabba'at . . . . site in Judea where several scrolls were found

Mur 1 or MurGen . . . . . Murabba'at, first scroll (Genesis)

nahal . . . . Hebrew for a streambed that is dry part of the year (= Arabic *wadi*)

Nahal Hever . . . . site in Judea where several scrolls were found

Nahal Se'elim . . . . site in Judean Desert where scrolls were found (= Arabic Wadi Seiyal)

Nash Papyrus . . . . early text with parts of the *Shema* Prayer and Ten Commandments

Nebi'im . . . . Hebrew for "Prophets," the second division of the Jewish Bible

new covenant . . . . made with God in Damascus, according to the *Damascus Document*

NETS . . . . New English Translation of the Septuagint (2007)

Nonaligned . . . . one grouping of biblical texts (Emanuel Tov)

NRSV . . . . New Revised Standard Version

oral law . . . . unwritten traditions, believed passed down since days of Moses

orthographic . . . . with respect to spelling

ostracon (pl. ostraca) . . . piece(s) of pottery with writing

Otot . . . . Hebrew for "signs" (4Q319)

outlier . . . . measurement that differs markedly without known cause

paleography . . . . analysis of ancient handwriting

paleo-Hebrew . . . . very ancient form of the Hebrew script

Palestinian Text . . . . . . one of the three biblical text-types (Frank Moore Cross)

papyrus (pl. papyri) . . . . type of paper made from plants

Paral(e)ipomena. . . . . . . books in Septuagint equivalent to 1 and 2 Chronicles

parchment . . . . treated animal hide

Pentateuch . . . . first five books of the Hebrew Bible

pesher (pl. *pesharim*) . . . commentary, interpretation

Peshitta. . . . . Syriac Bible (Old Testament with apocryphal books)

Philo of Alexandria . . . . Jewish writer in Egypt (about 20 B.C.E.–50 C.E.)

Pliny the Elder. . . . . Roman official, naturalist, and scholar (23–79 C.E.)

post-Herodian period . . from fall of the Temple to the Bar Kochba revolt (70 B.C.E.–135 B.C.E.)

Postscript period . . . . . . of the Qumran site after its destruction in 68 C.E.

pre-Masoretic. . . . . another word (and preferred term) for proto-Masoretic

pre-Rabbinic . . . . another word for pre-Masoretic

pre-Samaritan . . . . one grouping of biblical texts (Emanuel Tov)

proto-Jewish Period. . . . date for early script (about 250–150 B.C.E. = Archaic Period)

proto-Masoretic. . . . . . . one grouping of biblical texts (Emanuel Tov)

Psalms 154 and 155. . . . Syriac Psalms II and III

Pseudo-Daniel A **and** *B* . Pseudepigraphal texts featuring Daniel and the end times (4Q243–45)

Pseudepigraphon . . . . . . writing falsely attributed to an ancient author

Pseudepigrapha . . . . ancient Jewish works other than the OT and Apocrypha

Qohelet . . . . Hebrew name for the book of Ecclesiastes

Qumran . . . . site on the western shore of the Dead Sea; occupied by Essene community known as the *Yahad*, who hid scrolls in Caves 1 to 11

Qumran Essene . . . . Hypothesis: that Essenes met/lived at Qumran and hid scrolls in the caves

Qumran Practice . . . . . . method for grouping many biblical scrolls (Emanuel Tov)

Rabban. . . . . Our "teacher," used for patriarchs and presidents of the Sanhedrin

Rabbi . . . . means "teacher," a term for addressing Pharisees

Rabbinic Judaism . . . . . as practiced by the rabbis, sucessors of the Pharisees

Renewed Covenant . . . . alternative translation to New Covenant

resurrection . . . . physically coming back to life after death

Rule . . . . book of precepts of list of rules (as in the *Rule of the Community*)

S (1) . . . . *Rule of the Community*

S (2) . . . . Codex Sinaiticus (a Greek manuscript)

Sanhedrin (1) . . . . a kind of early Jewish Supreme Court

Sanhedrin **(2)** . . . . tractate in the Babylonian Talmud

scriptorium . . . . writing hall

SdeirGen . . . . Genesis scrolls from Wadi Sdeir (= Sdeir 1)

Se . . . . Wadi Seiyal

Secacah . . . . city in Judean wilderness mentioned in Joshua 15:61

Second Jewish Revolt . . . against Rome, also called the Bar Kokhba revolt (132–135)

Second Temple Period . . from its building (516 B.C.E.) to destruction by the Romans (70 C.E.)

Sectarian Period . . . . when the Qumran site was occupied by the *Yahad* Essenes

sectarian scrolls . . . . scrolls authored by the Essene movement or reflecting its ideas

Seleucid Empire . . . . Greek-Syrian Empire that included Judea

Septuagint (1) . . . . literally, by *the Seventy* (translators), abbreviated LXX

Septuagint (2) . . . . Greek OT and other books, used by some Jews and the Early Church

Serekh ha-Yahad . . . . . . Hebrew name for the *Rule of the Community*

Similitudes . . . . Parables

solar calendar . . . . calendar of 364 days (calculated by the sun)

SP . . . . Samaritan Pentateuch, with first five books of the Hebrew Bible

Strophe . . . . group of verses

Syriac Psalms II and III . . Psalms 154 and 155

Ta'amireh . . . . a Bedouin tribe

Talmuds . . . . compilations of rabbinic laws and writings

Tanakh . . . . acronym for Hebrew Bible (from *Torah, Nebi'im, Kethubim*)

Targum . . . . translation or paraphrase of Scripture in Aramaic

Teacher Hymns . . . . part of the *Hodayot* (*Thanksgiving Hymns*)

Temple of Onias IV . . . . built at Leontopolis in Egypt in 154 B.C.E. by an heir to the high priesthood

Torah . . . . "Law," first division of Jewish Bible (Genesis to Deuteronomy)

tractate . . . . treatise or long essay

triclinium . . . . dining room with three couches

uncial . . . . manuscript written in capital letters

Urtext . . . . original text

villa rustica . . . . country villa or wealthy manor house

Vorlage . . . . (Hebrew) text used by the (Septuagint) translator

Vulgate . . . . Latin translation of the Bible, mainly by Jerome (fourth century)

wadi . . . . Arabic for streambed that is dry part of the year (= Hebrew Nahal)

Wadi Seiyal . . . . site in Judean Desert where scrolls were found (= Hebrew Nahal Se'elim)

Wadi Sdeir . . . . site in the Judean Desert where scrolls were found

War . . . . Josephus, *Jewish War*

**Wisdom of Jesus
  ben Sira** . . . . name for Sirach (= Ecclesiasticus)

XIIev/Se 5 . . . . uncertain cave at Nahal Hever or Wadi Seiyal, fifth text

Yadayim . . . . Mishnah, *Tractate Yadayim*

Yahad . . . . Hebrew for "oneness" or "community," name for Essenes in some scrolls

Ancient Groups
and Figures

Aaron . . . . name for the priests in the *Rule of the Community* (1QS)

Aemilius . . . . Marcus Aemilius Scaurus, Roman governor in Syria

Alcimus . . . . Judean High Priest (162–159 B.C.E.)

Alexander Balas . . . . Syrian commander, became king of Seleucid Empire in 150 B.C.E.

Alexander Jannaeus . . . . . Judean king and high priest (103–76 B.C.E.)

Alexandra . . . . see Salome Alexandra

Anointed Prophet . . . . . . figure of the last days, perhaps Elijah

Antigonus . . . . Judean king and high priest (40–37 B.C.E.)

**Antiochus IV
Epiphanes** . . . . Seleucid king (about 215–164 B.C.E.)

Aristobulus I . . . . Judean king and high priest (104–103 B.C.E.)

Aristobulus II . . . . Judean king and high priest (66–63 B.C.E.)

Aristobulus III . . . . last Hasmonean high priest (53–36 B.C.E.)

Belial . . . . name for Satan in some sectarian scrolls

Booth of David . . . . one of many names for the royal Messiah

Branch of David . . . . one of many names for the royal Messiah

Children of Dawn . . . . . . another name for the Sons of Light (the *Yahad* Essenes)

Damascus . . . . features in *Damascus Document*, could be symbolic location

Darius the Mede . . . . Persian ruler mentioned in Daniel (possibly Cyaxares II or Cyrus)

Demetrius I . . . . Syrian king (reigned 161–150 B.C.E.)

Diodotus Trypho . . . . Seleucid general and king (142–138, co-ruler 145–142 B.C.E.)

Ephraim . . . . name for the Pharisees (= Seekers of Slippery Answers = Wall-Builders)

Essenes . . . . perhaps "Observers" of the Law. One main sect in early Judaism (early second century B.C.E. to later first century C.E.)

Gamaliel . . . . a Pharisee and leading member of the Sanhedrin (Acts 5:34)

Guardian . . . . Hebrew *Mabaqqer* or *Paqid*, possibly another name for the Instructor. Assessor of new candidates, overseer, teacher, presider over meetings

Hasidim . . . . ones pious or loyal to God, an earlier name for the Pharisees

Hasmoneans . . . . Hasmonean dynasty, high priests and kings descended from Maccabees

Herod Archelaus . . . . ruler of Roman provinces of Judea, and Idumea (about 4 B.C.E.–6 C.E.)

Herodians . . . . Jewish political party that supported Herodian rule

Herod the Great . . . . king of Judea (ruled 37–4 B.C.E.), rebuilt the Second Temple

Hyrcanus . . . . see John Hyrcanus I, John Hyrcanus II

Instructor . . . . The *Maksil* (Wise Leader who enlightens), possibly another name for the Guardian

Interpreter of the Law . . . name for the Teacher of Righteousness (sometimes messianic)

Israel . . . . name for the laymen in the *Rule of the Community* (1QS)

Jason . . . . Judean high priest (175–172 B.C.E.), brother of Onias III

Jedariah, etc. . . . . names of the priests and their courses (rotations)

Jehoshua ben Jehozadak . . . . first Zadokite priest after the exile

John Hyrcanus I . . . . Judean king and high priest (reigned 134–104 B.C.E.)

John Hyrcanus II . . . . Judean king and high priest (76–66, restored 63–40 B.C.E.)

Jonathan Apphus . . . . Judean high priest (152–143 B.C.E.)

Josephus . . . . Flavius Josephus, Jewish and Roman author (37–about 100)

Judas the Maccabee . . . . . led Maccabean revolt against Seleucid Empire (167–164 B.C.E.), a high priest according to the Groningen Hypothesis

King Jonathan . . . . *Prayer for King Jonathan* (4Q448). Most likely Alexander Jannaeus.

Kittim. . . . . Romans or wicked Gentiles in some sectarian scrolls

Leader of Congregation. . . one of many names for the royal Messiah

Levites . . . . from the tribe of Levi, had religious duties and included priests

Lion of Wrath . . . . Alexander Jannaeus (king and high priest; 103 to 76 B.C.E.)

Maaziah . . . . a priestly family. Maaziah is the twenty-fourth priestly group.

Manasseh . . . . possible name for Sadducees in some sectarian scrolls

Man of Mockery . . . . name for the Man of the Lie (= the Spewer of Lies)

Man of the Lie. . . . . opponent of the Teacher of Righteousness

Many, the. . . . . name used for the *Yahad* (or the general membership)

**Marcus Aemilius
   Scaurus** . . . . see *Aemilius*

Maskil . . . . Instructor (the Wise Leader who enlightens), possibly another name for the Guardian

Melchizedek (1) . . . . Hebrew Bible: king of Salem and priest of the Most High God

Melchizedek (2) . . . . *Melchizedek Text:* eschatological liberator, divine being, or angel

Men of Mockery . . . . group in Jerusalem that opposed the Teacher of Righteousness

Messiah of Aaron. . . . . . . name for the priestly Messiah

Messiah of Israel . . . . one of many names for the royal Messiah

Nebuchadnezzar . . . . king of Babylon (about 605–562 B.C.E.), destroyed Jerusalem in 587/586

New Covenanters. . . . . . . term for the Essenes, especially in the *Damascus Document*

Onias III . . . . Judean king and high priest (185–175 B.C.E.)

Peitholaus. . . . . Jewish officer executed in 53 B.C.E.

Pharisees (1). . . . . Separatists or the Separated Ones

Pharisees (2). . . . . one main sect in early Judaism; forerunners of the Rabbis

Philo of Alexandria . . . . . Jewish writer in Egypt (about 20 B.C.E.–50 C.E.)

Pliny the Elder. . . . . Roman official, naturalist, and scholar (23–79 C.E.)

Priest (1) . . . . name for the priestly Messiah

Priest (2) . . . . name for the Teacher of Righteousness

Prince of Congregation . . . one of many names for the royal Messiah

Prophet . . . . "Prophet like Moses," a messianic figure, or the Teacher of Righteousness

Prophetic Messiah . . . . . . features in the *Messianic Apocalypse* (4Q521)

Royal Messiah . . . . also called the Booth/Branch/Shoot of David, Messiah of Israel, and more

Sadducees. . . . . in early Judaism; *minim* (heretics) in some rabbinic writings

Salome Alexandra . . . . . . Judean Queen (76 to 67 B.C.E.), widow of Alexander Jannaeus

Scepter . . . . one of many names for the royal Messiah

Seekers . . . . of Slippery Answers, name for Pharisees (= Ephraim = Wall-Builders)

Shelamsion. . . . . name for Queen Salome Alexandra in *Historical Text C* (4Q331)

Shoot of David. . . . . one of many names for the royal Messiah

Simeon . . . . Judean high priest (142–134 B.C.E.)

Simon I . . . . Judean high priest (about 280–260 B.C.E.)

Simon II. . . . . Judean high priest (218–185 B.C.F.)

Sons of Darkness . . . . phrase for fallen angels and wicked humans in some scrolls

Sons of Light . . . . phrase for the Essenes in some scrolls

Spewer of Lies . . . . name for the Man of the Lie (= the Man of Mockery)

Star. . . . . Interpreter of the Law (the Teacher of Righteousness)

Teacher of Righteousness. . early and most prominent leader of the Essene movement (most likely active from 176–142 B.C.E.)

Therapeutae. . . . . Jewish sect in Egypt, described by Philo of Alexandria

Titus. . . . . Roman commander, then emperor (79–81)

Wall-Builders. . . . . name for the Pharisees (= Seekers of Slippery Answers = Ephraim)

Wicked Priest. . . . . opponent of the Teacher of Righteousness

Yahad . . . . Hebrew for "oneness" or "community," name for Essenes in some scrolls (esp. 1QS), hence the *Yahad* Essenes

Zadok. . . . . priest descended from Aaron's son Eleazar

Zadokite. . . . . high priests descended from Zadok, first to serve in the Temple

Zechariah s. of Barachiah . . . . Zechariah son of Baris (or Baruch), during First Jewish Revolt

Introduction

The Greatest Find of Our Times

On April 11, 1948, the Dead Sea Scrolls were announced to the world by Millar Burrows, one of America's leading biblical scholars, in the *Times* of London. Soon afterward, famed archaeologist William Albright confirmed the antiquity of the scrolls, praising them as "the greatest archaeological find of the twentieth century." How could Albright—a careful and learned professor—make such an extraordinary claim?

Before answering this key question, it will be helpful to describe very briefly here just what is meant by the "Dead Sea Scrolls."

Overview of the Dead Sea Scrolls

In late 1946 or early 1947, Bedouin shepherds found several scrolls in a cave near an ancient site called Qumran, about one mile inland from the western shore of the Dead Sea, and 13 miles east of Jerusalem. This cave became known as Cave 1, which contained seven scrolls altogether, including the *Great Isaiah Scroll* and the *Rule of the Community*. By 1956, a total of 11 caves had been discovered at Qumran. These yielded various artifacts, especially pottery, but most importantly scrolls (that is, rolled manuscripts). Almost 1,050 scrolls were found in the Qumran caves in about 25,000 to 50,000 pieces (a number that varies depending on how the fragments are counted), with many no bigger than a postage stamp. While a few are well-preserved, all the scrolls are damaged and most are fragmentary.

More scrolls were discovered at other locations in the vicinity of the Dead Sea, especially at Wadi Murabba'at (about 120 scrolls in 1951–1952), Nahal Hever (over 70 scrolls in 1951–1961), and Masada (15 scrolls in 1963–1965). Thus the term *Dead Sea Scrolls* refers not only to scrolls discovered at Qumran (the main site) but also to scrolls from all sites in the vicinity of the Dead Sea. However, most research and discussion among scholars has been centered on the Qumran scrolls.

The scrolls found near Qumran were written in Hebrew, Aramaic, and Greek, the three languages of the Bible. Scholars divide these into two general categories of writings: Biblical and Nonbiblical. Of these 1,050 or so manuscripts found at Qumran, approximately 300 (about 29 percent of the total) are classified as Biblical, which constitute our earliest witnesses to the text of Scripture. Many of the other 750 or so documents are of direct relevance to early Judaism and emerging Christianity: they anticipate or confirm numerous ideas and teachings found in the New Testament and in later rabbinic writings (the Mishnah and Talmud).

The Dead Sea Scrolls are very ancient indeed: the earliest ones found at Qumran date from about 250 B.C.E. or a little earlier; the latest were copied shortly before the destruction of the Qumran site by the Romans in 68 C.E. Scrolls from the other sites are somewhat later: Masada (up to 74 C.E.), Wadi Murabba'at (up to 135 C.E.), and Nahal Hever (up to 135 C.E.).

With this information at hand, five solid reasons emerge to confirm Albright's recognition of the supreme importance of the Dead Sea Scrolls.

The Significance of the Scrolls

(1) The Scrolls Were Found in the Holy Land

The ancient land of Palestine is holy to three faiths: Judaism, Christianity, and Islam, and indeed, to most readers of this book. However much we may care for our own countries, for Jews and Christians the land of Israel is the only true Holy Land because it is there that the prophets preached, there that Jesus lived, and there that the events of Easter took place. Prior to the discovery of the scrolls, virtually no writings dated before the destruction of the Second Temple had been found in Israel. With the Qumran scrolls we now have more than 1,000 documents from the land itself, all written while the Temple was still standing.

(2) The Scrolls Are Written in the Three Languages of Scripture

For biblical scholars, ancient languages (such as Latin or Syriac) and modern languages (such as English, French, and German) are important, but manuscripts written in the original Hebrew, Aramaic, and Greek are valued above all. The scrolls found near Qumran include ancient biblical books in Hebrew and Aramaic (portions of Daniel) and ancient fragments of the Septuagint in Greek, as well as nonbiblical compositions in all three languages.

(3) The Dead Sea Scrolls Include Our Oldest Biblical Manuscripts

The antiquity of the biblical scrolls is of supreme importance for biblical scholars. The oldest Hebrew manuscript known before the discovery of the scrolls was the Nash Papyrus, which is dated at 150–100 B.C.E. This fragment contains text from Exodus

20:2–17 and Deuteronomy 5:6–21. However, this piece contains very little text; the Hebrew Bible and translations made from it must be based on complete manuscripts, or at least very substantial ones. As we will explore further, all Hebrew copies of the Hebrew Bible used today are based on medieval manuscripts. The main Hebrew text (on which most modern English translations are based) is a single manuscript, the Leningrad (or St. Petersburg) Codex. Copied in 1008 or 1009 C.E., this is our earliest complete example of the traditional Hebrew Bible. Another very important Hebrew manuscript is the Aleppo Codex, which was copied in about 925 C.E., almost a century before the Leningrad Codex. However, this manuscript is damaged, with most of the Pentateuch missing. Now, quite incredibly, we have 250 or so biblical scrolls found at Qumran that are up to 1,175 years older than the Aleppo Codex. All are dated from 250 B.C.E. to 68 C.E., while the Second Temple was still standing, and are therefore our most extensive and important ancient copies of Scripture.

(4) The Scrolls Contain New Information About Early Judaism

Because the Qumran scrolls were all written before the Temple fell in 70 C.E., they are authentic source material for the study of early Judaism and confirm that there were several Jewish groups at this time. We already knew a good deal about the Pharisees and the Sadducees, the two main Jewish groups in the days of Jesus Christ. Some of the nonbiblical scrolls provide further information on these groups, but other nonbiblical scrolls (the sectarian scrolls) record the ideas and outlook of a very different group: the Community of the New Covenant, whom most scholars identify as the Essenes. Certain scrolls also contain fascinating insights on the intense competition among the various Jewish groups in ancient times to be the legitimate and chosen people of God. One such document is *Some of the Works of the Law*, which was found in Cave 4 at Qumran. In this manifesto, the Essenes or their predecessors spell out the rules and observances that make a person acceptable in the sight of God, in contrast to the more flexible observances promoted by their opponents, the Pharisees.

(5) The Scrolls Contain New Information About Early Christianity

The scrolls were not written by Christian authors and never mention any Christian individuals by name and thus have no direct relationship to Jesus and early Christianity. However, some key manuscripts are important for understanding Jesus' life and teaching, while others anticipate several New Testament doctrines. More specifically, these ancient documents throw welcome light on the Gospels by: (a) providing helpful information about Jewish society, groups, practices, and beliefs at the time of Jesus and the early Christians; (b) helping us see in sharper outline some of the basic differences between the message of Jesus and the messages of other Jewish groups; and (c) providing new texts with similarities to certain New Testament passages. Such texts are especially interesting, since they show that some of Jesus' teaching in the Gospels and other information in various New Testament books was anticipated in earlier Jewish texts, rather than being fabricated by the later church.

Some scrolls even contain wording that is very close to passages found in the New Testament, which shows that this material was known to some or many Jews in the first century B.C.E., thus supporting the ancient origin or authenticity of the relevant New Testament passages. New Testament themes that are anticipated in various scrolls include: lists of beatitudes; the Holy Spirit; Messiah as Priest, King, and Prophet; a messianic Son of God; the term *works of the Law*; the Battle of Armageddon (the eschatological war); and the New Jerusalem.

Since 1987, I have had the privilege of studying, seeing, and editing many of the Dead Sea Scrolls, as well as giving many lectures on these documents and serving as a consultant to several scrolls exhibitions at museums in the United States and Canada. During these years I have witnessed the attraction of the scrolls for hundreds of thousands of people and their lasting effect on many lives, museums, and even cities. Even after all these years, the scrolls remain new and impart a sense of awe and wonder.

The scrolls have had a mighty impact on scholarship of the Hebrew Bible (Old Testament), the New Testament, and Second Temple Judaism in general. It is remarkable to note that since the 1950s (when the scrolls began to be disseminated) thousands of books have been published, either on the scrolls themselves or making significant use of the scrolls in studies on biblical and other Second Temple subjects. This is in addition to the tens of thousands of scholarly articles on scrolls-related subjects. An entire society (the International Organization for Qumran Studies) is devoted to scrolls scholarship, as well as two scholarly journals (*Revue de Qumrân* and *Dead Sea Discoveries*) and four book series (Discoveries in the Judaean Desert, Dead Sea Scrolls Editions, Studies on the Texts of the Desert of Judah, and Studies in the Dead Sea Scrolls and Related Literature). Research on and discussion by scholars on the scrolls have readily been made available to the wider public in magazines such as the *Biblical Archaeology Review*, the world's best-selling archaeological publication. The effect of all these studies has been to overturn some older views (but also to confirm others) concerning the form and shape of the Hebrew Bible, the nature of early Judaism before the fall of the Temple, and the ideas that gave rise to early Christianity and the New Testament.

Albright's evaluation of the scrolls as "the greatest archaeological find of the twentieth century" has convincingly been confirmed, and is indeed appropriate. With the immense impact of the scrolls on scholarship of the Bible and Second Temple Judaism, and the fact that millions of people have viewed the scrolls in Jerusalem and millions more have seen them in exhibitions around the world (including many readers of this book), it is clear that the Dead Sea Scrolls have become a cultural icon.

1

The Discovery
of the Scrolls in the
Judean Desert

Introduction

The Dead Sea Scrolls are ancient manuscripts found at sites in the Judean Desert near the western shore of the Dead Sea. This chapter focuses on the major site, Qumran, with its 1,050 or so scrolls and many artifacts such as jars. A few details will also be given on three other important sites: Wadi Murabba'at, Nahal Hever, and Masada.

Since the discovery of the first scrolls in 1946 or 1947, Palestine has been a volatile region: sometimes dangerous, always exciting. Even the name is controversial: most scholars prefer *Palestine*, which denotes the larger area now called Israel and the Palestinian territories.

The first scrolls were found at a time of great turmoil and violence in the Middle East, with Palestine under a British Mandate that ended with partition of the land in May 1948. Tensions between Arabs and Jews did not end with Israel's independence and remain to this day. This political backdrop helps explain the actions of various key figures, whether Jewish (acquiring scrolls for the new State of Israel), or Bedouin (working secretly as treasure hunters), or Western (bringing scrolls to the United States and planning international exhibits).

1. The First Cave at Qumran and Its Seven Scrolls

The discovery of Cave 1 and the first scrolls has been told from several perspectives: the Bedouin shepherds, the Israelis, the archaeologists, and Western scholars. Each group, not always consciously, tends to follow an agenda, whether cultural, historical, or scientific. For the most complete accounts, we are grateful to two men, who interviewed many of

1

the early discoverers while preparing their books. The earlier is John C. Trever—the first American to see and photograph the scrolls—in *The Untold Story of Qumran* (1965), *The Dead Sea Scrolls: A Personal Account* (1977), and *The Dead Sea Scrolls in Perspective* (2004). The second is Weston W. Fields, managing director of the Dead Sea Scrolls Foundation, in his definitive work *The Dead Sea Scrolls: A Full History, vol. 1: 1947–60* (2009).

1.1 The Discovery

Cave 1 was discovered by a group of Bedouin (from the Ta'amireh tribe) near a spring on the northwestern shore of the Dead Sea called Ain Feshka, a frequent stopover point for watering flocks. Three shepherds, Khalil Musa, Jum'a Muhammed Khalil, and Muhammed edh-Dhib, or "the Wolf," were tending their herds near the adjacent Khirbet (ruin) of Qumran.

One day in late 1946 or early 1947, Jum'a threw a rock into an opening in the cliffs and heard the sound of shattering pottery. He summoned his two cousins, but they decided to come back later. However, the youngest, Muhammed edh-Dhib, returned early and entered the cave. (The Bedouin later described the interior of a cave whose walls were lined with several tall jars, some with lids and handles for tying to the jars.) Muhammed the Wolf saw a pile of rocks fallen from the ceiling and broken pottery strewn about the floor. There were two intact jars, one with a cover and containing a large leather scroll, the *Great Isaiah Scroll* (1QIsaᵃ). It also contained two greenish bundles, wrapped in linen and coated with a black layer of pitch or wax. These were later identified as the *Habakkuk Commentary* (1QpHab) and the *Community Rule* (1QS), first called the *Manual of Discipline*.

Edh-Dhib removed the three scrolls from the jar and brought them to his companions, who were displeased he had returned to the cave alone. Jum'a deposited the scrolls at a Ta'amireh site southeast of Bethlehem, where they remained in a bag suspended on a tent pole for several weeks. It is not surprising that some were damaged; for example, the cover sheet of 1QIsaᵃ broke off. In May and June, George Isha'ya Shamoun, a key figure in the sale of one group of scrolls, was brought twice to the cave by its discoverers; on his second visit, four more were removed, including the *Genesis Apocryphon* (1QapGen).

The four scrolls named so far (1QIsaᵃ, 1QpHab, 1QS, and 1QapGen) are grouped as the "St. Mark's Monastery Scrolls," for the first institution to purchase them. The other three—a second copy of *Isaiah* (1QIsaᵇ), the *Thanksgiving Hymns* (1QHᵃ), and the *War Scroll* (1QM)—form the "Hebrew University Scrolls," also named for the institution of purchase.

1.2 The Hebrew University Scrolls

In June 1947, Musa and Jum'a sold the three scrolls, together with two jars from the cave, to an antiquities dealer in Bethlehem named Faidi Salahi for seven Jordanian pounds (about $28).

Salahi's associate Nasri Ohan (an Armenian dealer in Jerusalem) contacted Eleazar Sukenik (1889–1953), professor of archaeology at the Hebrew University, and arranged to show him a sample. On November 25, they met near the Jaffa Gate in Zone B of partitioned Jerusalem, and Sukenik was shown a sizable piece. On this first encounter with the scrolls, his diary reads:

> As I gazed at the parchment, the letters began to become familiar, though I could make no immediate sense of the writing. . . . I had seen such letters scratched, carved and, in a few cases, painted on stone. But not until this week had I seen this particular kind of Hebrew lettering written with a pen on leather. (Yadin, *Message of the Scrolls*, 18)

A few days later, at great risk, Sukenik traveled to Salahi's shop in Bethlehem, where he received two scrolls: the *Thanksgiving Hymns* (1QH^a) and the *War Scroll* (1QM). Taking these back with him to Jerusalem, he promised to decide within two days whether to buy them.

Sukenik's trip to Bethlehem took place on a momentous day: Friday, November, 29, 1947, when the United Nations voted to partition Palestine into Jewish and Arab sections. Rioting broke out the following day, but on Monday, December 1, Sukenik contacted Ohan and confirmed his decision to buy. On December 22, he also bought the two jars and the Isaiah scroll (1QIsa^b).

By then, Sukenik had become aware of the four St. Mark's scrolls, but their contents were as yet unclear to him. So he set to work on the Hebrew University Scrolls, and already in 1948 published the first preliminary edition, with a second volume in 1950. Sukenik died in 1953, but all three scrolls and excerpts from his diary were published in a posthumous volume (Sukenik, 1954 and 1955).

1.3 The Saint Mark's Monastery Scrolls

The journey of the four St. Mark's Scrolls—the *Great Isaiah Scroll* (1QIsa^a), the *Habakkuk Commentary* (1QpHab), the *Community Rule* (1QS), and the *Genesis Apocryphon* (1QapGen)—makes fascinating reading.

In February or March 1947, Musa and Jum'a showed three of them (1QIsa^a, 1QpHab, and 1QS) to Ibrahim 'Ijha, an antiquities dealer in Bethlehem, but Jum'a also met with George Isha'ya Shamoun, a member of the Syrian Orthodox Church. The three scrolls were brought to Kando (Khalil Eskander Shahin, about 1910–1993), another antiquities dealer (with a shop near Nativity Square in Bethlehem) and a member of the same church. Kando agreed to pay five Jordanian pounds ($20) to the Bedouin.

The *Genesis Apocryphon* (1QapGen) was added to Kando's purchase soon afterward. All four scrolls were kept by Shamoun for Kando, who proceeded to seek a major buyer.

Thinking the four scrolls were written in Syriac, Shamoun contacted St. Mark's Syrian Orthodox Monastery in Jerusalem's Old City during Holy Week (April 13–17) of 1947. Athanasius Yeshue Samuel (1907–1995), a mar (or archbishop) associated with the monastery, was shown part of the *Community Rule* and decided to buy all four scrolls. On July 19, the scrolls were transferred to the Metropolitan, hence their collective title "The St. Mark's Monastery Scrolls." Samuel paid 24 Jordanian pounds (about $100) to Kando, who in turn paid the Bedouin 16 pounds ($64). In late July, Shamoun took to the cave a priest (Father Yusif), who observed one intact jar, several pieces of cloth wrapping, and scroll fragments on the floor.

Mar Samuel found it difficult to obtain a scholarly evaluation of the four scrolls. Both a visiting European scholar and Jewish scholar from the New City identified the largest scroll as containing Isaiah, but thought it to be medieval. Samuel then enlisted Anton Kiraz (a member of the Syrian Orthodox church) to help find a qualified scholar to authenticate his four scrolls.

On February 4, 1948, Kiraz met at the YMCA in West Jerusalem with Eleazar Sukenik, who had bought the three Hebrew University Scrolls two months earlier. Sukenik at once noted similarities in script between the *Great Isaiah Scroll* (1QIsa^a), the *Habakkuk Commentary* (1QpHab), and the *Community Rule* (1QS), and those he had purchased. Sukenik borrowed the three scrolls, and soon afterward secured funding from the Bialik Foundation to buy them. On February 10, Sukenik made an offer of 1,000 Jordanian pounds ($4,000) for all four St. Mark's scrolls, but Kiraz decided to seek an independent appraisal.

Meanwhile, also in February 1948, the St. Mark's scrolls were shown to John Trever and William Brownlee of the American School of Oriental Research (ASOR) in Jerusalem. Soon afterward, Trever photographed 1QIsa^a, 1QpHab, and 1QS. The American scholars were not supportive of selling the manuscripts to the Hebrew University and reminded the Metropolitan of the investment already made by ASOR in photographing the three scrolls and preparing them for publication.

1.4 The American School of Oriental Research, First Photographs, and Authentification

On February 18, 1948, Father Butrus Sowmy of St. Mark's telephoned ASOR, and spoke with interim director John Trever, a visiting Fellow from the United States. Trever was asked to examine what the Syrian priest described as some old manuscripts from the monastery library but, in fact, were the four St. Mark's scrolls. Trever describes the first time he—and any Western scholar—saw two of the scrolls (the *Community Rule* and the *Great Isaiah Scroll*):

> Father Sowmy . . . handed me a very brittle, tightly rolled scroll of cream-colored leather, less than two inches in diameter. Very gently I pulled back the end of the scroll and saw that it was written in a clear, square Hebrew script, not at all like archaic Hebrew. . . . [Then] they lifted from the satchel a large scroll, about 10 1/2 inches long and 6 inches in diameter, . . . made of thinner, softer leather and much more pliable. It was about the same color as the first one, but with a darkened center, evidence of much handling. It unrolled easily. (Trever, *The Untold Story*, 22)

Trever compared 1QIsa^a against some color slides he had of a few other Hebrew manuscripts. He noticed differences in the characters against a medieval Torah manuscript, but similarities with the much older Nash Papyrus (with text from the Ten Commandments and the *Shema' Yisrael* prayer, and dated to the second to first century B.C.E.). Before the Syrians left, he copied a few lines from column 51 of 1QIsa^a, which he later identified as Isaiah 65:1: "I let myself be sought out by those who did not ask me, be found by those who did not seek me."

Trever now suspected that the scrolls shown to him were very ancient—but was only the third person to perceive just how ancient. The first was Sukenik, who saw three scrolls on November 25 and 27, 1947. The second was Sowmy's brother Ibrahim, a customs official for the Mandate government. The scrolls, he suggested, were copied before 200 B.C.E. since they were wrapped like ancient mummies and belonged to an ancient sect called the Essenes, who had deposited them in the cave during a time of persecution.

February 21, 1948, marks a historic milestone: the first photographs of the Dead Sea Scrolls. Trever, Brownlee, Sowmy, and Samuel gathered in the basement of ASOR to photograph three of the four St. Mark's scrolls (1QIsaᵃ, 1QpHab, and 1QS; the *Genesis Apocryphon* was too damaged to be unrolled).

By day's end, the *Great Isaiah Scroll* and the *Habakkuk Pesher* had been photographed in black and white, and a few color shots were taken of 1QIsaᵃ. Trever's breathtaking photograph of columns 32–33, with the rolled manuscript visible on both sides, was to become the most famous image of a Dead Sea Scroll. On February 24, Trever also photographed the *Community Rule*. The ASOR scholars then urged the Syrians to move the scrolls to a safer place and have experts in the United States open the badly damaged *Genesis Apocryphon*.

News of the St. Mark's scrolls reached the outside world via a photograph of 1QIsaᵃ and a letter from Trever to William F. Albright in the United States on February 25. The next day, ASOR director Millar Burrows confirmed that the American School would fund the publication of the St. Mark's scrolls. Trever also secured permission to rephotograph 1QIsaᵃ and 1QpHab in order to improve picture quality for publication.

On March 5, 1948, Mar Samuel and Father Sowmy disclosed to Trever the true origin of their scrolls, as purchased from Bedouin in Bethlehem the previous August, shortly after which Father Yusif had visited the cave of origin accompanied by the Bedouin. With the correct details of the discovery site now established, plans for an official excavation of Cave 1 commenced. Trever and Brownlee applied for an excavation permit from the Jordanian Department of Antiquities, but canceled their plans due to growing danger and military activity in the vicinity of the cave. Trever also rephotographed all of 1QIsaᵃ in color, which he completed by March 13.

The strongest authentication of the scrolls' antiquity came on March 15 in a letter from Albright, who was teaching at Johns Hopkins University and was America's greatest archaeologist at the time:

> Dear Trever,
>
> My heartiest congratulations on the greatest MS discovery of modern times! There is no doubt whatever in my mind that the script is more archaic than that of the Nash Papyrus, standing very close to that of the third-century Egyptian papyri and ostraca in Aramaic. Of course, in the present state of our definite knowledge about Hebrew paleography it would be safe only to date it in the Maccabaean period *i.e.*, not later than the ascension of Herod the Great. I should prefer a date around 100 B.C. (Trever, *The Untold Story*, 85)

A few days later, Sowmy was sent with the precious manuscripts to Beirut and deposited them in a bank vault for safekeeping. The first international press report announcing the discovery appeared in the *Times* of London on April 12, 1948:

> Yale University announced yesterday the discovery in Palestine of the earliest known manuscript of the Book of Isaiah. . . . dating to about the first century B.C., . . . a commentary on the Book of Habakkuk, . . . a manual of discipline of some comparatively little-known sect or monastic order, possibly the Essenes. The third scroll has not yet been identified.

1.5 The St. Mark's Scrolls in the United States and Their Final Purchase

On April 26, Professor Sukenik called a press conference, announcing the three scrolls recently acquired by the Hebrew University and that these and the St Mark's Monastery Scrolls were from the same cave near Qumran.

With the authenticity of his four scrolls now confirmed, Samuel's asking price rose to one million dollars, and Sukenik's hopes of acquiring them faded. Sukenik's son, Yigael Yadin, deeply regretted that his father, who died in 1953, did not live to witness the purchase of the St. Mark's scrolls for the State of Israel on June 15, 1954.

On May 14, 1948, the British Mandate over Palestine expired, and the State of Israel was declared. Burrows and Trever, having already returned to the United States, had invited Mar Samuel over to finalize the publication of the St. Mark's scrolls and to get expert help in unrolling the damaged *Genesis Apocryphon*. Samuel was also appointed Apostolic Delegate of the Syrian Church to the United States and Canada. In December (or early January 1949), he sailed from Beirut to Jersey City, carrying the four scrolls with him.

The first ASOR publication appeared in March 1950: *The Dead Sea Scrolls of St. Mark's Monastery*, volume 1, with photographs and transcriptions of the Isaiah manuscript and the *Habakkuk Commentary*. The next year volume 2 appeared, with photographs and transcriptions of the *Community Rule*.

The Metropolitan set about seeking a buyer for Mar Samuel's scrolls, holding exhibits at the Library of Congress (October 1949) and Duke University (1950) and the University of Chicago (1950). Still no buyer came forward, perhaps dissuaded by the asking price (initially one million dollars) or questions as to legal ownership of the manuscripts. Mar Samuel's final attempt to sell was through an advertisement in the *Wall Street Journal*, which first appeared on June 1, 1954:

The Four Dead Sea Scrolls

Biblical manuscripts dating back to at least 200 B.C. are for sale.
This would be an ideal gift to an educational or religious institution
by an individual or group.

Box F 206, *Wall Street Journal*

Earlier that summer, Yigael Yadin was to lecture at Johns Hopkins University and learned from Albright of Mar Samuel's attempts to sell his scrolls. Albright estimated the real price at around $500,000, and encouraged Yadin to buy them for the new State of Israel. After Yadin was alerted to the *Wall Street Journal* advertisement, his agent managed to bid the price down to $250,000. On June 15, Yadin's purchase of the St. Mark's Monastery Scrolls was finalized.

In early February 1955, the four scrolls were flown to Israel, and on February 13, Israel's purchase was announced by Premier Moshe Sharett, together with plans for a museum to house all seven scrolls from Cave 1. Ten years later, on April 20, 1965, the Shrine of the Book in Jerusalem was inaugurated.

Were it not for Yadin's success, the St. Mark's scrolls would most likely have been sold to an American group that included John Trever, who envisaged housing them at the Palestine Archaeological Museum in East Jerusalem (then part of Jordan). His planned international project included future exhibitions around the world, with the funds raised being used for the Syrian Orthodox Monastery in Jerusalem and for humanitarian and educational projects.

2. The Other Ten Qumran Caves and Their Scrolls

Between 1952 and 1956, ten more caves were discovered in the vicinity of Qumran, not all of which contained scrolls. Surveys to find caves were conducted by archaeologists, most notably G. Lankester Harding (1901–1979), director of the Jordanian Department of Antiquities, and Pére Roland de Vaux (1903–1971), director of the École Biblique (the French Archaeological School) in Jerusalem. Archaeologists found seven minor caves (3–5, 7–10), none of which contained extensive manuscript remains, but the Bedouin (with their intimate knowledge of the terrain) discovered the three richest caves (1, 4, 11) and two minor ones (2 and 6).

2.1 The Five Caves Found in 1952

Cave 2. In February 1952, a short distance south of Cave 1, some Bedouin found a second cave containing fragments from over thirty scrolls. With the agreement of the Department of Antiquities, these pieces were purchased from Kando by the Palestine Archaeological Museum and the École Biblique. From March 10 to 29, an archaeological team explored Cave 2 and the surrounding region and found two more small scroll fragments and pieces of cylindrical jars.

Cave 3. On March 14, the archeologists found a third cave. It yielded at least 15 manuscripts, including the *Copper Scroll* and many cylindrical jars.

Cave 4. In August, Bedouin explorers made a momentous discovery: Cave 4 at Qumran—which contained the remnants of well over 700 scrolls. They reportedly were alerted to the cave by an older tribesman, who recalled as a young lad chasing a partridge into a cavity that turned out to be the opening of a cave near Khirbet Qumran. Several youths, he remembered, had entered it and found pottery and other objects.

On September 20, 1952, de Vaux contacted Harding to say that the Bedouin had offered him a huge quantity of fragments and that he had purchased some for 1,300 Jordanian pounds ($5,200). Traveling to the Qumran area, Harding caught the Bedouin at work and stopped them from removing further material from the cave. An official excavation was conducted from September 22 to 29, 1952. De Vaux later wrote that the Bedouin had already removed more than half the cave's contents and had worked so carefully that only a few small fragments were found in their debris. Most of the scrolls had been scattered in ancient times, probably by the Romans who entered the cave and trashed it. The archaeologists also explored the cave and gathered almost a thousand fragments.

The many fragments already taken by the Bedouin would have to be purchased. De Vaux was confident these were from Cave 4 because the pieces found by the archaeologists belonged to about 100 different manuscripts that were almost all represented among those bought from the Bedouin.

The vast number of fragments from Cave 4 (more than 700 scrolls in some 20,000 pieces) changed the way archaeologists and government agencies approached the Qumran discoveries. At Harding's suggestion, the government turned to foreign institutions to purchase fragments with the understanding that once fragments were assembled into documents and then published, the originals would be divided among the purchasing bodies. Four universities responded (Oxford, Manchester, Heidelberg, and McGill), as well as the Vatican Library, one seminary (McCormick, Chicago), and one wealthy church (All Souls, New York).

In the end, the texts remained in East Jerusalem, but the institutions were reimbursed. These foreign bodies provided crucial funding for the Cave 4 scrolls at a very vulnerable time and ensured that the vast majority were not dispersed all over the world.

Cave 4 is located near the buildings at Khirbet Qumran, which raises the question of these ruins' relationship to the scrolls the cave contained, since one almost has to pass through them to reach it.

Caves 5 and 6. While excavating Cave 4, the archaeologists found Cave 5 a short distance north. It contains the remains of some 25 manuscripts, several of which have still not been identified. Also in September, in the cliffs west of Qumran, the Bedouin found Cave 6, which contained remains of about 33 scrolls, most written on fragile papyrus.

2.2 Five More Caves Found in 1955 and 1956

Caves 7–10. During an excavation from February 2 to April 6, 1955, archaeologists discovered four more caves near Khirbet Qumran. They contained relatively few scrolls: 19 in Cave 7, five in Cave 8, one in Cave 9, and only an ostracon in Cave 10. Cave 8 also contained about 100 items used for fastening scrolls.

Cave 11. The final discovery of a scroll-bearing cave in the Qumran area was by the Bedouin in January 1956. Farther north than the other caves (except Cave 3), Cave 11 contained the remains of 31 scrolls. Several preserved large amounts of text, most notably:

the *Paleo-Leviticus Scroll* (11QpaeloLev^a), the *Great Psalms Scroll* (11QPs^a), the *Targum of Job* (11QtgJob), and the *Temple Scroll* (11QT^a).

3. Dead Sea Scrolls from Other Sites in the Judean Desert

Several other sites were found with caves containing scrolls and artifacts. Moving south (from Qumran) along the western shore of the Dead Sea, the most relevant are: Wadi Murabba'at, Nahal Hever, and Masada.

Wadi Murabba'at (11 miles south of Qumran. Found by Bedouin, 1951; excavated, 1952). During the Second Jewish Revolt against Rome (132–135 C.E.), led by Simon bar Kokhba (d. 135 C.E.), Jewish fighters hid out in several of the caves. These contain about 120 documents from the Roman period, including: contracts, a writ of divorce, letters signed by Bar Kokhba, biblical scrolls (Pentateuch, Isaiah, Minor Prophets), and phylacteries (with portions of Exodus and Deuteronomy).

Nahal Hever (Found by Bedouin, 1952; excavated 1960–1961). Also during the Second Revolt, caves were used here as hiding places for Jewish fighters. The Romans erected siege camps in the cliffs above, and the rebels and their families died in the caves, most notably Cave 8 (the Cave of Horrors). A large number of scroll fragments were found in Cave 5/6 (the Cave of Letters), and a few in Cave 8. Most are letters and legal documents from the second century, but a few are biblical (Pentateuch and Psalms in Cave 5/6; the Greek Minor Prophets Scroll in Cave 8).

Masada (On the edge of the Judean Desert and the Dead Sea valley; excavated, 1963–1965). This fortress atop a huge rock became the rebels' base following the fall of Jerusalem (70 C.E.) in the First Jewish Revolt (68–73). It was besieged by the Romans, resulting in the mass suicide of the defenders, but two women and a few children survived. The site yielded more than 700 ostraca, mostly in Hebrew or Aramaic. Fragments of 15 scrolls were also found, seven of them biblical (Pentateuch, Psalms, Ezekiel). The nonbiblical scrolls include *Ben Sira*, *Jubilees*, and the *Songs of the Sabbath Sacrifice*.

4. The Quest for Further Caves and Scrolls

In more recent times, archaeologists and Bedouin have searched for more caves in the Qumran area that might contain written material, even using ground-penetrating radar (GPR) to detect underground caves and archaeological remains. In 2004, some Bedouin made the first scroll discovery in 40 years, in a cave used by rebel fighters during the Second Revolt: four fragments with text from Leviticus 23–24. They were acquired and published in 2005 by Israeli scholar Hanan Eshel (who was then arrested).

In the 1980s, scholars became aware of more scrolls in private hands that were being offered for sale. Most turned out to be from Cave 4, were being kept outside Israel, and were being offered by the Kando family. In this "underground market," dealings are often clandestine and complicated, and most scholars do not get involved. It appears that most or all of these scrolls were found in the caves near Qumran, including the following:

- 2000–2005: Martin Schøyen (a Norwegian collector of manuscripts) purchased about 40 Dead Sea Scrolls. Most are biblical fragments and include Genesis (two scrolls), Exodus (one), Leviticus (one), Deuteronomy (two), Joshua (two), Ruth (one), Samuel (three), Kings (one), Nehemiah (one), Psalms (two), Proverbs (one), Isaiah (one), Jeremiah (four), Daniel (two), the Minor Prophets (one), Tobit (2), and *1 Enoch* (3).

- 2009: Azusa Pacific University (Azusa, California) acquired five fragments with text from Leviticus and Daniel, two from Deuteronomy, and one possibly from Exodus. These were featured in a successful exhibit, Treasures of the Bible: The Dead Sea Scrolls and Beyond (August 21–29, 2010).

- 2010: Southwestern Baptist Theological Seminary (Fort Worth, Texas) bought an ancient pen used at Qumran and fragments of Exodus, Leviticus, Deuteronomy, Psalm 22, and Daniel. These were the centerpiece of a powerful exhibit, The Dead Sea Scrolls and the Bible: Ancient Artifacts, Timeless Treasures (July 2, 2012–January 13, 2013).

- 2011: The Green Collection (Oklahoma City) purchased 12 scrolls, with text from the Pentateuch, Prophetic books, Psalm 11, Nehemiah, and a nonbiblical scroll known as 4QInstruction. These have been featured in several *Passages* exhibits, for example at Atlanta (November 19, 2011–June 30, 2012) and the Vatican (March 1–April 15, 2012).

2

Archaeology of the Qumran Site: The Caves, Buildings, and Cemeteries

Archaeologists have played a vital role in acquiring, identifying, and dating the Dead Sea Scrolls; they have had even more important roles in researching jars and artifacts found together with many scrolls, as well as sites and nearby settlements with which many scrolls are associated. Within a year after the first scrolls were found (late 1946 or early 1947), archaeologists took an increasing interest in them.

The first Jewish scholar to examine a scroll was Eleazar Sukenik, professor of archaeology at the Hebrew University, who at once recognized the great age and immense importance of these manuscripts. The first American scholar to study a scroll was John C. Trever. Soon afterward, archaeologist William F. Albright of Johns Hopkins University confirmed that scrolls found in Cave 1 were ancient and authentic and proclaimed in a letter to the American School that the Dead Sea Scrolls were "the greatest manuscript discovery of modern times."

Since so many objects have been found at or near Qumran, many opposing views have been put forward by scholars. Discussion here will be limited to the archaeology of the Qumran caves and the site of Khirbet (or ruin of) Qumran; of course, more could be said about the excavations of other sites where scrolls were found (Wadi Murabba'at, Nahal Hever, and Masada).

1. Archaeology and the Qumran Caves

1.1 Excavations of Caves 1–11

From February 15 to March 5, 1949, archaeologists excavated Cave 1 under the auspices of the Jordanian Department of Antiquities, the École Biblique et Archéologique

Française, and the Palestine Archaeological Museum. The leaders were G. Lankester Harding, director of antiquities in Jordan, and Pére Roland de Vaux, director of the École. De Vaux reported the size of the cave as about eight meters long and four meters high, with a varying width. Although the Bedouin and Syrians had removed the complete manuscripts and larger pieces, the excavators found about 600 scroll fragments and the remains of at least 50 jars and covers, some bowls, a pot, a pitcher, four lamps, three phylactery cases, a wooden comb, and about 50 linens.

Between 1952 and 1956, ten more caves were discovered in the vicinity. Searches led by de Vaux and Harding yielded five minor caves (5, 7–10), none of which contained extensive manuscripts, and Cave 3, which yielded about 15 scrolls and several jars. Bedouin explorers were far more successful, discovering two scroll-rich caves (4 and 11) and two minor ones (2 and 6).

Cave 2 (February 1952). The Bedouin found about 30 scroll fragments. An archaeological team (March 10–29) discovered two scroll fragments and pieces of cylindrical jars.

Cave 3 (March 14, 1952). Archaeologists found at least 15 manuscripts, including the *Copper Scroll*, and many cylindrical jars.

Cave 4 (August, 1952). The Bedouin discovered at least 15,000 fragments. An archaeological excavation (September 22–29) found they had removed more than half the cave's contents. The cave was described by de Vaux as an oval chamber opening onto two smaller ones (4a and 4b). Almost all the texts and pottery (from jars and other objects) came from Cave 4a. Archaeologists explored the lower levels and a small underground room, discovered the original entrance, gathered almost 1,000 scroll fragments, and found the scrolls had been scattered in an ancient upheaval (most likely trashed by the Romans).

Caves 5 and 6 (September 1952). Archaeologists excavated Cave 5 from September 25 to 28, finding remains of some 25 manuscripts. A little earlier, the Bedouin found Cave 6 in cliffs west of Qumran, with remains of about 33 scrolls.

Caves 7–10 (February 2 to April 6, 1955). Archaeologists discovered these caves near Qumran, all carved from the marl terrace and collapsed. They yielded few scrolls: 19 in Cave 7, five in Cave 8, one in Cave 9, and an ostracon in Cave 10. Cave 8 also contained items used for fastening scrolls (about 100 leather thongs and leather tabs with eyelets).

Cave 11 (January 1956). The Bedouin found this very northern cave containing the remains of 31 scrolls.

1.2 Caves Near Qumran and Elsewhere

In 1984–1991, J. Patrich of the University of Haifa re-excavated five caves (including 3 and 11). He sought the remains of huts or tents, since de Vaux had thought most members of the Qumran group had lived in such dwellings. Patrich confirmed de Vaux's view that the caves in the cliffs did not serve as dwellings for the members of the Dead Sea Sect, but rather as stores and hiding places. He concluded that all members of the community lived inside Khirbet Qumran. Patrich found that two caves (Cave 24 between Caves 3 and 11, and FQ37 south of Qumran) could have been used for living quarters, but showed no sign of long-term habitation.

In 1995–1996, Israeli archaeologists Magen Broshi (Shrine of the Book, Jerusalem) and Hanan Eshel (Bar Ilan University) carried out further excavations north of Qumran. They reported additional caves not examined by Patrich, which they believed served as dwellings for the inhabitants of Qumran along with other artificial caves that had eroded away from the limestone cliffs. In a small ravine, they found 280 potsherds in Cave C and 110 potsherds in Cave F.

2. Archaeology of the Qumran Buildings

2.1 Early Surveys and Descriptions of the Site

The ruins of the Qumran site are visible aboveground and have attracted the attention of passing travelers for centuries. Piles of stones, a cistern or reservoir, an aqueduct, and a cemetery with many graves could be seen. Several early visitors to the site recorded their observations, well before the scrolls were found in 1946/1947. For example:

- (1850–1851) Félicien de Saulcy coined the name Qumran (or Gumran) and declared it the site of the notorious biblical city of Gomorrah.

- (1855) Henry Poole excavated burials in the cemetery at Qumran, but found no bones.

- (1873) C. Clermont-Ganneau surveyed the ruin, and concluded the site was not important. His description of the cemetery and a grave he excavated are of note.

- (1914) Gustav Dalman decided that the ruins were left from a Roman fort.

- (1938) Martin Noth was first to suggest that Qumran was the City of Salt (Josh 15:62).

- (1940) D. C. Baramki noted the ruined buildings, reservoir, boundary wall, and more than 700 graves. He concluded that the graves resemble Bedouin ones, but are not orientated like Muslim graves.

- (1946) S. Husseini surveyed the site, noting the ruins, plastered reservoir, corner towers, cemetery, aqueduct, and "extensive garden walls" between Khirbet Qumran and Ain Feshkha to the south. The pottery, he added, was "Byzantine and Arab including one Iron Age fragment."

2.2 The De Vaux-Harding Excavations (1951–1956) and De Vaux's Hypothesis

(a) Overview

Until the discovery of the first scrolls in 1946/1947, the site was considered of little significance. The first caves containing manuscripts (Cave 1) were located within 1.5 kilometers of the site, and as several more caves were unearthed near Qumran, some relationship between the scrolls and the site became evident: Caves 4, 5, 6, 7, 8, 9, and 10 are all within several hundred yards of Qumran.

While excavating the first cave in 1949, Roland de Vaux, from the École Biblique; and Lankester Harding, director of Antiquities in Jordan, visited Qumran, but found no archaeological evidence linking the site and the cave. Since they had managed only a quick surface examination and opened two tombs, they decided to return later. From 1951 to 1956, de Vaux and Harding—assisted by many local workers—spent five "seasons" excavating Khirbet Qumran, under the auspices of the Jordanian Department of Antiquities, the École, and the Palestine Archaeological Museum. They were first to make the connection between the manuscript discoveries and Qumran explicit and to identify it as the Essene settlement described by Pliny the Elder in his *Natural History*.

(b) The Buildings

With each season, more of the site and buildings were uncovered, and de Vaux gradually wrote up his findings. Some were published in French in the journal *Review Biblique* and a book (1961), and twelve years later in English (*Archaeology and the Dead Sea Scrolls*, 1973). However, this volume provides only an overview of the archaeology of Qumran and is not a complete, scientific report. When de Vaux passed away in 1971, the material finds from the site were passed to the École Biblique, the Dominican institution to which he was attached. The final report of the excavation, overseen by archaeologist Jean-Baptiste Humbert of the École, is projected in five volumes, of which three were published by 2003.

De Vaux proposed and refined a hypothesis that has become accepted, though not in every detail, by most scholars who study the Dead Sea Scrolls and the archaeology of the Qumran site (for others who disagree, see below). He identified three overall Periods in which the site was occupied or at least in use, with the main one (the Sectarian Period and its Aftermath) in the first century B.C.E. Many scholars refer to the stages of occupation within this Period also as *periods*, which is confusing. For greater clarity I follow James VanderKam (2010) by using *phases* instead, and reserve *periods* for three more general time spans (see below).

(c) De Vaux's Hypothesis for Interpreting the Qumran Site

The Israelite (or Iron Age) Period. In the eighth to seventh centuries B.C.E., a small dwelling stood on the site. Pottery and the remains of a rectangular building were discovered, as well as a large courtyard with a row of rooms. Excavators also found a jar handle with a Hebrew inscription meaning "of the king" and an ostracon that had writing in paleo-Hebrew. De Vaux associated the site with 2 Chronicles 26:10, where King Uzziah of Judah "built towers in the wilderness and hewed out many cisterns." It could also be the remains of a city named *Secacah* in Joshua 15:61.

The Sectarian Period and Its Aftermath. The site was abandoned for several centuries, after which comes de Vaux's second main period. He distinguished three phases of settlement. **Phase I** (subdivided into **Ia** and **Ib**) and **Phase II** form the Sectarian Period, when the site was occupied by the *Yahad* Essenes (who are associated with the sectarian scrolls). **Phase III** is the Aftermath, featuring military occupation by Roman forces (after the community was destroyed or expelled) from 68 C.E. to near the end of the first century.

Phase Ia. De Vaux found it difficult to date these constructions, since very few survive due to later construction and destruction. No coins survive nor any distinctive pottery (possibly a few pots in the southern part). He began this phase in about 140 B.C.E., with coins and pottery from the next phase as his main evidence, admittedly making it difficult to distinguish this phase from the next.

Phase Ib. This phase probably began in the reign of the Hasmonean king and high priest John Hyrcanus (134–104 B.C.E.), but the site was certainly occupied during the reign of Alexander Jannaeus (103–76 B.C.E.). The archaeological remains show significant expansion, and that the number of people associated with the site had rapidly grown. During this time the site assumed its most definitive shape. Upper stories were added, and the buildings were extended to the west and south. De Vaux identified the most prominent new additions as a two-story tower, a communal assembly hall or dining room, and an adjacent pantry. The impressive water system was extended. The main addition was an aqueduct (bringing winter rainwaters from the wadi), which de Vaux considered the most striking characteristic of Khirbet Qumran. The large pools were equipped with steps, the upper part divided by a low partition. De Vaux initially believed they were used as ritual baths, but later he concluded they were probably simple cisterns, with the steps to facilitate drawing water. This phase ended in an earthquake and a fire, which damaged the buildings. De Vaux equated the earthquake to the one that struck Judah in 31 B.C.E. (Josephus, *Jewish War* 1.370–80; *Antiquities* 15.121–47), but admitted that the case for connecting the disasters shown by the ruins and reported by Josephus is circumstantial. The site then lay abandoned for a time, which is suggested by the absence of coins of King Herod the Great (37–4 B.C.E.).

Phase II. Around the time Herod Archelaus began his reign (about 4 B.C.E.–6 C.E.), the site was rebuilt. Debris was cleaned, structures and cisterns were repaired, and the buildings were reoccupied by the same group that had earlier used it. The base of the tower was reinforced, and de Vaux identified the remains of a second story to the largest room in the building. On this floor, the long table, one or two shorter tables, low seats along the walls, a low platform, and two inkwells pointed to a scriptorium (writing hall). Some later critics would charge that de Vaux, a Dominican priest, was influenced by his Catholic roots to view Qumran as an early Jewish monastery. Phase II ended with the final destruction of the site in 68 C.E. by Roman troops of Vespasian's Tenth Legion who were putting down the First Jewish Revolt of 66–73. Several iron arrowheads were found, as well as widespread evidence of a massive fire. De Vaux's date of 68 is very plausible, in light of numismatic evidence (coins) found in the layers of Qumran: 83 from the second year of the Revolt (67–68), only five from the third year (68–69). Also, the iron arrowheads were of the type used by Roman soldiers in the first century C.E.

Phase III. Following its devastation, Roman soldiers occupied the site, and constructed a few barracks in the southwestern corner of the central building. They most likely remained there until near the end of the century, to judge by a series of coins lasting until about 90 C.E.

The Postscript Period. The site lay abandoned for many years, but de Vaux also found 13 coins from the Second Jewish Revolt (or Bar Kokhba period, 132–135 C.E.). He concluded that these did not signify another period of occupation, only a brief time of use, after which the site was finally abandoned for good.

2.3 Modifications from Scholars Who Support De Vaux's Overall Hypothesis

De Vaux's interpretation of the Qumran buildings as being used by Essenes has prevailed to the present day, but often with some modification.

(a) Should Phase Ia Be Eliminated?

Ernest Laperrousaz, a scholar also associated with the École Biblique, participated in the excavations of Qumran and interpreted the archaeological evidence differently. For example: what he called "Phase Ia" began in 104/103 B.C.E. and soon developed into Phase Ib, thus doing away with de Vaux's earlier Phase Ia. On this point, many archaeologists and other scholars agree (for example, Jodi Magness [2002]).

Jean-Baptiste Humbert of the École Biblique has published results of the Quamran excavation. One key volume, *The Excavations of Khirbet Qumran and Ain Feshkha*, vol. 1B, 2003, is in English. Like de Vaux, he accepted an earlier occupation of the site, but as a villa or manor house for agricultural purposes. Humbert believes that it begins in de Vaux's Phase Ia and was destroyed in 57 B.C.E. by the Roman Gabinius or in 31 B.C.E. by King Herod. This time line, he adds, helps explain the presence of Hasmonean coins at Qumran.

(b) The Beginning of Phase Ib

For Magness, de Vaux's argument for beginning Phase Ib by the reign of Alexander Jannaeus (103–76 B.C.E.) or even earlier is not convincing. She proposes, instead, that the site was probably resettled only in the first half of the first century (between 100 and 50 B.C.E.). For Humbert, however, Phase Ib began when Essenes took over the site in 31 B.C.E.

(c) Little or No Gap Between Phases I and II

Laperrousaz also challenged de Vaux's view that Phase Ib ended with the earthquake of 31 B.C.E., proposing instead a Hasmonean attack between 67 and 63; thus, for him, the period between Phases I and II was even longer. In 1992, archaeologist Magen Broshi focused on the 561 silver coins found by de Vaux's excavators. He accepted that Phase Ib ended with the earthquake of 31 B.C.E. and the fire that followed, but by 26 B.C.E. the site was most likely settled and the land cultivated. Thus Broshi eliminated all or most of the gap between Phases I and II.

Magness reached a different conclusion by reassessing the silver coins. Almost all are from Tyre, and the latest is dated to 9/8 B.C.E. Whereas de Vaux assigned these coins to the *beginning* of Phase II, Magness assigned them to the *end* of Phase Ib, which eliminates a long period of abandonment between Phases I and II. Rather than being deserted for more than 20 years due to the earthquake, she argued, the site was abandoned for only a short period due to destruction by fire.

Magness agrees with de Vaux's view that Phase II began early in the reign of Herod Archelaus (4 B.C.E.–6 C.E.), when the same group returned to the site, cleared it, and rebuilt it.

(d) The Site and Buildings Used by a Sectarian Movement (the *Yahad* Essenes)

A major issue for scholars is whether the Qumran site was settled by a specific Jewish group. De Vaux's conclusion that it was occupied by Essenes who used the buildings for religious and other purposes during Phases I and II is supported by most scholars. Evidence includes sectarian items such as ritual baths (*mikva'ot*) and signs of the custom of depositing animal bones outside buildings. Moreover, the communal assembly hall and adjacent pantry identified by de Vaux tie in nicely with key sectarian scrolls that feature religious community life (such as the *Rule of the Community*). Some features from Humbert's version of the archaeological results will be helpful:

- Essenes took over the site in 31 B.C.E.

- The Essenes turned it into a cultic center for their other settlements in the area.

- This cultic center was on the north side of the complex, the one facing Jerusalem, and included a court and an altar. There the Essenes offered sacrifices.

- There was no break during the Essene occupation, but the site was modified.

- Only 10 to 15 "guardians" lived permanently in the buildings at Qumran, while others working at the site came from outside.

- The site was destroyed by the Romans in 68 C.E.

Thus Humbert supports de Vaux's overall thesis, but is more controversial in some specifics. For example, no evidence for the offering of sacrifices in the buildings of Qumran has been found by other archaeologists.

2.4 Scholars Who Propose Different Interpretations of the Buildings

For some scholars, this was never a sectarian site, and so the buildings had very different purposes. Their proposals have at times led to marked disagreements at academic meetings and in the pages of popular magazines such as the *Biblical Archaeology Review*.

(a) The Ruins of a Fortress

As mentioned above, some early explorers of the Qumran site—such as Gustav Dalman—took it to be a small fortress of some sort. Norman Golb of Chicago University has argued (1995) that the Qumran site was a fortress erected by the Hasmoneans and maintained by Jewish garrisons until its destruction by the Romans in 68 C.E. Consequently his belief is that the scrolls have no connection to the site, but were hastily deposited in the caves by fleeing residents of Jerusalem during the First Jewish Revolt, especially the siege of Jerusalem in 70 C.E. These residents, Golb maintains, were from various Jewish groups, and any attempt to reconstruct a system of beliefs or practices from the scrolls is artificial since they are writings from a diverse range of libraries and collections in Jerusalem. Golb's theory has not met with much favorable support among the scholarly community, for several reasons:

- There is no reference to such a fortress in the ancient sources.

- The layout of Qumran is unlike all fortresses of the time.

- Only the tower was sufficiently sturdy for military needs.

- The buildings are poorly located for military security.

However, Golb has heightened interest in a period of military occupation of the site before it was settled by the Essenes.

(b) A Country Villa (or Manor House)

A different proposal came from Belgian scholars Robert Donceel and Pauline Donceel-Voûte (1994), with three main features:

Qumran was a place of industry, including work with balsam and bitumen, and integrated into the regional economy. Fine glassware, stoneware, metalwares, and coins suggest that its residents were wealthy traders, with connections to the upper classes and the wealthy in Jerusalem.

Qumran was a *villa rustica* (country villa or wealthy manor house), possibly a winter or second home to a rich family from Jerusalem. Thus it was not a sectarian site.

The furniture from the second story of the largest building belonged to a *triclinium* (a dining room with three couches, on which reclining banqueters ate), as found in many archaeological sites along the eastern Mediterranean. Thus the inkwells found there had no relationship to the furniture. In contrast, de Vaux had concluded this room to be a scriptorium.

These proposals have been rejected by most scholars. First, the Donceels fail to explain why any wealthy family would want to spend the winter at dry and rugged Qumran when the lush destination resort of Jericho was so close by. Second, as Donceel-Voûte conceded, this precise type of "dining couch" has not been found at any other archaeological site.

(c) A Site with One or More Functions

An Early Field Fort or Road Station. Several scholars believe that Qumran had different functions over the centuries. For Yizhar Hirschfeld (2004), the site was occupied during the Hasmonean period (before 37 B.C.E.), but only as a field fort or road station. This view is supported by Lena Cansdale and Alan Crown (1995), and by Yizhak Magen and Yuval Peleg (2006).

An Early Villa. The view of Jean-Baptiste Humbert was discussed above: the site was first occupied as a villa or manor house for agricultural purposes. (But his belief is that it was later occupied and used by Essenes.)

A Commercial Center. Donceel-Voûte argued that Qumran was place of industry and integrated into the regional economy. For Hirschfeld, too, it was a fortified house or agriculture-based trading station during the Herodian period. For Cansdale and Crown, Qumran became a port town on the shores of the Dead Sea and a commercial site on a major north-south trade route. Magen and Peleg suggest a more specific industrial purpose: a pottery production plant, with the water system bringing in clay-laced water. David Stacey (2007) proposes that Qumran served as a tannery and a facility for producing pottery, both of them seasonal due to the scarcity of year-round water.

Part of the Wider Region. According to Rachel Bar-Nathan (2006), the settlement is best seen as part of the wider Jordan Valley, with the same type of pottery found at several other sites, such as Masada and Jericho. More specifically, David Stacey associates the site with an estate at Jericho.

2.5 Is the Qumran Site Connected to the Caves and the Scrolls?

(a) Finding Connections

Most scholars accept de Vaux's finding of a connection between Qumran and the caves and that Essene sectarians from the site deposited scrolls in the caves, most likely before it was destroyed by Roman troops in 68 C.E. For others who believe Qumran was never a sectarian site, there is no connection. Golb and Hirschfeld, for example, believe that the texts were hastily deposited in the caves by fleeing residents of Jerusalem just before its destruction in 70.

It is very reasonable to find connections between the Qumran site and the caves in which manuscripts were found, since they are mostly close to each other. For example, Caves 7–9 are accessible only by passing through the settlement, and Cave 4—which contained about 90 percent of the Qumran scrolls—is about 300 yards away. The other caves are farther, most notably 1, 3, and 11. For archaeologist Eric M. Meyers (2010), to ignore the scrolls when studying the Qumran site—even if one believes they were deposited in the caves during the First Revolt—seems to avoid the obvious. The majority of scholars now see in the site, the caves, and the scrolls a unique opportunity: the site where a community lived, the places where they deposited their sacred texts, and the contents of those writings can all be studied together. Here is a very special instance in which the archaeological material and textual finds closely complement one another. Confidence in real connections between the site and the scrolls is bolstered by the next four points of evidence (b through e).

(b) The Water System and the Ritual Baths

First, the extensive water system at the site is best explained in light of the concern for ritual purity that is evident in the sectarian scrolls. For Magen Broshi (2000), the presence of ten ritual baths (*miqva'ot*) in such a compact area confirms that it was a center for ritual purification. Broshi calculates that these occupy 17 percent of the entire site, the highest density for any site in Israel. For Meyers (2010), too, the *miqva'ot* represent a disproportionate amount of space and effort for the settlement's size, showing that religious practice was a central component of the occupants' lifestyle.

(c) A Concern for Purity

The concern for ritual purification at the site corresponds closely with the desire for purity in the sectarian literature from Qumran. Jonathan Klawans (2010) finds four main points of agreement: (i) the centrality of purity law for the Qumran sect; (ii) the integration of purity laws with the group's dualism and sectarian social structure, notably in the *Rule of the Community*; (iii) correspondence between the literary evidence and archaeological evidence, notably the *miqva'ot*; and (iv) the contrast between the Qumran sectarians and the later rabbis, who had more lenient views.

Many relevant passages may be cited from the sectarian scrolls. For example, the *Damascus Document* mentions the need to abstain from "defiling the sanctuary" (CD 4:18; 5:6; and 12:1), which most likely involved ritual cleansing. The idea of purity is also reflected in the *War Rule* (1QM) and in *Some of the Works of the Law* (4QMMT).

> [Co]ncerning streams of liquid, we have determined that they are not intrinsically [p]ure. Indeed, streams of liquid do not form a barrier between the impure and the pure. For the liquid of the stream and that in its receptacle become as one liquid (section B, lines 55–58). (*Dead Sea Scrolls: A New Translation*, 458–59)

Purification Liturgy (4Q284) and *Rituals of Purification A* (4Q414) and *B* (4Q512) describe some of the rituals and shed light on their significance. For example, 4Q512 directs that when the member has completed "the seven days of [his] puri[fication," he is to wash his clothes in water, cover his nakedness with his clothes, and say "Blessed are You], O God of Isr[ae]l" (frg. 11 x.2–5).

(d) Physical Evidence Connecting the Site to Caves That Contained Scrolls

The Scroll Jars. The same type of jar in which several scrolls were deposited was found at the Qumran site and in some of the caves. These cylindrical, widemouthed containers were named *scroll jars* by de Vaux because of their close resemblance to the jar from Cave 1 that contained the book of Isaiah (1QIsaᵃ), the *Rule of the Community* (1QS), and the *Habakkuk Commentary* (1QpHab). Various purposes for these jars have been suggested; Jodi Magness, for example, believes they were used for storing food and to ensure its purity.

This type is extremely rare outside of Qumran, since the vast majority of jars found at other archaeological sites in Israel have much narrower necks and mouths. However, a very small number of similar jars have been found at Jericho, Masada, and possibly Qalandiya near Hebron. Jan Gunneweg, an archaeologist and archaeometrist (who measures aspects of ancient remains) at the Hebrew University is part of the Material and Bio Culture Qumran Project 1998–2010. Using Instrumental Neutron Activation Analysis, his research traces pottery by its chemical composition to the place where it was manufactured. Gunneweg reported that some of the scroll jars were made using clay found at Qumran and others using Motsa (or terra rosa) clay from Hebron, farther southwest.

The fact that the scroll jars are almost exclusive to the Qumran site and the nearby caves, and at least some were made from clay found at Qumran, strengthens the case for a connection between the site and the caves.

Ancient Pathways. The relationship between the caves, their contents, and the site is bolstered by the discovery of an ancient network of paths that connected the caves and the site. These pathways (for which Broshi and Eshel found evidence in coins and nails from sandals dated to the first century C.E.) indicate that there was considerable human traffic between Khirbet Qumran and the caves.

(e) Sectarian Scrolls Found in the Caves and the Site Plan Envisage a Communal Group

Evidence that the sectarian scrolls were products of a communal group or movement is found in several key texts, including the *Damascus Document*, the *Rule of the Community* (CD), the *Rule of the Congregation* (1Q28a), and *Some of the Works of the Law*. The authors of many scrolls present a mind-set that corresponds with the function of Qumran as a communal site. This is evident in key words for denoting themselves, especially *Yahad* (Community) and *Congregation* (CD 7:20; 10:4, 8; 13:13; 14:10; 1QSa 1:16–17, 19, 23–25). The layout of the site also has a community in mind. Most notable is the large assembly hall or dining room, with an adjacent pantry stacked with 708 bowls and 210 plates, which indicates enough room for a large number of people to meet there.

3. The Qumran Cemeteries

3.1 Early Excavations

The first known excavation in the cemetery at Qumran was conducted in 1855 by explorer Henry Poole, who found no bones. For C. Clermont-Ganneau in 1873, the most interesting feature of the site was the tombs, one of which he excavated. These are distinguished by their N-W orientation (with the buried person's head facing south and feet facing north) from more recent Muslim graves whose axes point E-W (the head facing Mecca). This feature, he wrote, indicated that they belonged to non-Muslims, most likely an early pagan Arab tribe. He also observed that the graves were constructed with some care and respect for their occupants but were not Christian since they lacked Christian marks or emblems. Over 60 years later in 1940, D. C. Baramki agreed, noting that the graves are not correctly orientated for Muslim graves.

3.2 The De Vaux-Harding Excavations of the Qumran Cemeteries

From 1949 to 1955, de Vaux and Harding opened and excavated tombs in three cemeteries near Khirbet Qumran. While excavating the first cave in 1949, they visited the site and opened two tombs in the Main Cemetery.

In the first official season of excavation (1951), they opened nine more, and concluded that bodies were buried there during the time the main building was occupied. De Vaux later observed that the buildings and cemetery were the central meeting place for the living and the resting place for the dead "of a community which practiced a strict discipline to which the arrangement of the cemetery attests."

In the second season (1953), several more tombs were opened. During the fourth (1955), de Vaux and Harding spotted a second small cemetery north of the ruins, containing a dozen tombs that were grouped and others that were haphazard. They excavated two graves, which proved similar to those in the Main Cemetery. In the fifth season (1956), 18 more tombs from the large cemetery were excavated. De Vaux and Harding also found to the south of Khirbet Qumran a third cemetery containing 30 graves, four of which they opened.

So by 1956, about 1,200 tombs had been found in three cemeteries: the Main Cemetery (tombs aligned N-S) with its Extension to the east (tombs less carefully arranged, often differently oriented), the North Cemetery, and the South Cemetery.

A total of 43 graves were excavated. Bones from 14 tombs in the Main Cemetery were sent to Professor Henri-Victor Vallois, director of the Musée de l'Homme in Paris, for analysis. Later, Gottfried Kurth of Göttingen examined several skeletons from the Main Cemetery, finding them all to be males and in N-S tombs. Additional tombs in the Extension contained four skeletons of women in E-W graves, one of a child (E-W), and one of undetermined sex (N-S). Kurth also identified five skeletons from four graves in the South Cemetery to include one female (E-W) and three infants (one N-W, two E-W). From the North Cemetery, the two opened graves contained a woman of 30–35 years and a man of over 50 years.

On the basis of this early evidence, de Vaux drew several tentative conclusions:

- All the graves are of the same type, and seem connected with the occupation of Qumran in Phases I and II.

- The well-ordered section of the Main Cemetery contains only tombs of males, except for one female in tomb 7.

- The Extension of the Main Cemetery to the east includes four women and one infant.

- The North Cemetery contains males and females.

- The South Cemetery includes four children and a woman.

- None of the graves containing males had objects with the body, whereas three of the women's tombs had some ornaments.

- Tombs 17 and 19 (opened in 1953) and 32 and 36 (1956) had the remains of wooden coffins, suggesting that the bodies may have been brought from elsewhere.

- Three tombs (11, 24, 37) contain disjointed skeletons, perhaps indicating reburial. These could be from another site, or were burials of victims of the earthquake by those who reoccupied the site.

3.3 Scientific Analysis of the Skeletons Excavated at Qumran

In April 1966, with the permission of the Jordanian Department of Antiquities, journalist Solomon Steckoll excavated a tomb at Qumran and later (December 1966 and March 1967) 10 or 11 more in the Main Cemetery. The first skeleton was studied by physical anthropologists and for many years remained the only one to receive full scientific examination.

The 1990s saw renewed interest among scholars for a modern scientific analysis of the Qumran tombs and the skeletal remains. However, with the conquest and occupation of the West Bank by Israel in June 1967, digging up Jewish burials and working with human remains became virtually impossible, since these activities are forbidden in Jewish law.

In 2001, the Main Cemetery was remapped using GPR (Ground Penetrating Radar), locating several additional graves and finding several tombs that had been clandestinely excavated. Hanan Eshel, Magen Broshi, Richard Freund, and Brian Schultz (2002) report a total of 1,054 tombs in the Main Cemetery, of which 999 are N-S in orientation and 55 are E-W. The estimated total for all three cemeteries is 1,213, of which 995 are unexcavated graves, 82 are excavated ones (with or without a permit), and 136 are potential burials. The number of excavated graves is approaching 100, since a further three were dug up by Broshi and Eshel (1995–1996 or later), and nine more by Yitzhak Magen and Yuval Peleg (1996–1999 or later). The number of documented tomb excavations is 68 (one by Clermont-Ganneau, 43 by de Vaux, 12 by Steckoll, three by Broshi and Eshel, and nine by Magen and Peleg).

From de Vaux's 43 tombs, about 14 skeletons had been sent to Henri-Victor Vallois in France and 22 to Gottfried Kurth in Germany. These seem to have disappeared for several decades but came to light in the 1990s.

The French Collection features bones from 20 skeletons dug up by de Vaux (those sent to Vallois and several more at the École Biblique in Jerusalem). Scientific analysis was carried out by Susan Guise Sheridan, a specialist in biological and forensic anthropology at the University of Notre Dame. She reports (2002) that the sample size of exhumed individuals is poorly preserved and too small to make generalizations about the larger community at Qumran, such as how they adapted, their daily life, diet, health, longevity, or demographics. She collected data for creating a bio-cultural model of life at Qumran, hoping that comparison to bodies found elsewhere in the region and future excavations at the site will provide a more complete picture.

Sheridan found that interesting life histories can be constructed for some of the buried individuals, who were mostly male (except for one woman in tomb 15 and possibly another in tomb 5), over 30 years of age (except for one boy in tomb 15), and highly religious.

The German Collection has been examined by Olav Röhrer-Ertl, now at the University of Munich. He expresses the limitations of working with such a small and poorly preserved sample, but has some interesting results (1999). Rohrer-Ertl has "resexed" several skeletons to produce the following numbers: 17 from the Main Cemetery (nine males, seven females, one young girl) and five from the South Cemetery (one female, three boys, one child of undetermined sex).

These findings from French and German collections are important for determining whether the community at Qumran was a male celibate society. While most of the opened tombs contained male skeletons, the presence of females and children—even in the Main Cemetery—raises questions about the nature of the community.

In 2006, Brian Schultz reassessed all published results on the cemeteries, and identified 32 excavated tombs he believes can be confidently dated to the Second Temple period. These include skeletons of five women, each of which presents challenges or is open to dispute.

Schultz concluded that the three cemeteries support the view of most scholars that Qumran was a community center for a predominantly male sectarian group in the first century B.C.E. and first century C.E. His evidence includes a "total absence of children" in the Main Cemetery (but see above, on the German Collection) and that this cemetery shows greater uniformity with respect to burial orientation than any other Second Temple cemetery. He accepts that some women were buried by the sectarians, which suggests special treatment of certain women by this male-dominated community.

3.4 Intrusive Burials: Do All the Graves at Qumran Date from the Second Temple Period?

Joe Zias, curator of archaeology and anthropology for the Israel Antiquities Authority from 1972 to 1997, raises the important issue of "intrusive burials" (whether the Qumran cemeteries were reused in later times). Pointing to the beads, a finger ring, and earrings found in some of the tombs, Zias questioned whether all were ancient burials, since beads are not found in Second Temple Jewish graves. Also noting five Bedouin burial practices (such as E-W orientation and grave goods), Zias concludes that graves in the Qumran cemeteries with an E-W orientation are Muslim ones, containing Bedouin who were buried in the fifteenth century C.E.

Another reason Zias doubts certain burials were from ancient times is that the bones of women and children, normally the least likely to be preserved intact, are the best preserved at Qumran. He uses dental evidence from the excavated skeletons to suggest that the males in the Main Cemetery (with relatively good teeth) came from different areas (such as cities) to the desert, whereas the women in the other cemeteries (with much poorer teeth) were desert-dwellers whose teeth show greater damage due to an abrasive and sandy diet.

In the Main Cemetery, Zias cites the lack of extended family tombs comprising several generations (found in nearby Jewish sites such as Ein Gedi and Jericho) and the absence of females and children as attesting to a celibate community of males. (However, Rohrer-Ertl's identification of several females and a young girl in this cemetery challenge these results.)

Zias also observes that the strict orientation of these graves along a N-S axis deviates from other Jewish burial norms and suggests this may be due to the community's opposition toward the priestly class in Jerusalem. If Zias is correct, his evidence for a community of males living at Qumran must be confined to the Main Cemetery, since many burials in the Extension and the other two cemeteries would not be ancient.

In his reassessment, Schultz also compared the Qumran burials with Muslim burial practices. He found that the E-W orientation of some Qumran graves does not always mean they are Muslim ones, and that a N-S orientation does not always signify burials by the Qumran sectarians. For example, of the 14 burials that he identifies as intrusive (that is, long after the Qumran period), six are oriented N-S.

3.5 Population Estimates and the Qumran Cemeteries

Using archaeological data, several scholars have tried to estimate the population of Qumran. For de Vaux, the length of time the community was there, the number of graves, and the average lifetime of the residents (deduced from study of the skeletons), showed that the group numbered not many more than 200. Most, he believed, lived in tents or huts in the area. De Vaux also suggested that some bodies were brought from elsewhere, so not all tombs in the cemeteries held the remains of members of the Qumran group. Laperrousaz, using the number 1,200 for the tombs and a mortality rate of 7 percent at Qumran, concluded that there were about 300 to 350 people at Qumran in Phase Ib and 340 to 400 in Phase II. Broshi, using the seating capacity of the meeting hall at 120 to 150, concluded that the community was no bigger than 150 to 200 members.

Much lower estimates have been proposed. In Patrich's resurvey of the area covered during the caves expedition of 1952, he excavated five caves (including 3 and 11). Patrich concluded that the membership lived mostly on the upper story at Qumran, and numbered no more than 50 to 70. Humbert's number is even lower: only ten to 15 "guardians" lived permanently in the Qumran complex, while others working at the site came from outside.

However, the number of graves in the three Qumran cemeteries (1,213) indicates a far higher number of community members than estimated by Patrich and Humbert. Even if some or many tombs are Muslim or other intrusive burials, it is reasonable to conclude that the majority of graves contained Qumran residents.

3.6 Is the Main Qumran Cemetery Unique?

At least one other cemetery has characteristics of the Main Cemetery at Qumran and is from the same time period. This is at Ain el-Ghuweir (about 10 miles to the south), and well over 800 yards from the nearest building. Nineteen graves were excavated by P. Bar Adon, who reported (1977) that he found skeletons of 13 males, six females, and one child. Bar Adon took this to be another Essene settlement, but de Vaux was skeptical and Broshi concluded that pottery from the two sites was not produced in the same place.

Farther south, another cemetery at Hiam el-Sagha contains about 20 N-S tombs. Two were examined, one containing a young child and the other a 25-year-old man. Some scholars find similarities between certain shaft tombs found in Jerusalem, one at Talpiot, another at Mamila, and about 25 at Beth Zafafa. Israeli scholar Boaz Zissu (1998) has shown that one type of tomb at Beit Safafa in southern Jerusalem resembles the Qumran method of burial and suggests that these may be tombs of Essenes living in Jerusalem.

Rachel Hachlili (2000) finds no real proof that the tombs at Beit Safafa in Jerusalem and Hiam el-Sagha are Jewish graves, but recognizes their strong similarity in form to the Qumran burials. Finally, in 1996 and 1997 excavations were carried out at Khirbet Qazone near the southern end of the Dead Sea in Jordan. About 3,500 tombs, most of them previously looted, were identified, all having similar characteristics to the Qumran graves. Twenty-three undisturbed burials were examined and found to hold Nabateans (an Arabian tribe best known for their city of Petra in modern Jordan).

Concluding Comments

With some modifications by later scholars, a new time line for de Vaux's three periods is:

- *The Israelite (or Iron Age) Period* (eighth to seventh centuries B.C.E.).

- *The Sectarian Period and Its Aftermath.*

- **Phase Iab.** Began late in the reign of John Hyrcanus (about 104 B.C.E.) or Alexander Jannaeus (103–76 B.C.E.); there was most likely no gap. Continued until 31 B.C.E. or as late as 8 B.C.E.

- **Phase II.** Began between 4 and 1 B.C.E. and continued until 68 C.E.

- **Phase III.** Roman soldiers occupied the site briefly after its destruction in 68 C.E.

- *The Postscript Period.* Brief use of the site during the Second Jewish Revolt (132 to 135 C.E.).

We may conclude that the site and buildings were used by a sectarian movement known as the *Yahad* Essenes, even if it initially served as a road station and pottery was produced there (by the *Yahad* Essenes). This group also hid all or most of the scrolls in the caves, most likely before Qumran was destroyed by Roman troops in 68 C.E.

From the three cemeteries, the skeletal remains studied so far support the view of most scholars that Qumran was a community center for a predominantly male sectarian group in the first century B.C.E. and first century C.E. A very small number of women were also likely buried by the sectarians, perhaps to show special treatment of certain women by this community. Bodies of later Bedouin were also buried at the site ("intrusive burials"), especially in the North and South Cemeteries and mostly in Muslim fashion (facing E-S).

With respect to population estimates, the cemeteries and buildings indicate that the community at Qumran numbered between 150 and 200. Perhaps 50 lived at the site itself, the others in nearby tents or huts.

3

Dating the Scrolls Found at Qumran

One major reason why the Dead Sea Scrolls are so important is the knowledge that these documents are ancient, not medieval. Most people who study the scrolls found at Qumran believe they were written or copied in the last few centuries B.C.E. and the first century C.E. If so, the scrolls are major witnesses to the late Second Temple period, early Judaism, the biblical text, and Christian beginnings. If the scrolls were copied much later (in medieval times), they would still be significant but far less so. It is crucial, therefore, that the Dead Sea Scrolls, especially those found at Qumran, be dated as accurately as possible. Another reason is to place the scrolls in their proper historical context, which is of vital importance for interpreting them.

None of the scrolls found at Qumran reveals exactly when or by whom it was written, so dating is no simple task. This chapter discusses four dating methods: archaeology, internal datings in the scrolls, paleography, and carbon-14 (radiocarbon) techniques.

1. Dating the Scrolls and the Qumran Site by Archaeology

Between 1949 and 1956, Caves 1–11 near Qumran were excavated by Roland de Vaux and Lankester Harding, and between 1984 and 1991 five caves (including 3 and 11) were re-excavated by Joseph Patrich. De Vaux and Harding also excavated the Qumran site and buildings over five seasons from 1951 to 1956. By studying physical remains such as layers of use or occupation, pottery, and coins from each layer, de Vaux arrived at a chronology for the Qumran site.

These studied remains are nonwritten ones, not the scrolls themselves. However, since most scholars believe the scrolls found near Qumran and the physical remains are related, the archaeological evidence is helpful for dating when many scrolls were written or were being used.

2. Internal Datings in the Scrolls

On rare occasions, some scrolls mention known historical figures or events from the Second Temple period. By providing such information, a particular Qumran scroll could not have been written before the named person lived or the event took place, but must have been written afterward (but no later than 68 C.E., when the Romans destroyed the site).

One important scroll for reconstructing the history behind the *Yahad* Essenes whose foremost community was at Qumran is the *Pesher on Nahum* (4QpNahum = 4Q169).

Jannaeus ruled over Israel as king and high priest from 103 to 76 B.C.E. (Josephus, *Antiquities* 13.375–76; *Jewish War* 1.90–92), and was affiliated with the Sadducees and priestly groups. However, he was resented for laxity in religious observance by some groups led by the Pharisees. Jannaeus' response was to suppress dissent by executing or banishing the rebels. In about 88 B.C.E., his enemies formed an alliance with King Demetrius III Eucarus of Syria, inviting him to invade Israel and depose their king. Demetrius complied and put Jannaeus to flight in a battle near Shechem. But now, with the threat of Gentile dominance over the Holy Land, many allies of the Pharisees switched sides to assist Jannaeus. Demetrius accordingly withdrew his armies. The *Pesher on Nahum* quotes and interprets Nahum 2:11b:

> *Wherever the old lion goes, there is the lion's cub* [2]*[without fear].* (Nahum 2:12b) [The old lion is Deme]trius, king of Greece, who sought to come to Jerusalem through the counsel of the Seekers of Slippery Answers, [3] [but the city never fell into the] power of the kings of Greece from Antiochus until the appearance of the rulers of the Kittim; but afterwards it will be trampled [4][by the Gentiles . . .] (frgs. 3–4 col. i.2–4) (Adapted from *The Dead Sea Scrolls: A New Translation*, 245)

Here the lion is most likely Demetrius III, the Seekers of Slippery Answers are the Pharisees, Antiochus is Antiochus IV Epiphanes (who sacked Jerusalem in 168 B.C.E.), and the Kittim are the Romans, whose army under Pompey conquered Jerusalem in 63 B.C.E. A bit further on (lines 6–7), the pesher mentions the Lion of Wrath (Jannaeus), who took vengeance against the Seekers of Slippery Answers (Pharisees) "because he used to hang men alive." This squares with Josephus' report that Jannaeus crucified 800 Pharisees, who were then forced to watch from their crosses as their wives and children were slaughtered (*Antiquities* 13.379–80).

A few more references to historical persons or events are found in several scrolls:

- Shelamsion (Queen Salome Alexandra, who ruled Judea from 76 to 67 B.C.E.), in *Historical Text C* (4Q331) frg. 1 col. 2.7.

- Hyrcanus (Hyrcanus II, who ruled with his mother from 76 to 67 B.C.E., and held some power from 63 to 40), in *Historical Text D* (4Q332 frg. 2.6) and *On Writing Exercises* (4Q341 frg. 1.7).

- Aemilius (Marcus Aemilius Scaurus, Roman governor in Syria from 65 to 62 B.C.E.), in *Hodayot-like Text A* (4Q433 frg. 1.4, 8).

- King Jonathan (Alexander Jannaeus, whose Hebrew name was Jonathan), in the *Hymn to King Jonathan* (4Q448).

- Peitholaus (a Jewish officer who joined Gabinius in his campaign against Alexander, son of Aristobulus II, and was executed in 53 B.C.E.; cf. Josephus, *Jewish War* 1.162–63, 180; *Antiquities* 14.84–85, 120), in *Historical Text F* (4Q468e) line 3.

3. Dating Dead Sea Scrolls Using Paleography

3.1 Early Work

The first scholars to date the scrolls made extensive use of paleography (the analysis of ancient handwriting). Paleography assumes that the ways in which scribes formed letters changed over time, and so many or most scrolls can be dated as earlier or later relative to each other. This method seems very reasonable; compare, for example, the United States *Declaration of Independence* or the *First Folio* (1623) of Shakespeare's plays with modern English writing. However, it was at first controversial and untested with respect to the Dead Sea Scrolls, since almost no other examples of Hebrew texts on parchment or papyrus from ancient Israel have survived. Of course, many ancient stone inscriptions have been found; Eleazar Sukenik was able to date the scrolls he purchased to the late Second Temple period because their scripts were similar to the writing styles on ossuaries from that time.

One rare manuscript from the period is the Nash Papyrus (acquired in Egypt in 1898), which contains the Ten Commandments and the *Shemaʿ* ("Hear, O Israel") from Deuteronomy 6:4. In 1937, William F. Albright compared the script with several other documents and inscriptions and was first to outline the development of the Aramaic (or Hebrew) script in the late Persian Empire and early Jewish handwriting that evolved from it. Albright dated the Nash Papyrus as between 150 and 100 B.C.E. John Trever was able to date the *Great Isaiah Scroll* by comparing its script to the Nash Papyrus and a few other texts that had been found.

Other early scholars who examined the scrolls paleographically are Solomon Birnbaum and Nahman Avigad. Both dated the scrolls from the second century B.C.E. to the first century C.E. (although Avigad dated 4QSamuel[b] to the third century B.C.E.).

3.2 The System of Dating Scrolls Developed by Frank Moore Cross

The most important system of dating Dead Sea Scrolls was developed by Frank Moore Cross (1921–2012). His landmark article "The Development of the Jewish Scripts" (1961)—updated as "Palaeography and the Dead Sea Scrolls" in *The Dead Sea Scrolls After Fifty Years* (Flint and Vanderkam, 1999)—remains the standard reference work on the scripts of the scrolls and other Jewish texts from the last few centuries of the Second Temple period.

Cross consulted the ancient texts available to him for comparison, mostly from Qumran but also from other sites (such as Nahal Hever and Wadi Murabba'at) and inscriptions. He distinguished three paleographic periods in which the Qumran scrolls were written and a fourth period that features later scrolls:

- The Archaic or Proto-Jewish Period (about 250–150 B.C.E.). The relatively few examples include 4QExod^b (275 to 225) and 4QSam^b (about 250).

- The Hasmonean Period (150–30 B.C.E.). Cross called this period "the heyday of sectarian composition," since the major sectarian texts were most likely composed during it. Examples include 4QDeut^a (175–150) and the *Rule of the Community* (100–75).

- The Herodian Period (30 B.C.E.–68/70 C.E.). The largest number of scrolls were copied during this period, including the Nahal Hever Psalms scroll (5/6HevPs, 301-1 C.E.), the *Pesharim* (*Commentaries*), and 4QPs^b (50–68 C.E.).

- The Post-Herodian Period (70–135 C.E.). One example is a Hebrew contract from Murabba'at (Mur 24, 133 C.E.).

Cross also distinguished four writing styles: formal, semiformal, cursive, and semicursive. A fifth should be added: the paleo-Hebrew script, an archaic form rarely used at Qumran. Most examples are of pentateuchal books (such as 4QpaleoExod^m). However, in several other scrolls (including the *Psalms Scroll*, 11QPs^a) the names for God were written in paleo-Hebrew letters—compare the translation "LORD" for the Hebrew *Yahweh* in many English Bibles.

3.3 Precise Datings Are Not Possible

None of the 1,050 or so Qumran scrolls discloses exactly when it was written, which means virtually all should be assigned relative dates. Thus paleography is a helpful tool for approximate dating of texts, usually within 50 or even 25 years. One exception is an ostracon with a partial date found more recently at the Qumran site, which mentions "the second year of" (perhaps the First Jewish Revolt against Rome, which is 67 C.E.).

4. Radiocarbon Methods of Dating

In 1949, Willard Libby and colleagues at the University of Chicago invented radiocarbon dating of organic objects. Virtually all the Dead Sea Scrolls were copied on parchment (treated animal hide) or papyrus (from plants), which are both organic, so carbon-14 analysis may be used to date them. To be precise, radiocarbon analysis supplies the number of years between the death of the plant or animal and the present time.

4.1 Early Radiocarbon Testing of Dead Sea Scrolls

On November 14, 1950, Libby received four ounces of linen from one of the Cave 1 scroll wrappers from G. Lankester Harding, director of the Jordanian Antiquities Authority. In January 1951, Libby announced that his carbon-14 test dated the linen at 33 C.E., plus or minus 200 years (and so between 167 B.C.E. and 233 C.E.).

Although this result was not very precise, it proved that the linen wrapper was ancient and not medieval, leading to the conclusion that the scroll or scrolls wrapped in it were ancient as well. The importance of this result was summed up by Ovid R. Sellers of McCormick Theological Seminary, who had proposed the test: "[E]pigraphy, archaeology, and nuclear physics now combine to support the genuineness and antiquity of the material found in the cave" (1951:29).

Libby tested only a linen wrapper, not a scroll, because at that time carbon-14 testing entailed the destruction of a large amount of material (two to five grams to get one gram of carbon for processing). Testing an actual text would entail losing too much of the precious scroll.

4.2 Accelerator Mass Spectrometry (AMS) Testing

Radiocarbon dating methods have advanced and become much more refined. Accelerator mass spectrometry (AMS) requires the loss of a tiny amount of material (0.02–0.1 gram), which makes it possible to subject scrolls and scroll fragments to testing.

In the 1990s, two sets of Dead Sea Scrolls were dated using AMS. In 1991, samples from 14 manuscripts from Qumran and five other sites were tested at the Institut für Mittelenergiephysik in Zurich, Switzerland. In 1994–1995, samples from 22 scrolls were tested at the University of Arizona's NSF Accelerator Mass Spectrometry Facility in Tucson, Arizona. Of the scrolls involved, only one (the *Great Isaiah Scroll*) was tested at both Zurich and Tucson.

The results from these two groups are presented in **Table 1**. Of the 35 scrolls, seven (none from Qumran) had their own ("internal") dates, which helps assess the effectiveness of the AMS dates.

These results are very encouraging. For six scrolls, the internal dates and the 1-s AMS dates correspond, with the internal dates falling at or near one end of the AMS range. The notable exception is the Deed of Sale in Aramaic (XHev/Se 8a), with more than a 100-year discrepancy. However, for this text the 2-s range is 140–390 C.E. (denoting 95 percent confidence). So even XHev/Se 8a fits the pattern of the internal date (134/35 C.E.) being near one extreme of the AMS date.

The two laboratories also tested 19 scrolls from the Qumran caves, all of which have no internal dates. The 22 results appear in **Table 2**, with one scroll (1QIsaᵃ) tested at both facilities, another (4Q258) tested twice at Tucson, and one (4Q22 or 4QpaleoExodᵐ) and its repair patch both tested. In **items 23–25** the dates for three more scrolls are included: 4Q342 (a letter), 4Q344 (an acknowledgment of debt), and 4Q345 (a bill of sale of land). However, these may not be from Qumran, so they are listed last.

All these scrolls—except for item 18 (4Q317, cryptA) which features a lunisolar calendar—have been given paleographic dates by scholars, which may be compared to the AMS dates:

Of these results, for the *2s-column* (95 percent certainty of the correct date), only seven fall outside the paleographic date range. However, four of these (**items 11, 12, 16, and 19**) are within a few years of being included, and one (**item 20**) is within 26 years. For the more restrictive *1s-column* (68 percent certainty), ten results are outside

Table 1.			
Text	**Internal Date**	**AMS Date: 1-s**	**AMS Date: 2-s**
1. WDSP 2	352/351 B.C.E.	(T) 399–357 or 287–234 C.E.	408 B.C.E.–203 C.E.
2. 5/6Hev 19	128 C.E.	(Z) 131–240 C.E.	84–322 C.E.
3. 5/6Hev 21	130 C.E.	(T) 132–324 C.E.	80–389 C.E.
4. XHev/Se 11	130/131 C.E.	(Z) 32–129 C.E.	2–220? C.E.
5. Mur 30	134/135 C.E.	(Z) 77–132 C.E.	32–224? C.E.
6. XHev/Se 8a	134/135 C.E.	(T) 237–340 C.E.	140–390 C.E.
7. Mird	744 C.E.	(Z) 676–775 C.E.	660–803 C.E.

Key: (T) = test done in Tucson (Z) = test done in Zurich
1-s = 68 percent confidence that correct date falls within proposed limits
2-s = 95 percent confidence
Adapted from VanderKam and Flint, *The Meaning of the Dead Sea Scrolls* (2002), 29

Table 2.			
Text	**Paleographic Date**	**AMS Date: 1-s**	**AMS Date: 2-s**
1. 1QIsaiah[a]	125–100 B.C.E.	(Z) 201–93 B.C.E.	351–296 or 230–48 B.C.E.
2. 1QIsaiah[a]	125–100 B.C.E.	(T) 341–325 or 202–114 B.C.E.	351–295 or 230–53 B.C.E.
3. 1QS	100–50 B.C.E.	(T) 164–144 or 116 B.C.E.–50 C.E.	344–323 B.C.E. or 203 B.C.E.–122 C.E.
4. 1QH[a]	30–1 B.C.E.	(Z) 37 B.C.E.–68 C.E.	47 B.C.E.–118 C.E.
5. 1QapGen	30 B.C.E.–30 C.E.	(Z) 47 B.C.E.–48 C.E.	89 B.C.E.–69 C.E.
6. 1QpHab	1–50 C.E.	(T) 88–2 B.C.E.	160–148 B.C.E. or 111 B.C.E.–2 C.E.
7. 4Q22 (paleoEx[m])	100–25 B.C.E.	(T) 164–144 or 116 B.C.E.–48 C.E.	203 B.C.E.–83 C.E. or 105–115 C.E.
8. 4Q22 (repair patch)	—	(T) 51 B.C.E.–47 C.E.	161–146 or 113 B.C.E.–70 C.E.
9. 4Q53 (Sam[c])	150–30 B.C.E.	(Z) 196–47 B.C.E.	349–318 B.C.E. or 228 B.C.E.–18 C.E.

Table 2 (continued).			
10. 4Q171 (pPs[a])	1–70 C.E. (?)	(T) 29–81 C.E.	3–126 C.E.
11. 4Q208 (Enastr[a])	225–175 B.C.E.	(T) 167–53 B.C.E.	172–48 B.C.E.
12. 4Q213 (Levi)	50–25 B.C.E.	(Z) 197–105 B.C.E.	344–324 or 203–53 B.C.E.
13. 4Q249 (cryptA)	190–150 B.C.E.	(T) 196–47 B.C.E.	349–304 or 228 B.C.E.–18 C.E.
14. 4Q258 (S[d])	30–1 B.C.E.	(T) 133–237 C.E., 1st sample	129–255 C.E. or 303–318 C.E.
15. 4Q258 (S[d])	30–1 B.C.E.	(T) 36 B.C.E.–81 C.E., 2nd sample	50 B.C.E.–130 C.E.
16. 4Q266 (Dam-Doc[a])	100–50 B.C.E.	(T) 4–82 C.E.	44 B.C.E.–129 C.E.
17. 4Q267 (Dam-Doc[b])	30–1 B.C.E.	(T) 168–51 B.C.E.	198–3 B.C.E.
18. 4Q317 (cryptA)	?	(T) 166–48 B.C.E.	196–1 B.C.E.
19. 4Q365 frg. 3	40–10 B.C.E.	(Z) 339–327 or 202–112 B.C.E.	351–296 or 230–53 B.C.E.
20. 4Q521 (MessAp)	125–75 B.C.E.	(T) 39 B.C.E.–66 C.E.	49 B.C.E.–116 C.E.
21. 4Q542 (Qahat)	125–100 B.C.E.	(Z) 385–349 or 317–208 B.C.E.	395–181 B.C.E.
22. 11Q19 (Temple)	30 B.C.E.–30 C.E.	(Z) 53 B.C.E.–21 C.E.	166 B.C.E.–67 C.E.
23. 4Q342	1–30 C.E.	(T) 25–127 C.E.	43 B.C.E.–214 C.E.
24. 4Q344	after 70 C.E. (probably)	(T) 68–131 C.E.	24–226 C.E.
25. 4Q345	60–10 B.C.E.	(T) 361–168 or 141–125 B.C.E.	392–51 B.C.E.

Key: (T) = test done in Tucson (Z) = test done in Zurich
1-s = 68 percent confidence that correct date falls within proposed limits
2-s = 95 percent confidence
Adapted from VanderKam and Flint, *The Meaning of the Dead Sea Scrolls* (2002), 30

the paleographic range, but three are within a few years. These figures show that for the vast majority of scrolls from Qumran that were tested, the paleographic and AMS dates overlap, and in a few cases very nearly so.

In two cases, however, there is a marked discrepancy. For **item 14**, the 134-year discrepancy in the Zurich test of 4Q258 (*Rule of the Community*[d]) may be due to contamination. The later Tucson test (**item 15**) yielded 2s-results within the paleographical date range of 30–1 B.C.E. and 1s-results within just a few years. For **item 21** (4Q542, the *Testament of Qahat*), the discrepancy is at 56 years. This AMS result may be an *outlier* due to contamination; even a scholar's fingerprint can have this effect.

The only scroll to be included in both the Zurich and the Tucson tests was the *Great Isaiah Scroll* (**items 1 and 2**). The 2s-results reported by the two laboratories are almost identical, while for the 1s-results the Tucson numbers are at 341–325 or 202–114 B.C.E., which encompass the Zurich figures of 201–93 B.C.E. The strong agreement between these results from the two laboratories is significant and reinforces confidence in the AMS method of dating.

4.3 Significance of the Radiocarbon Results

The results of the Zurich and Tucson tests are significant since they confirm the view of most scholars that the Qumran scrolls are ancient and were written or copied in the last few centuries B.C.E. and the first century C.E. Radiocarbon testing also shows high correspondences with the dates of manuscripts assigned by scholars on paleographical grounds, although there are a few exceptions.

As mentioned above, radiocarbon analysis supplies the number of years between the death of the plant or animal and the present time, which is not necessarily the date of a text. Thus the texts written on the scrolls are a little more recent in age. However, this is a minor obstacle, since the gap between the animal's death and the leather being used as a writing surface most likely was not a large one.

Concluding Comments

The four methods for dating materials from Qumran indicate that the scrolls found there were copied between the third century B.C.E. and the first century C.E. (radiocarbon dating allows even the fourth century B.C.E.). There is little or no likelihood that the scrolls and the buildings at the Qumran site belong to any other period. The datings for each method are as follows:

- Archaeology: second century B.C.E.–first century C.E.
- Internal Datings (allusions to historical figures): second century B.C.E.–first century C.E.
- Paleography: third century B.C.E.–first century C.E.
- Radiocarbon Dating / Accelerator Mass Spectrometry (AMS): 1-s (68 percent confidence): fourth B.C.E.–first C.E. 2-s (= 95 percent confidence): fourth B.C.E.–third C.E.

4

The Bible Before
the Scrolls

This title of this chapter is a tease. First, here the term *Bible* denotes only the Hebrew Bible/Old Testament, since the earliest books of the New Testament were being written down only when Qumran was destroyed by the Romans in 68 C.E. Second, there *was* no Hebrew Bible or Old Testament before the scrolls were written or copied, including those found at Qumran (dating up to 68), Masada (to 74), or even Murabba'at and Nahal Hever (to 135). However, there were three main ancient Bibles long before the first scrolls were discovered in 1946 (or 1947).

The following pages explore the texts of the Hebrew Bible/Old Testament available to us before the discovery of the Dead Sea Scrolls: the Masoretic Text (written in Hebrew and Aramaic), the Samaritan Pentateuch (in Hebrew), and the Septuagint ([LXX] in Greek). Other, later, collections include the Latin, Syriac, and Aramaic Bibles.

1. The Masoretic Text

1.1 Definition, Origins, and Growth

Almost all modern English translations of the Hebrew Bible or Old Testament are based on the Masoretic Text (MT). This term covers many manuscripts rather than a single one, so Masoretic Group or Masoretic Family would be more accurate. In its broader sense, the MT refers to any text of the Hebrew Bible produced by the Masoretes and to any copy of such a text. In its narrower—and more usual—sense, the MT denotes the standard text of the Hebrew Bible finalized by the Masoretes of Tiberias (in the Tiberian Tradition).

The Masoretes were a group of Jewish scholars from the eighth century C.E. onward who maintained ancient traditions and developed new ones for copying the biblical text for liturgical or scholarly use. Earlier scholars who had maintained these traditions, known as scribes, had as their chief concern establishing and preserving the correct form of the biblical text. Many scholars refer to the early form of the text that the Masoretes took over as the pre-Masoretic or proto-Masoretic Text.

The Hebrew Scriptures were originally written and copied in consonantal form only, that is, without vowels. Many words could thus be read in more than one way, leading to different meanings (*dg* in English could be *dig*, *dog*, or *dug*, depending on which vowels are used). As Jews dispersed to many areas in the early centuries of the Common Era, different understandings of many consonantal Hebrew words arose. In order to standardize the biblical text, the Masoretes added vowel signs and other components, which fixed the meaning of each group of consonants (that is, only *dig*, not *dog* or *dug*).

The Masoretic Text is by far the largest among all our textual witnesses of the Hebrew Bible. It underwent three periods of transmission (that is, being copied and handed down):

- The first period originated among Babylonian Jews, the Pharisees, or "temple circles," and ended with the destruction of the Temple in 70 C.E. or with the end of the Second Jewish Revolt (135). (The terms *pre-Masoretic* or *proto-Masoretic* are used for precursors of the MT in this period.)

- The second period of transmission extends from the destruction of the Temple 70 C.E. to the eighth century, with documents that show a high degree of textual consistency. (The terms *pre-Masoretic* and *proto-Masoretic* are also used for precursors of the MT in this period.)

- The third period extends from the eighth century until the end of the Middle Ages, and is characterized by almost complete textual unity. The complete apparatus of the Masorah (markings and marginal notes) is usually included, together with biblical quotations in the writings of medieval commentators. Since the addition of vowels and accents and the Masorah-demanded fixation of consonants, the MT became almost completely standardized.

1.2 Manuscripts of the Masoretic Text

There are many prominent Masoretic manuscripts, several with interesting stories of discovery and preservation.

Scrolls from the first period of transmission (up to 70 C.E.) include many Hebrew texts from Qumran (about 250 B.C.E. to 68 C.E.), Masada (before 74 C.E.), and ancient translations such as *kaige-Theodotion* (mid-first century B.C.E.).

Documents from the second period (70 to the eighth century C.E.) are several biblical scrolls from the Judean Desert and some translations into other languages. The earliest scrolls—all written before 135—were found at Murabba'at (parts of the Torah, Isaiah, the Minor Prophets) and at Nahal Hever (Genesis, Numbers, Deuteronomy, Psalms). The 600-year period that followed (third through eighth centuries) often called the "silent era," since almost no Hebrew manuscripts from that time survived. Reasons include continuing persecution of Jews and the related destruction of Hebrew manuscripts. Biblical manuscripts exist from this period in Greek, Latin, and other languages, but Hebrew texts in significant numbers date only from the ninth century onward.

Manuscripts from the third period of transmission (seventh or eighth century onward) are in two groups: from the early Middle Ages (up to about 1100) and later ones. Although differences between these manuscripts involve minute aspects, the earlier ones are more reliable.

The Rediscovery of an Important Early Masoretic Manuscript

In 2007, the Israel Museum in Jerusalem unveiled a rare text dated to the seventh or eighth century: the *Song of the Sea,* or *Ashkar Manuscript,* part of a Torah scroll containing Exodus. This section of the scroll was soon joined by another part, the darkened *London Manuscript* from the Stephan Loewentheil Collection in New York (which had been known for some 60 years). The *London Manuscript* was brought to Jerusalem, and in 2010 the Israel Museum announced the exhibition of the reunited fragments of the Hebrew scroll. The *London Manuscript* section features text from Exodus 9:18–13:1 (the seventh to tenth plagues, the Passover, and the exodus), and the *Song of the Sea* section has text from Exodus 13:19 to 15:27 (the exodus, the crossing of the Red Sea, the drowning of Pharaoh's armies, the Song of the Sea, the Song of Miriam, and the sweetening of the bitter water). This rare and important scroll may well have come from the Cairo Genizah.

- **The Cairo Genizah.** The largest number of earlier texts are from this collection. In the late nineteenth century, almost 250,000 Jewish manuscript fragments were found in the *genizah* of the Ben Ezra Synagogue in Fustat (Old Cairo). Later supplemented by additional fragments from other parts of Cairo and the Basatin cemetery to the east, the wider collection has about 280,000 manuscripts. The Genizah documents were written from about 870 (or earlier if the London *Song of the Sea Manuscript* is included) to as late as 1880. Most are biblical manuscripts, almost all of them Masoretic. The collection is dispersed among several libraries, including the libraries of Cambridge University, Oxford University, and the University of Manchester in Great Britain, the Jewish Theological Seminary of America in New York, and St. Petersburg in Russia.

- **The Aleppo Codex.** Copied in about 925 C.E., this manuscript forms the basis of the Hebrew University Bible Project (HUBP) based in Jerusalem. A substantial portion, however, has been lost, which means that for some books the HUBP must rely on other manuscripts. The first volume published was *Isaiah* (1995), followed by *Jeremiah* (1997) and *Ezekiel* (2004).

Many scholars consider the Aleppo Codex to be the most authoritative copy of the Masoretic Text, in both its consonants and its vowels. (The sage Maimonides described it as trusted by all Jewish scholars.) The consonants were copied by Shlomo ben Buya'a in Israel in about 920, and the text was given vowel signs and provided with Masoretic notes by Aaron ben Moses ben Asher. Ben Asher (d. 960) was the most prominent member of the Ben Asher dynasty of grammarians (from Tiberias on the western shore of Galilee), who shaped the most accurate version of writing vowel sounds and thus the Hebrew Bible. (In 1976, a facsimile was published [*The Aleppo Codex: Provided with Massoretic Notes and Pointed by Aaron Ben Asher the Codex, Considered Authoritative by Maimonides*], with editor Moshe Goshen-Gottstein describing it as the oldest known Masoretic Bible in a single volume and the first complete Hebrew Bible to be produced by one or two people in a consistent style.)

The Codex was purchased by the Karaite Jewish community of Jerusalem about 100 years after it was made. During the First Crusade (1095–1099), the Karaite synagogue was plundered, and the Codex was removed. It was later sent to Egypt after Jews there paid a hefty price for its ransom. In 1375, one of Maimonides' descendants took it to Aleppo in Syria (hence Aleppo Codex). In December 1947, rioters—enraged by the decision at the United Nations to establish a Jewish state in Palestine—burned down the synagogue where it was kept, and the Codex disappeared. In 1958, it was smuggled into Israel, presented to President Yitzhak Ben-Zvi, and entrusted to the Ben-Zvi Institute and the Hebrew University in Jerusalem.

The Israelis were dismayed to find that large parts had been lost. Only 294 of the original 487 pages survived, with the following texts missing: almost the entire Torah, three pages each from Kings and Jeremiah, much of the Minor Prophets (half of Amos, all of Obadiah and Jonah, the beginning of Micah), two pages from the Psalms, and all of Ecclesiastes, Lamentations, Esther, Daniel, and Ezra-Nehemiah.

Members of the Jewish community of Aleppo said that the missing leaves were destroyed when the synagogue housing the Codex was burned, but there is no evidence that fire reached it. At least some pages were torn off, including two "missing" leaves ending up in the United States that have been reunited with the scroll: in 1982, a page containing 2 Chronicles 35:7–36:19 was brought to Israel, and in 2007, a piece of a page containing Exodus 8. Scholars believe that members of the Aleppo Jewish community still hold many of the missing pages and other pages may be in the hands of antiquities dealers.

Some photographs exist of pages of the Aleppo Codex that are now missing. In 1887, English scholar William Wickes published a book with a photograph of Genesis 26:35–27:30 from the Codex, and in 1910, Joseph Segall published two facing pages containing Deuteronomy 4:38–6:3.

- **The Leningrad Codex.** Almost all modern English translations of the Old Testament are based on the Leningrad (or St. Petersburg) Codex. The manuscript is housed in the National Library of Russia (which prefers the name *Leningrad Codex*), and is cataloged as Firkovich B19A, after its former owner. Abraham Firkovich left no word on where he had acquired the Codex, which was taken to Odessa in 1838 and later transferred to the Imperial Library in St. Petersburg.

The Leningrad Codex was copied in 1008 or 1009 (almost a century after the Aleppo Codex) and is our earliest complete example of the traditional Hebrew Bible, or Masoretic

Text. It is also a primary source for the recovery of text in the missing parts of the Aleppo Codex. According to the colophon, the Leningrad Codex was copied in Cairo from manuscripts written by Aaron ben Moses ben Asher; however, it appears that ben Asher himself never saw it. Unlike the Aleppo Codex, the same scribe (Samuel ben Jacob) wrote the consonants, vowels, and Masoretic notes. Apart from the Aleppo Codex, the Leningrad Codex is the manuscript most faithful to ben Asher's scribal tradition. Numerous alterations and erasures suggest that the scribe was using an existing text that did not follow ben Asher's rules and was heavily emended to make it conform to these rules. The Leningrad Codex is used by most biblical scholars in its published edition, *Biblia Hebraica Stuttgartensia* (*BHS*), and now *Biblia Hebraica Quinta* (*BHQ*).

1.3 Shape of the Masoretic Text

Pre-Masoretic and Masoretic manuscripts are close to each other with respect to the text of Scripture, but among those large enough to contain several books, there are differences in order. The same overall shape for the Hebrew Bible is consistent: the threefold arrangement that was developed by the rabbis. The first two sections are the *Torah* (Genesis to Deuteronomy) and the *Prophets* (Joshua, Judges, Samuel, Kings, Isaiah, Jeremiah, Ezekiel, and the Book of the Twelve Minor Prophets).

The third section is the *Writings,* for which the order varies between manuscripts for the following books: (1) Chronicles; (2) Psalms, Job, and Proverbs; and (3) the Five Scrolls (Song of Songs, Ruth, Lamentations, Ecclesiastes, and Esther). For example, the Aleppo Codex and Leningrad Codex place Chronicles as the first book of the Writings and end it with Ezra-Nehemiah, while the most widely used edition of the Hebrew Bible (*Biblia Hebraica Stuttgartensia* [*BHS*]) places Chronicles at the very end after Ezra-Nehemiah. Here the Leningrad Codex reflects the traditional order of books as in modern printed editions, notably the Koren Bible (1962), other Masoretic manuscripts, and lists in rabbinical works such as *Baba Bathra* 14b in the Babylonian Talmud.

The Aleppo and Leningrad codices differ from the traditional order of several more books in the Writings, as detailed below in **Table 1.**

2. The Samaritan Pentateuch

2.1 Introducing the Samaritan Pentateuch

The Samaritan Pentateuch (SP) is not a translation, but the Samaritan version of the first five books of the Hebrew Bible, the Torah. For Samaritan Jews, who still exist as a group in Israel today, notably in Nablus (in the West Bank) and Holon (near Tel Aviv), the SP constitutes their entire Bible.

The SP was rediscovered by European scholars only in the seventeenth century, when Renaissance traveler Pietro della Valle sent a copy (Codex B) to Europe in 1616. This was published in the *Paris Polyglot* of 1629–1645, and again (with corrections) in the *London Polyglot* of 1657–1669. Appended to the *London Polyglot* is Edmund Castell's *Lexicon*

Table 1.			
Aleppo Codex (925) and Leningrad Codex (1008/9)	***BHS* (1968–1976)**	***Koren Bible* (1962)**	**Various Hebrew Manuscripts and *Baba Bathra* 14b**
Chronicles	Psalms	Psalms	Ruth
Psalms	Job	Proverbs	Psalms
Job	Proverbs	Job	Job
Proverbs	Ruth	Song of Songs	Proverbs
Ruth	Song of Songs	Ruth	Ecclesiastes
Song of Songs	Ecclesiastes	Lamentations	Song of Songs
Ecclesiastes	Lamentations	Ecclesiastes	Lamentations
Lamentations	Esther	Esther	Daniel
Esther	Daniel	Daniel	Esther
Daniel	Ezra-Nehemiah	Ezra-Nehemiah	Ezra-Nehemiah
Ezra-Nehemiah	Chronicles	Chronicles	Chronicles

Heptaglottum (1669), which includes some 6,000 variant readings against the Masoretic Text—1,900 of which agree with the Septuagint.

2.2 Manuscripts, Editions, and Translations of the Samaritan Pentateuch

The text of the Samaritan Pentateuch is preserved in three kinds of sources: biblical manuscripts (of the SP); translations of the SP in Greek, Aramaic, and Arabic; and citations in other Samaritan literature. While the biblical manuscripts are all medieval, the other two sources bear witness to the Samaritan text during the first millennium of the Common Era and interpret obscure passages in the Samaritan Pentateuch.

The oldest manuscript is Codex Add. 1846 (copied about 1100 C.E.), which is housed at the University Library in Cambridge. For the Samaritan religion, the most sacred text is the *Abisha' Scroll*, which is used in the Samaritan synagogue of Nablus. The manuscript introduces itself as written by "Abisha', son of Phineas, son of Eleazar, son of Aaron" (cf. 1 Chron 6:35) in the thirteenth year after the Israelites entered the land of Canaan under Joshua's leadership. However, modern scholars believe it was written much later and includes material by as many as nine scribes, with the oldest parts dating to the twelfth century. Five manuscripts are listed in **Table 2**.

There is to date no full critical Hebrew edition of the Samaritan Pentateuch, but four Hebrew editions and one English translation have been published:

- August F. von Gall, *Der hebräische Pentateuch der Samaritaner* (1914–1918). This edition attempts to reconstruct the original form of the SP by selecting readings from various manuscripts, but tends to follow Codex B. It is generally accurate, but contains several errors, is too reliant on the MT, and lacks important sources such as the *Abisha' Scroll*. It includes critical notes and readings from other manuscripts, which are highly valued by scholars.

Table 2. Some Manuscripts of the Samaritan Pentateuch		
Manuscript	**Date**	**Other Details**
Codex Add. 1846	1100	University Library, Cambridge
Codex B	1345/46	Purchased by Pietro della Valle
Codex C	1204	Highly regarded by scholars
Manuscript E	1219	Book of Exodus
Abisha' Scroll	12–13th c.	Text revered by the Samaritans
Cotton Claudius B VIII	1362–1363	British Library

- Avraham and Ratson Sadaqa, *Jewish and Samaritan Versions of the Pentateuch with Particular Stress on the Differences between Both Texts* (1961–1965). Based on the *Abisha' Scroll*, this edition contains many unique forms and misprints, so must be used with caution.

- Luis F. Giron Blanc, *Pentateuco Hebreo-Samaritano: Genesis. Edición crítica sobre la base de Manuscritos ineditos* (1976). This is the first volume of a new critical edition by the Biblia Poliglota Maritense, Madrid. Containing the text of Codex Add. 1877 (University Library, Cambridge) and variant readings from 15 unpublished manuscripts, this full critical edition of Genesis has been carefully and expertly executed.

- Abraham Tal, *The Samaritan Pentateuch, Edited According to MS 6 (C) of the Shekhem Synagogue* (2010). This is the edition of a manuscript copied in Damascus by the scribe Phinhas ben Elazar in 1204. Tal's text is well laid out and viewed by many scholars as the most accurate one so far, but it is not a full critical edition. An electronic version, with tagged text, is available from Accordance Bible Software at www.accordancebible.com.

- Benyamim Tsedaka and Sharon Sullivan, *The Israelite Samaritan Version of the Torah: First English Translation Compared with the Masoretic Version*, 2013. At least one more is in preparation.

2.3 Character of the Samaritan Pentateuch

Readings of the SP that differ from the traditional Masoretic Text may be classified in eight groups. Four involve copying and Hebrew grammar and interest scholars of the Hebrew language and Bible rather than the more general reader:

(1) Scribal errors

(2) Differences in grammar

(3) Replacement of old Hebrew forms with later ones

(4) Removal of grammatical difficulties, replacement of rare constructions with more frequent ones

The other four differences between the SP and the MT are more significant with respect to the content and meaning of the biblical text:

(5) Interpretation and clarification of the text by small changes

(6) Corrections to remove historical difficulties and objectionable passages

(7) Additions and interpolations from parallel passages

(8) Addition of Samaritan features or adaptation to Samaritan ideology

Group 6: Corrections to Remove Historical Difficulties and Objectionable Passages

One example is in Genesis 50:23, where the SP changes "on the knees of Joseph" (MT) to "in the days of Joseph," since it seemed improper for Joseph's grandchildren to be borne upon his knees. Another is in Deuteronomy 25:11, where "his genitals" (MT) is changed to "his flesh," since it seems obscene for a woman to grab a man's genitals during a fight.

Group 7: Additions and Interpolations from Parallel Passages

One example is the insertion after Exodus 6:9, concerning the Israelites' complaint to Moses in Egypt. This complaint is quoted later in Exodus (14:12), but the MT and LXX versions of 6:9 have no record of it. However, it is provided in the SP with material from 14:12 (in bold italics):

> Moses told this to the Israelites, but they would not listen to Moses, because of their broken spirit and cruel slavery. ***And they said to Moses, "Please, leave us alone, and let us serve the Egyptians; for it would be better for us to work for the Egyptians than to die in the wilderness."***

Longer interpolations include Genesis 31:11–13 after 30:36, and passages from Deuteronomy before or after the corresponding passage in Numbers (for example, Deut 1:6–8 before Num 10:11, and Deut 3:24–28 after Num 20:13). Another example is the additional commandment (with text from Deuteronomy and Exodus) after the Ten Commandments in Exodus 20:17.

Group 8: Addition of Samaritan Features or Adaptation to Samaritan Ideology

Some readings contain specifically Samaritan features; for example, the defense of God's honor and the honor of Moses and other ancient heroes; legal differences from the MT; and the specification of Mount Gerizim rather than Jerusalem as the center for worshiping Yahweh.

One example is Deuteronomy 11:30, where the SP emphasizes Shechem, following the "blessing on Mount Gerizim" in verse 29. The Samaritans eventually built their temple on this mountain, which was near Shechem. Another example is Deuteronomy 12:14, where the implied reference to Shechem means God has already chosen this site, rather than Jerusalem, which is chosen in the MT.

Table 3.	
Deut 11:30 in the Samaritan Pentateuch	*Deut 11:30 in the Masoretic Text (NRSV)*
As you know, they are beyond the Jordan, some distance to the west, in the land of the Canaanites who live in the Arabah, opposite Gilgal, beside the oak of Moriah **opposite Shechem.**	As you know, they are beyond the Jordan, some distance to the west, in the land of the Canaanites who live in the Arabah, opposite Gilgal, beside the oak of Moriah.
Deut 12:14 in the Samaritan Pentateuch	*Deut 12:14 in the Masoretic Text (NRSV)*
But only at **the place that the Lord has chosen** in one of your tribes—there you are to offer your burnt offerings and there you are to do everything I command you.	But only at **the place that the Lord will choose** in one of your tribes—there you are to offer your burnt offerings and there you are to do everything I command you.

2.4 Evaluation of the Samaritan Pentateuch

In Edmund Castell's appended volume to the *London Polyglot*, the SP contains about 6,000 variant readings against the MT, 1,900 of which agree with the Septuagint. Most are minor with respect to the text's meaning since they involve scribal and grammatical forms. Many others are more significant (groups 5–8 in the numbered list above), including a large portion of the 1,900 that agree with the Septuagint. But how important is the SP for understanding the text of the Hebrew Bible/Old Testament or for establishing the best text from which translations are to be made?

German scholar Wilhelm Gesenius (1786–1842) regarded the SP of little worth for establishing the text of Scripture. In 1815, he proposed that the Samaritan sect and its text began when Alexander the Great allowed the Samaritans to build their temple on Mount Gerizim. Gesenius believed that Samaritan priests introduced sectarian readings into the Hebrew text, and he attributed the many agreements between the SP and the Septuagint to similar Hebrew manuscripts used by the Samaritans in Palestine and by Jews in Alexandria who translated the Septuagint. He referred to this common source as the Alexandrino-Samaritanus Text, which was of little value for establishing the most ancient form of Scripture since it was a text that had been simplified, corrected, and expanded (a "vulgar" text). This was in marked contrast to the Judean text (the precursor to the MT) produced by the Jews of Jerusalem, who tried to preserve the ancient Hebrew text unchanged. Gesenius' negative view of the SP was followed by most scholars for the next century.

In 1915, Paul Kahle (1875–1964) offered a far more positive view: the SP preserves many genuine old readings, is one ancient form of the Pentateuch, and several versions of the Hebrew Bible were used by Jews in the Second Temple period. Kahle also proposed that the Septuagint derives from several of these translations (including the ancient SP) and was later standardized by the church. He regarded the MT not as representing the original text (*Urtext*) of Scripture, but as a late creation from older sources. Kahle identified an early pre-Samaritan text because of agreements between the SP and the Septuagint, *Jubilees, 1 Enoch,* the *Assumption of Moses,* and parts of the New Testament. This more favorable view of the SP has been adopted by many modern scholars, even though most still view the MT as a better text.

2.5 The Samaritan Pentateuch, the Dead Sea Scrolls, the Septuagint, and the New Testament

The discovery of the scrolls has enabled scholars to appreciate the antiquity of the SP and its value for understanding the biblical text. The existence of Kahle's early pre-Samaritan text is confirmed by several Qumran biblical scrolls, which are classified as Palestinian or pre-Samaritan in form since they preserve a text similar to the SP. The most prominent examples are three scrolls from Cave 4: 4QpaleoExod^m, 4QExod-Lev^f, and 4QNum^b. Distinctive readings of this type are found in many more biblical scrolls, but because they also feature other textual forms they are not classified as pre-Samaritan. This form of the biblical text is dated by scholars to the second century B.C.E. or earlier. However, it does not include the "sectarian readings" that were later inserted into the SP to bolster distinctive views of the Samaritan community.

The SP is of value to Septuagint studies since it agrees with the Greek Bible against that of the MT in about 1,900 readings. Many are minor, but many others are quite substantial. One is in Genesis 4:8, where the MT reads "And Cain said to his brother Abel," but the SP (supported by the Septuagint, Vulgate, and some Targums) adds *"Let us go out to the field."* Another example is in Exodus 1:22, on the Hebrew male infants who are to be put to death around the time of Moses' birth. Here the MT has a shorter text: "Then Pharaoh commanded all his people, '*Every boy that is born to you* will be thrown into the Nile.'" However, the SP (supported by the Septuagint and Targums) reads *"Every boy that is born to the Hebrews . . ."*

Several passages in the New Testament support an Old Testament text that is similar to the SP. One example is in Acts 7:4, where Stephen states that Abraham left Haran and came to Canaan *after* the death of his father, Terah. This agrees with the SP's statement in Genesis 11:32 that Terah died in Haran at the age of 145 years. (Abraham was born when Terah was 70 [Gen 11:26], and Abraham moved to Canaan when he himself was 75 [Gen 12:4].) In contrast, the MT of Genesis 11:32 states that Terah died in Haran at the age of 205—60 years *after* Abraham had left for Canaan.

A second example is in Galatians 3:17, which understands the law to have been given 430 years after Abraham: "[16]Now the promises were made to Abraham and to his offspring; . . .[17]My point is this: the law, which came 430 years later, does not annul a covenant previously ratified by God, so as to nullify the promise."

This agrees with the version of Exodus 12:40 in the SP (supported by the Septuagint), which includes the three generations from Abraham to Jacob: "The time that the people of Israel and their fathers lived *in the land of Canaan and in the land of Egypt* was 430 years." In contrast, the shorter MT confines this period to the time in Egypt alone, thus excluding the three patriarchs: "The time that the Israelites had lived in Egypt was 430 years."

3. The Septuagint or Greek Bible

3.1 The Term Septuagint *and the Origins of the Septuagint*

The Septuagint was originally only the Greek translation of the Pentateuch. For most scholars, the term *Septuagint* is more wide-ranging and includes Greek translations of the Hebrew Bible, the additions to some books (for example, Daniel), books among the Apocrypha (for example, 1 Maccabees and Judith), and books not among the Apocrypha of the Roman Catholic Church but recognized by Orthodox churches (for example, the Prayer of Manasseh and Psalm 151).

The term comes from the Latin *Septuaginta*, meaning "seventy" (hence the abbreviation LXX in Roman numerals), and is derived from a fascinating story. According to the *Letter of Aristeas* (written sometime between 150 and 100 B.C.E. by Aristeas, a Jew from Alexandria), the Egyptian king Ptolemy II (285–247) ordered his librarian, Demetrius of Phalerum, to collect all the books in the world for his famous Library at Alexandria. Demetrius believed that this collection should include a copy of the Jewish law translated into Greek. In response to an invitation, the high priest Eleazar sent six elders from each of the twelve tribes, for a total of 72. Following their arrival in Alexandria, drafts of the translation were made, and the final version was completed in exactly 72 days:

> [301]Three days later Demetrius took the men and passing along the sea-wall, seven stadia long, to the island, crossed the bridge and made for the northern districts of Pharos. There he assembled them in a house, which had been built upon the sea-shore, of great beauty and in a secluded situation, and invited them to carry out the work of translation, since everything that they needed for the purpose [302]was placed at their disposal. So they set to work comparing their several results and making them agree, and whatever they agreed upon was suitably copied out under the direction of Demetrius. . . .
>
> [307][T]hey met together daily in the place which was delightful for its quiet and its brightness and applied themselves to their task. And it so chanced that the work of translation was completed in 72 days, just as if this had been arranged of set purpose. (Charles, *The Letter of Aristeas* [1913], 301–7)

The translation was read to the Jewish community, and the leaders pronounced a curse on anyone who might seek to change it since this was the authorized Greek translation of God's Law. The translators returned home with a guard of honor, a letter, and gifts for the high priest Eleazar.

The *Letter of Aristeas* is mostly fictitious but is the earliest text to mention the Library of Alexandria. It is also important for understanding the origins of the Septuagint (70, rounding off the number of translators from 72), for five reasons:

(1) "Septuagint" originally applied only to the five books of the Pentateuch. The others were translated later, some as late as the first century C.E.

(2) Many Greek-speaking Jews needed a translation of the Scriptures, since they spoke little or no Hebrew.

(3) At least some Jews viewed the Septuagint as authoritative Scripture. One of the author's goals was to establish the superiority of the Septuagint text over other translations of the Hebrew Scriptures.

(4) The *Letter of Aristeas* seems to be a work typical of Jewish apologetics and propaganda, in which case it was directed to Greeks.

(5) However, it may have been written for Jewish readers, in order to promote the Septuagint as inspired and authoritative Jewish scripture.

3.2 Manuscripts and Editions of the Septuagint

Copies of the Septuagint may be listed in five groups:

(a) Papyri

These preserve some of the earliest copies of the Greek Bible, but most are very fragmentary. Important examples include the Chester Beatty Papyri from Egypt (second to fourth centuries), with fragments from Genesis, Numbers, Deuteronomy, Isaiah, Jeremiah, Ezekiel, Daniel, Esther, and Ecclesiastes.

(b) Uncials

In contrast to most early Hebrew ones, several early Greek manuscripts preserve much or all of the Old Testament. These include a few uncials. Since they were preserved and handed down by church leaders, these manuscripts contain both the Old and the New Testaments. The three most important uncials are:

- *Codex Sinaiticus* (abbreviated S or ℵ), fourth century. Sinaiticus originally contained the entire Greek Bible, but only half of the OT remains. Most of the manuscript was brought to Russia in the late 1850s from St. Catherine's Monastery in the Sinai Desert by German archaeologist Constantin von Tischendorf, but not without controversy. By far the largest portion now resides at the British Museum and a smaller portion at Leipzig in Germany.

- *Codex Vaticanus* (B), fourth century, housed at the Vatican Library since before 1481. It originally contained the whole Greek Bible, but the beginning has been lost (up to Gen 1:1–46:27; Pss 106–138, and Heb 9:14 through Revelation).

- *Codex Alexandrinus* (A), fifth century, and housed at the British Museum in London. Like Sinaiticus and Vaticanus, this manuscript originally contained the entire Greek Bible. In the OT section, several passages are missing (notably 1 Kingdoms [= 1 Samuel] 12:18–14:9 and Pss 49:19–79:10).

(c) Minuscules or Cursives

Hundreds of Greek manuscripts, copied in medieval times, are in the cursive script found in printed editions. Used by scholars today, they bear witness to all or parts of the Septuagint.

(d) Printed Editions

There are several printed editions of the Septuagint. The three most important are:

- The shorter edition published by Alfred Rahlfs, with later versions edited by Robert Hanhart: *Septuaginta. Id est Vetus Testamentum Graece iuxta LXX interpretes* (1935).

- The Göttingen Edition. This multivolume critical edition is published by the Septuginta-Unternehmen in Germany: *Septuaginta Vetus Testamentum Graecum. Auctoritate Academiae Scientiarum Gottingensis editum.* About 40 volumes are planned; the first (*Psalmi cum Odis*) appeared in 1931, over two-thirds were published by 2012, and completion is scheduled before 2020.

- The Cambridge Edition. This critical edition was published by Henry Barclay Swete as *The Old Testament in Greek*. Volume 1 (Genesis–IV Kings) appeared in 1887, Volume 2 (1 Chronicles–Tobit) in 1891, and Volume 3 (Hosea–*4 Maccabees*) in 1894.

(e) English Translations of the Septuagint

Two English translations have appeared in recent times. The most authoritative is by a team from the International Organization for Septuagint and Cognate Studies: Albert Pietersma and Benjamin G. Wright (eds.), *The New English Translation of the Septuagint* (2007). The second is *The Orthodox Study Bible* (1993), which has its merits and is more devotional in nature.

Before these translations of the Septuagint, very few were available in English. For some 150 years the most widely used was Sir Lancelot Brenton's *The Septuagint Version: Greek and English* (1844). Another translation, one very difficult to obtain, is Charles Thomson's *The Holy Bible, Containing the Old and New Covenant, Commonly Called the*

Old and New Testament: Translated from the Greek (1808). Thomson (1729–1824) served as secretary to the American Continental Congress from 1774 to 1789.

3.3 The Shape and Contents of the Septuagint

The content of the Old Testament section in Christian (Protestant) Bibles is almost identical to the MT, but the order of books differs from that in Jewish Bibles. Whereas Jewish Bibles contain Genesis through Ezra-Nehemiah and Chronicles, Christian Bibles contain Genesis through Malachi. This is because the structure of the Christian Bible is not based upon the Hebrew Bible, but largely upon the Septuagint that was used by the New Testament writers and the early church.

Greek manuscripts also differ with respect to the **order of books** in the latter part of the Septuagint. Codex Vaticanus, for example, ends with Ezekiel and Daniel (see **Table 4** on page 51). It is possible, but not certain, that the order of Genesis to Malachi adopted in Christian Bibles may have been finalized by Christians rather than Jews.

With respect to **contents**, the Septuagint contains a text that is close to some books of the MT, but very different from others. In many cases, these differences are because of the translator's free technique; for example, in the case of Proverbs (see **Table 5** on pg. 51).

In other cases, however, the Septuagint translates a Hebrew text (called the *Vorlage*) that differs from the MT. There are many examples, one of which is in Psalm 145:13:

> (13a) Your kingdom is a kingdom of all the ages, and your dominion is in every generation and generation.

> (13b) *Faithful is the Lord in all his words, and devout in all his works.*

This verse is longer in the Septuagint than in the MT, since the latter contains only the Hebrew text for verse 13a. Most scholars believe that the LXX translator here produced verse 13b because the translator was using a longer Hebrew *Vorlage*.

The Septuagint also contains many books not found in the MT (LXX manuscripts differ as to which are included). Nine are found in Roman Catholic Bibles and are known as the *Apocrypha* ("Hidden Books") or *Deuterocanonicals*:

(1) Tobit (fourth or third century B.C.E.)

(2) Judith (second or first century B.C.E.)

(3) Additions to Esther (second or first century B.C.E.)

(4) 1 Maccabees (late second or early first century B.C.E.)

(5) 2 Maccabees (124 B.C.E.)

(6) The Wisdom of Solomon (about 40 C.E. or earlier)

(7) Ecclesiasticus (about 180 B.C.E., prologue about 132 B.C.E.). Also known as Sirach or the Wisdom of Jesus ben Sira.

(8) Baruch (between 200 and 60 B.C.E.)

(9) Additions to Daniel, in three sections (all third to second centuries B.C.E.):

   • The Prayer of Azariah and the Song of the Three Young Men, between Daniel 3:23 and 3:34

   • Susanna (ch. 13 of the Greek version)

   • Bel and the Dragon (ch. 14 of the Greek version)

Several more books are found in various Septuagint manuscripts, and are included in the Bibles of various Orthodox churches:

(1) *The Prayer of Manasseh* (probably first century B.C.E.)

(2) *Psalm 151* (Hellenistic period, but from earlier Hebrew sources)

(3) *1 Esdras* (also called *2 Esdras*), probably second century B.C.E.

(4) *2 Esdras* (also called *3 Esdras*), late first to third centuries C.E. (Slavonic Bibles only)

(5) *3 Maccabees* (30 B.C.E. to 70 C.E.)

(6) *4 Maccabees* (first century B.C.E. to late first century C.E. [Greek Orthodox Bibles only])

4. Other Versions (Translations) of the Hebrew Bible/Old Testament

Other translations were made of the Hebrew Bible so that Jews and Christians who knew little or no Hebrew could read the Old Testament Scriptures in their own languages. The most important of these versions are:

   • The Aramaic Targums (which began before the Common Era). The term *Targum* means "Translation" or "Paraphrase."

   • The Old Latin (began late second century)

   • The Syriac Peshitta (second–third century)

   • The Latin Vulgate (390–405). This version was translated by Jerome and became the Bible of the Western church.

Comparison against the biblical texts from the Judean Desert suggests that among these versions, significant ancient readings are occasionally preserved especially in the Old Latin and the Peshitta. However, the Masoretic Text, Samaritan Pentateuch, and Septuagint remain our most significant witnesses to the biblical text or texts of Antiquity.

Table 4. Contents of the Septuagint According to Three Manuscripts		
[Bracket] means not preserved. *Paraleipomena* is equivalent to Chronicles.		
Codex Sinaiticus	**Codex Vaticanus**	**Codex Alexandrinus**
Genesis–[Deuteronomy] [Joshua–4 Kingdoms] 1 [+2] *Paraleipomena*	Genesis–Deuteronomy Joshua–4 Kingdoms 1–2 *Paraleipomena*	Genesis–[Deuteronomy] Joshua–4 Kingdoms 1–2 *Paraleipomena*
[1 Esdras = Ezra] 2 Esdras (Nehemiah) Esther Tobit Judith 1–4 Maccabees Isaiah Jeremiah Lamentations [Esther] [Judith] [Tobit] [Hosea]–Malachi Psalms Proverbs Ecclesiastes Song of Songs Wisdom of Solomon Sirach Job	1 Esdras (= Ezra) 2 Esdras (Nehemiah) Psalms Proverbs Ecclesiastes Song of Songs Job Wisdom of Solomon Sirach Esther Judith Tobit Hosea–Malachi Isaiah Jeremiah Baruch Lamentations Letter of Jeremiah Ezekiel Daniel	Hosea–Malachi Isaiah Jeremiah Baruch Lamentations Letter of Jeremiah Ezekiel Daniel Esther Tobit Judith 1 Esdras (= Ezra) 2 Esdras (Nehemiah) 1–4 *Maccabees* Psalms Job Proverbs Ecclesiastes Song of Songs Wisdom of Solomon Sirach *Psalms of Solomon*

Table 5.	
Prov 30:1–3 in the Masoretic Text (NRSV)	**Prov 30:1–3 in the Septuagint (NETS)**
(1) The words of Agur son of Jakeh. An oracle. Thus says the man: I am weary, O God, I am weary, O God. How can I prevail? (2) Surely I am too stupid to be human; I do not have human understanding. (3) I have not learned wisdom, nor have I knowledge of the holy ones.	(1) My son, fear my words, and repent when you receive them; this is what the man says to those who believe in God: Now I stop, (2) for I am the most foolish of all people and I have not the prudence of people. (3) God has taught me wisdom, and I have gained knowledge of holy things.

5

The Biblical Scrolls

Counting recently acquired ones, there are over 1,250 Dead Sea Scrolls, of which more than 1,050 were found at Qumran. The Qumran copies may be divided into the Biblical Scrolls (almost 300), the Apocrypha and *Pseudepigrapha* (about 150 scrolls), and the Nonbiblical Scrolls (about 600).

This chapter gives an overview of the Biblical Scrolls, that is, copies of the books found in the Hebrew Bible and the Protestant Old Testament. The order of books in the Hebrew Bible or Old Testament was still not fixed by the end of the Second Temple period (70 C.E.), but it will be helpful to cover the various books in the order (Genesis to Malachi) and four divisions (Pentateuch, Historical Books, Poetical Books, and Prophets) found in most English Bibles.

For each book, the following information is provided: the number of scrolls, the number of chapters represented in these scrolls, comments on selected manuscripts, the textual form(s) of the book these scrolls contain, and at least one interesting reading.

1. The Pentateuch (or Torah)

Books of the Pentateuch are found in 127 separate scrolls, of which 116 were discovered at Qumran and 11 at other sites in the Judean Desert. Twelve of these scrolls preserve text from more than one book.

Genesis

With its creation of the heavens and earth, the primeval history, and the saga of the patriarchs, Genesis was one of the three most popular books among the *Yahad* Essenes at Qumran, with 30 scrolls discovered there, two or three more at Wadi Murabba'at, which was used as a hideout by rebels in the Bar Kokhba revolt (132–135 C.E.), and one further south at Masada. Most Genesis scrolls are fragmentary, with only 34 of the 50 chapters represented (1–6, 8, 10, 12, 17–19, 22–24, 26–27, 32–37, 39–43, 45–50).

The oldest is 4QpaleoGen^m (mid-second century B.C.E.), which was written in the ancient paleo-Hebrew script. Another features the title *Genesis*—the only biblical scroll to do so—and is abbreviated 4QGen^h-title (though it may be part of 4QGen^k).

The book was generally stable by the Qumran period, since these scrolls reveal a text generally close to the consonants in the traditional Masoretic Text and the Samaritan Pentateuch. Eleven contain variant readings worth noting, and may be classified as mixed or nonaligned (no consistent alignment with other texts). Other Genesis scrolls, notably those found at Murabba'at (early second century C.E.) are virtually identical to the MT.

One interesting variant reading is in Genesis 41:16. In the MT, Joseph answers Pharaoh: "It is not in *me*: God will give Pharaoh an answer of peace," which could be interpreted as arrogant (That is, "Without *me* [Joseph], God will give no answer concerning Pharaoh's welfare"). In 4QGen^j, supported by the SP and the Septuagint, Joseph is more respectful: "Apart from [*Go*]d, Phar[aoh's] welfare will receive no answer." It could be argued that an ancient scribe removed "me" to protect Joseph's character, but 4QGen^j most likely represents the original version.

Exodus

This book features the exodus from Egypt, the events leading to Mount Sinai, the covenant, the tabernacle, and instructions for worship. It was popular at Qumran: Thirty scrolls were found there, and one more at Murabba'at. Between them, these manuscripts preserve parts of all 40 chapters of the biblical book. The oldest is 4QExod-Lev^f (mid-third century B.C.E.), one of the two earliest (the other being 4QSam^b).

Most Exodus scrolls found at Qumran contain a text similar to the consonantal MT, while the one from Murabba'at (MurExod, early second century C.E.) conforms even more closely. At least two (4QpaleoExod^m and 4QExod-Lev^f) are close to the consonantal SP, while 4QExod^b is nearer to the Septuagint.

Written in the archaic paleo-Hebrew script, 4QpaleoExodus^m is the most extensive scroll found in Cave 4 and a good example of a different edition of a biblical book. Before the scrolls were discovered, many scholars attributed the major differences between the SP and the MT to later editing by the marginalized Samaritans. However, many variant readings preserved in the SP are also found in 4QpaleoExod^m, which shows that the book of Exodus circulated in early Judaism in two editions: the first close to the MT (and translated in the Septuagint), the second as an expanded version with features characteristic of the Samaritan version.

One striking illustration is at Exodus 7:18. Here 4QpaleoExod^m and the SP have a longer text, with Moses and Aaron repeating to Pharaoh God's command given in verses 16–18. In contrast, the shorter version is found in two scrolls (4QGen-Exod^a and 4QExod^c), the MT, and the LXX (see **Table 1**).

Leviticus

With its regulations for worship, sacrifices, the priesthood, and religious festivals, and its theme of holiness, Leviticus was an important book for the Yahad. Twenty-two

Table 1.	
Exodus 7:18 in 4QpaleoExodᵐ SP	**4QGen-Exodᵃ, 4QExodᶜ MT LXX**
(18) "[And the fish] *in the mi[dst]* of the Nile will die, [and the Nile will stink; and] the Egyptians will weary of drinking water from the Nile." [*And Moses and Aaron went to Pharaoh] and [s]aid to him, The Lo[RD God of the Hebrews sent us to you saying*], *"Let my people go so that [they] may serve [me in the wilderness." And behold, you have not listened until now]. Thus the* Lord *has said, "By [this you shall know that I am the* Lord. *Behold I am] s[trikin]g [the water which is in the Nile] with the rod that [is in my land and it will be turned to blood] and [the f]ish that are in the mi[dst of the Nile will die and the river shall stink and the] E[gy]ptians [will weary] of dri[nking water from the Nile."*	(18) "The fish in the river will die, the river itself will stink, and the Egyptians will be unable to drink water from the Nile."

Leviticus scrolls were found in the caves at Qumran and two more at Masada. All 27 chapters of the book, with the exception of chapter 12, are represented.

The oldest manuscript is 4QExod-Levᶠ (mid-third century B.C.E.). Four Leviticus scrolls (most notably 11QpaleoLevᵃ) were written in the ancient paleo-Hebrew script and two in Greek: 4QLXXLevᵃ and pap4QLXXLevᵇ (the latter on papyrus, far more fragile than the leather on which most scrolls were written).

The text was quite stable by the Qumran period, since the Leviticus scrolls reveal a text generally close to the consonantal MT and the SP; the two Masada scrolls (mid-first century C.E.) are especially close to the traditional MT. Most of the Qumran manuscripts contain variant readings against the MT and the SP, and several are best described as mixed or nonaligned. One example is at Leviticus 3:11, where the MT and the SP describe what the priest burns on the altar as a "food offering by fire to the LORD"; however, pap4QLXXLevᵇ and the Septuagint read "f[ood, for a pleasing od]or [of the offering by fire to the LORD]."

There is one translation of Leviticus into Aramaic among the scrolls (two more are of Job): the *Targum of Leviticus* (4QtgLev), copied about 150 B.C.E.

Numbers

This book covers the Israelites' 40 years of wandering in the Sinai Desert, closing with the people in the plains of Moab, poised to cross over the Jordan into the promised land. Eighteen Numbers scrolls were discovered: fifteen Qumran, two at Nahal Hever, and one at Murabba'at. While most are fragmentary, only chapters 6 and 14 of the book's 36 chapters are not represented.

One important—and the best preserved—Numbers scroll is 4QNumᵇ (about 30 B.C.E.), which contains text from chapters 11 to 36. 4QNumᵇ may be described as an early Jewish Living Bible, since it features many interpolations and expansions of the biblical text. The book of Deuteronomy contains several speeches not actually found in the MT of Numbers, but which were uttered during events also recounted in Numbers. So where these speeches are not included in the traditional book, 4QNum^b imports them from Deuteronomy at the appropriate place. One example is at Numbers 21:21, where 4QNum^b and the SP have imported God's command to fight the Amorites from Deuteronomy 2:24–25, whereas the MT and the Septuagint have a shorter text:

Table 2.	
Numbers 21:21 in 4QNum^b SP 4QNum^b SP	**Numbers 21:21 in MT LXX**
(21) And [the LORD] *spoke* [*to Moses, Rise up, get on your way, and pass through the valley of the Arnon. Behold, I have given into your hand*] Sih[*on the Amorite, king of Heshbon, and his land; begin to possess it, and contend with him in b*]*attle.* [*This day will I begin to put the dread of you and the fear of you on the peoples that are under the whole heaven, who shall hear the report of you, and shall tremble and be in anguish because of you.* And Israel sent messengers to Sihon king of the Amorites, saying]:	(21)
	And Israel sent messengers to Sihon king of the Amorites, saying:

Thus there were at least two editions of Numbers circulating in Judaism during the Second Temple period: one close to the MT and the other (represented by 4QNum^b) a longer version with many features characteristic of the Samaritan version.

Deuteronomy

Deuteronomy contains several addresses by Moses to the Israelites in the land of Moab as they prepared to enter the promised land and closes with the last words and death of Moses. It also features the Law and God's covenant through Moses with Israel, two themes that were prominent in *Yahad*'s own writings. Among the Essenes at Qumran, this was the most popular book of all.

There are 42 Deuteronomy scrolls altogether, with 39 found at Qumran, one more at Nahal Hever, one at Murabba'at, and one at Masada. Most are fragmentary, but all 34 chapters of the biblical book are represented among them. Two scrolls (4QpaleoDeut^r and 4QpaleoDeut^s) were written in the ancient paleo-Hebrew script, one (4QLXXDeut) in Greek, and one (pap6QDeut) on papyrus.

Many Deuteronomy scrolls are close to the consonantal MT and the SP. Some, however, are more textually independent (for example, 4QDeut^b and 4QDeut^c), and at least one (4QDeut^q) agrees most often with the Septuagint. Sometimes material found in other biblical manuscripts is omitted; for example, in Deuteronomy 3:20 where 4QDeut^d, the MT, and the SP merely read "until *the* LORD gives rest to your countrymen," 4QDeut^m and the Septuagint have "until *the* LORD *your God* gives rest to your countrymen"—thus reminding the Israelites who the LORD is.

We saw above how 4QNum[b] features interpolations and expansions of the biblical text. The same happens in some Deuteronomy scrolls, notably 4QDeut[j] and 4QDeut[n]. For example, in 4QDeut[j], Deuteronomy 11:21 (which describes the result of keeping God's commandments) is followed directly by Exodus 12:43–51 (though only vv. 43 and 44 actually survive). This longer reading is unique to 4QDeut[j], and not found in the other witnesses (the MT, the SP, or the Septuagint):

> (11:21) "[so that your days may be multiplied, and the days of your children, in the land which] the LORD [swore to your fathers to give them, like the days of the heavens above the earth]." (Exod 12:43) *And [the LORD] s[aid to Moses and Aaron, "This is the ordinance of the Passover]; n[o] fore[igner shall eat of it; (44) but every man's servant that is bought for money, when you have circumcised him], then he shall e[at of it]."* (*The Dead Sea Scrolls Bible*, 588–89)

So there were at least two editions of Deuteronomy circulating in Judaism during the Second Temple period: a shorter version close to the MT and a longer one (represented by 4QDeut[j] and 4QDeut[n]). The latter is characteristic of the SP; however, the example above shows that some key longer readings are not found even in the SP.

2. The Historical Books

The Historical Books are represented in 29 scrolls, all of which were found in the caves near Qumran.

Joshua

This book features the conquest of Canaan under Joshua's leadership and the division of the land among the tribes and ends with the renewal of the covenant at Shechem. Only three Joshua scrolls were found, both in Cave 4 at Qumran; a third relevant scroll is 4QpaleoParaJoshua (4Q123), but its contents are difficult to identify. The earliest is 4QJosh[a] (about 100 B.C.E.). Of Joshua's 24 chapters, only nine (2–8, 10, and 17) are represented.

Before the discovery of the scrolls, Joshua was known to exist in two different literary editions: an earlier, shorter edition found in the Septuagint, and the later, fuller edition in the traditional MT. Individual textual variants found in 4QJosh[a] and 4QJosh[b] sometimes agree with the Septuagint, sometimes with the MT, and on occasion have their own distinctive readings. The original contents of 4QJosh[a] were shorter than even the Greek text; this scroll most likely contains a third literary edition.

4QJosh[a] helps solve a problem that has long baffled scholars. In the traditional narrative, the MT has Joshua leading the Israelites across the Jordan (ch. 3), the Israelites encamping at Gilgal (ch. 4), fighting the battle for Jericho (6:1–27), and gaining another victory over Ai (8:15–29). Straight afterward, Joshua marches some 20 miles north to Shechem to build an altar on Mount Ebal, which is opposite Mount Gerizim, later to become the holy mountain of the Samaritans (8:30–35). Joshua then unexpectedly journeys back south to deal with Gibeon, which was below Ai (ch. 9). He thus inexplicably abandons his newly built altar in enemy territory.

Joshua's apparently unwise movements are explained by 4QJosh[a]. In this scroll, the end of the altar-building episode is directly followed by chapter 5, where the Israelites are encamped at Gilgal. This means that he constructed the first altar here (not at Ebal), immediately after crossing the Jordan and before beginning the conquest, which is what we would expect. In thanksgiving for the fulfilled promise of the land and in order to sanctify it, Joshua erected an altar at Gilgal (which continued to be an important place for worship. In contrast, Mount Ebal is never referred to again as a worship site for Israel). This sequence of events in 4QJosh[a] is confirmed by the historian Josephus (first century C.E.), who describes Joshua's building of an altar immediately after crossing the Jordan (*Antiquities* 5.16–20).

But why was the Joshua passage later altered? In Deuteronomy 27:4, the MT has Moses commanding the building of the first altar on Mount Ebal, but the SP puts it on Mount Gerizim. In light of 4QJosh[a], a three-stage development of the command to Joshua and its fulfillment now emerges. First, the altar was to be built after the people crossed the Jordan, and Joshua did so at Gilgal. Second, northerners, perhaps the Samaritans, changed the site to Mount Gerizim in order to support their claims to the land. Finally, Jewish scribes discounted this claim by changing Mount Gerizim to the otherwise insignificant Mount Ebal so as to promote their own claims to the land.

Judges

This book spans Israel's history from the invasion of Canaan to just before the monarchy, and features national leaders called *judges*, most of whom were military heroes. Only five copies were discovered at Qumran. Of the 21 chapters in the traditional form of Judges, only five (6, 8?, 9, 19, and 21) are represented. The earliest scroll is 4QJudg[a] (about 50–25 B.C.E.).

4QJudg[a] reveals an earlier text that is shorter than the Masoretic and the Septuagint forms, since it does not yet include a theological passage (Judg 6:7–10) found in these later versions and may represent a separate edition of the book. 4QJudg[b] was probably also a shorter version, although the missing text is no longer preserved.

Ruth

This romantic story features Ruth, a Moabite woman whose loyalty to her mother-in-law and devotion to God lead her to follow Naomi back to Israel after her husband's death in Moab. She finds a new husband, Boaz, and becomes the great-grandmother of King David. Five Ruth manuscripts were found at Qumran, which between them preserve material from all four of its chapters. The earliest are 2QRuth[a] and 4QRuth[b] (mid-first century B.C.E.).

These scrolls contain a text very much like the one in the traditional MT and the Septuagint. There are a few minor variant readings; for example, in Ruth 3:17, 2QRuth[a] and a much later Greek manuscript read *"How are you,* my daughter?,*"* while the MT and the Septuagint read *"Who are you"* and yet other Masoretic manuscripts read *"You are . . ."*

1 and 2 Samuel

A single book in the Hebrew Bible, 1 and 2 Samuel present Israel's history from the time of Samuel to the later events in David's reign, featuring Samuel's career, Israel's first king, Saul, and its greatest monarch, David. Only seven Samuel scrolls were discovered at Qumran. Except for six chapters (1 Sam 13, 22, 29; 2 Sam 1, 9, 17), these manuscripts preserve text from all 31 chapters of 1 Samuel and all 24 chapters of 2 Samuel.

The oldest is 4QSam^b (about 250 B.C.E., thus one of the two earliest scrolls). The most important is 4QSam^a (mid-first century B.C.E.). One of the largest biblical scrolls from Qumran, it preserves text ranging from the first chapter of 1 Samuel to the final chapter of 2 Samuel (thus containing both parts of the book).

It is unclear if there were two separate editions of the entire book in antiquity or only of specific passages. One example is the narrative of David and Goliath in 1 Samuel 17–18, for which two scrolls (1QSam and 4QSam^b) are very close to the traditional MT, but 4QSam^a contains many agreements with the Septuagint (plus several independent readings). Moreover, several agreements with 1 and 2 Chronicles show that this was the type of Samuel manuscript used by the Chronicler when composing his books (or, rather, book).

Some variant readings in 4QSam^a are superior to the traditional MT and to the Septuagint. The most striking is the end of 1 Samuel 10, where an additional paragraph describes the atrocities perpetrated by King Nahash of the Ammonites, thus explaining his cruel behavior in chapter 11. (Josephus, writing in the second half of the first century C.E., confirms key details in his *Antiquities* 6.68–72.)

> [Na]hash king of the [A]mmonites oppressed the Gadites and the Reubenites viciously. He put out the right [ey]e of a[ll] of them and brought fe[ar and trembling] on [Is]rael. Not one of the Israelites in the region be[yond the Jordan] remained [whose] right eye Naha[sh king of] the Ammonites did n[ot pu]t out, except seven thousand men [who escaped from] the Ammonites and went to [Ja]besh-gilead.
>
> (11:1) Then after about a month, Nahash the Ammonite went up and besieged Jabesh-[gilead]. (Adapted from *The Dead Sea Scrolls Bible,* 225)

So our two most ancient witnesses (4QSam^a and Josephus) confirm that the longer ending of chapter 10 was present in at least some ancient biblical manuscripts. This long-lost paragraph has now been restored in the New Revised Standard Version.

Scrolls such as 4QSam^a also help us to reassess the Septuagint. Its frequent agreements with the Greek Bible where the latter differs from the MT confirms that the translator was using an ancient Hebrew text similar in form to some Qumran manuscripts.

1 and 2 Kings

1 and 2 Kings (also a single book in the Hebrew Bible) recount Israel's history from the end of David's reign to the reigns of Jehoshaphat of Judah and Ahaziah of Israel (1 Kings), and then from the prophet Elisha to the fall of Jerusalem and the release of King Jehoiachin from prison (2 Kings). Only five Kings scrolls were discovered at Qumran, which preserve text from six chapters (1, 3, 7, 8, 12, and 22) of the 22 in 1 Kings, and six (5, 6, 7, 8, 9, and 10) of the 25 in 2 Kings. The oldest scrolls are 5QKings and pap6QKings (late second century B.C.E.), the latter written on fragile papyrus.

The Kings scrolls preserve numerous small variant readings and a few significant ones. Some are superior, but in other cases the MT has the best reading. One example of a superior reading is in 4QKings, where 1 Kings 8:16 preserves a longer passage also found in 2 Chronicles 6:5b–6a. As the example shows, the two clauses in italics were lost from the MT when a scribe's eye skipped from the first occurrence of "my name to be there" to the second. However, the Septuagint omits the first clause and retains only the second ("but I chose Jerusalem for my name to be there"):

Table 3.	
1 Kings 8:16–18 (= 2 Chron 6:5b–6a) in 4QKings	**In MT LXX**
(16) "[From the day I brought my people Israel out from Egypt, I did not choose a city from among the tribes of Israel to build a house for my name to be there, *nor did I choose any one*] *to be a leader over* [*my*] *people* [*Israel*, *but I chose Jerusalem for my name to be there*, but I chose David] to be over my people, over [Israel]."	(16) "Since the day that I brought my people Israel out of Egypt, I have not chosen a city from any of the tribes of Israel in which to build a house for my name to be there; [*but I chose Jerusalem for my name to be there*—LXX] but I chose David to be over my people Israel."

1 and 2 Chronicles

First and Second Chronicles (another single book)—a retelling of the events recorded in Samuel and Kings, but from a different viewpoint. Written after the exile, Chronicles shows that despite the destruction of Israel and Judah, God was still keeping his promises and blessing his returned people. Other prominent themes are worship, the Temple rituals, and the figures of David and Solomon.

Just one small fragment of Chronicles was discovered at Qumran (4QChron). Dated about 50–25 B.C.E., it preserves only parts of 2 Chronicles 28:27 and 29:1–3, which is four verses of all the 65 chapters in 1 and 2 Chronicles. Likely, 4QChron contained both 1 and 2 Chronicles, since the Chronicler's work forms a single book. However, it is also possible that the preserved text is from a smaller composition, in which case the existence of the entire book at Qumran is called into question.

Ezra and Nehemiah

Ezra-Nehemiah (yet another single book) deals with the return of some exiles to Jerusalem from Babylon, and the process of starting over. Ezra covers the rebuilding of the Temple and the restoration of true worship, while Nehemiah features rebuilding the city walls and a program of religious and social reforms.

Only one scroll of Ezra was found in Cave 4 at Qumran. For many years, scholars thought there was no copy of Nehemiah among the scrolls, but shortly after 2000 a Nehemiah scroll from Cave 4 emerged and was bought by Martin Schøyen, a Norwegian collector of manuscripts. In 2011, a second Nehemiah scroll came to light and was purchased by the Green Collection in Oklahoma City. For more on these scrolls, see chapter 1.4, above.

4QEzra (mid-first century B.C.E.) contains text from chapters 4, 5, and 6 of the ten in Ezra. The preserved text is almost identical to the consonantal MT, with only four minor variant readings. The two Nehemiah scrolls are most likely from Cave 4 at Qumran and copied in the late first century B.C.E. or early first century, 68 C.E. Of the book's 13 chapters, the Green Fragment preserves text from Nehemiah 2:13–16, and the Schøyen piece contains text from 3:14–15.

The book of Ezra provides a key term that the Essene movement appropriated for itself: the *Yahad* (Community, Ezra 4:3). Unfortunately, the actual word is no longer preserved in the key fragment of 4QEzra.

Esther

Esther is the only book in the traditional Hebrew Bible not represented among the scrolls from the Judean Desert. While it could be argued that this absence is due to chance and its relatively small size (ten chapters), it seems that Esther was rejected by the Essenes for theological reasons.

Scholars have proposed various explanations: this book makes no mention of God, Esther's marriage to a Gentile Persian king, and an emphasis on retaliation in the later chapters (which conflicts with some of the Qumran community's own writings). However, the most convincing reason for the decision to reject Esther involves the movement's religious feasts. This book introduces a new festival named Purim (Esther 9:20–32), which is not mentioned in the books of Moses and not included in the *Yahad*'s calendrical texts that list their feasts. It thus seems that they objected to the book that inaugurates Purim for the Jewish people.

3. The Poetical Books

The five Poetical Books are represented in 57 scrolls, of which 54 were found at Qumran and three at other sites in the Judean Desert.

Job

The book of Job is a powerful drama that deals with the problem of underserved suffering and disaster and why good people often experience great adversity.

Only six Job manuscripts were discovered at Qumran. Of the book's 43 chapters, 11 (8, 9, 13, 14, and 31–37) are represented, a number that rises to 33 if we include the two Job Targums (adding chapters 3–5, 17–30, and 38–42). The largest scroll is 4QJob^a, and the oldest 4QpaleoJob^c (about 225–150 B.C.E.) in the ancient paleo-Hebrew script. The two Targums, or Aramaic translations, were found in Cave 4 (4QtgJob), and Cave 11 (11QtgJob). The Cave 11 copy (early first century C.E.) is very extensive, preserving text from Job 17–42.

Of all these scrolls, 4QJob^a is closest to the consonantal MT. Most variant readings are quite minor, but a few are noteworthy. In Job 33:26, for example, 4QJob^a uses a form of the word *God* (*El*) that is more familiar than the one in the MT (*Eloah*). The Job scrolls also show that the Elihu speeches (chs. 32–37), which many scholars believe were not part of the original composition, were already part of this book before the Common Era.

Psalms

For Jews and Christians alike, the book of Psalms, or Psalter, is the prayer book of the Bible, the "Hymn Book of the Second Temple Period." The traditional Masoretic Psalter contains 150 psalms in five books or collections, most likely in imitation of the five books of Moses that make up the Pentateuch. The Greek Psalter has an additional psalm (151). Seventy-three psalms are associated with David, especially by their headings; several are attributed to groups such as the Sons of Asaph or figures such as Solomon; and several are untitled (the 34 "orphan" psalms).

There are 42 Psalms scrolls plus at least one more that incorporates a psalm, ranging in date from the mid-second century B.C.E. (4QPs^a) to about 50–68 C.E. Thirty-seven were found at Qumran, and three more farther south: one at Nahal Hever and two at Masada. Of all the works among the scrolls, Psalms are represented by the second-greatest number of manuscripts (after Deuteronomy, with 41). Most are very fragmentary, but several are very substantial, notably the *Great Psalms Scroll* (11QPs^a), followed by 4QPs^a, 5/6HevPs, 4QPs^b, 4QPs^c, and 4QPs^e (in descending order).

Of the 150 psalms in the traditional Hebrew Psalter, 127 are preserved in the Psalms scrolls and a few other manuscripts such as the *Pesharim*. The remaining 23 were most likely included, but are now lost. Of Psalms 1–89, 19 no longer survive, but of Psalms 90–150, only five are not represented.

At least 14 "apocryphal" psalms or compositions are included in four Psalms scrolls (4QPs^f, 11QPs^a, 11QPs^b, and 11QapocrPs). Six of these were previously familiar to scholars: Psalms 151A, 151B, 154, 155, David's Last Words (= 2 Sam 23:1–7), and Sirach 51:13–30. The other eight or nine were completely unknown prior to the discovery of the scrolls. These are, in alphabetical order: the *Apostrophe to Zion*, the *Eschatological Hymn* and the *Apostrophe to Judah*, the *Catena*, *David's Compositions*, the *Hymn to the Creator*, the *Plea for Deliverance*, and *Three Songs Against Demons*. Following are short descriptions of two of these fascinating works:

- The *Eschatological Hymn* and the *Apostrophe to Judah* are found in 4QPs^f. The *Hymn* offers praise to God, but with an eschatological emphasis, while the *Apostrophe* is also eschatological, but with a focus on Judah. Both may be parts of one broken acrostic poem. Translation:

  > [5]Then let heavens and earth give praise together; [6]then let all the stars of twilight give praise! [7]Rejoice, O Judah, in your joy; [8]be happy in your happiness, and dance in your dance. [9]Celebrate your pilgrim feasts, fulfill your vows, for no longer is [10]Belial in your midst. May your hand be lifted up! [11]May your right hand prevail! See, enemies will [12]perish, and all [13]evildoers will be scattered. But you, O LORD, are forev[er]; [14]your glory will be forev[er and ev]er. [15]Praise the LORD! (*The Dead Sea Scrolls Bible*, 588–89)

- *David's Compositions* is a prose epilogue to the Psalter in 11QPs^a, although found in the second to the last column (27) of the scroll. It asserts that David is the author of this scroll (and thus its Psalter), and that its arrangement and compositions were inspired by God himself (line 11: "All these he composed through prophecy . . . "). The numbers used (for example, 364, 52, and 30) show that this Psalter was arranged in accordance with the year, weeks, and months of the 364-day solar calendar, which was followed by the *Yahad*, rather than the lunar calendar, which had 354 days. Translation:

  > [2]And David, the son of Jesse, was wise, and a light like the light of the sun, and literate, [3]and discerning and perfect in all his ways before God and men. And the Lord gave [4]him a discerning and enlightened spirit. And he wrote [5]3,600 psalms; and songs to sing before the altar over the whole-burnt [6]perpetual offering every day, for all the days of the year, 364; [7]and for the offering of the Sabbaths, 52 songs; and for the offering of the New [8]Moons and for all the Solemn Assemblies and for the Day of Atonement, 30 songs. [9]And all the songs that he spoke were 446, and songs [10]for making music over the stricken, 4. And the total was 4,050. [11]All these he composed through prophecy which was given him from before the Most High. (*The Dead Sea Scrolls Bible*, 583–84)

The presence of these compositions in four Psalms scrolls reminds us that the book of Psalms at Qumran should not automatically be equated with the Psalter that appears in Bibles. Many Psalms scrolls are of little help for determining the ancient shape or contents of the book of Psalms. Some preserve little or almost no text, including 1QPs^c, 2QPs, 3QPs, 4QPs^j, 4QPs^p, 4QPs^r, 4QPs^u, and 4QPs^v; yet a few are helpful for showing early sequences (such as Psalms 49–51 in 1QPs^j). Others originally contained only small collections of psalms, often for liturgical use, most notably: 1QPs^a; Psalm 119 in 4QPs^g, 4QPs^h, 5QPs; and the *Psalms of Ascent* (120–34) in 1QPs^b.

For Psalms 1–89 or so, the Psalms scrolls contain material very much in the sequence that is familiar in Jewish and Christian Bibles. Evidence includes 4QPs^a and 4QPs^q, although Psalm 31 is followed by Psalm 33 in 4QPs^q, and Psalm 38 by Psalm 71 in 4QPs^a.

For Psalms 91 onward—90 is not preserved—the form of the Psalter is considerably different among several scrolls. Five main arrangements become evident:

- The *11QPs^a-Psalter* (Psalms 1–89 plus the order found in 11QPs^a) is evident in 11QPs^a, 11QPs^b, and probably 4QPs^e. The largest manuscript is the *Great Psalms Scroll* (11QPs^a), which was copied in about 50 C.E. and preserves 49 compositions in an arrangement beginning with Psalm 101 and ending with 151B. This Psalter differs from the Masoretic one with respect to the order of psalms and the inclusion of eleven compositions (the *Apostrophe to Zion, Catena, David's Compositions, David's Last Words, Hymn to the Creator, Plea for Deliverance*, Psalms 151A, 151B, 154, 155; and Sirach 51:13–30).

- The *MT-150 Psalter* (Psalms 1–150) as found in the MT is not unambiguously confirmed by even one Psalms scroll from Qumran. However, it seems to be attested in the second Psalms scroll from Masada (MasPs^b), which ends with Psalm 150.

- *Three Smaller Arrangements* are also found: the *Four Psalms Against Demons* in 11QapocrPs (three previously unknown psalms followed by Psalm 91); 4QPs^b (text from Psalms 91 to 118, but with 103 followed by 112); and 4QPs^f (Psalms 22, 107, and 109 followed by the *Apostrophe to Zion, Eschatological Hymn*, and *Apostrophe to Judah*).

This evidence suggests that two major editions of the book of Psalms are preserved in the scrolls: the *MT-150 Psalter* (in the traditional MT and the Septuagint, although the Greek Bible has many variant readings and ends with Psalm 151); and the *11QPs^a-Psalter* (Psalms 1–89 plus the arrangement found in 11QPs^a). For many scholars, the *11QPs^a-Psalter* is a genuine edition, indeed the foremost edition, of the book of Psalms in the scrolls. In contrast, many others maintain that the Psalms scrolls confirm an early form of the Psalter now represented by the MT (with 11QPs^a and several other Psalms scrolls containing collections based on the *MT-150 Psalter* for liturgical or instructive purposes).

The Psalms scrolls also contain numerous readings of passages in the Psalter, which help clear up difficulties in the traditional MT. Some have been included in most modern Bible translations.

One example will have to suffice: the missing verse from Psalm 145. A verse is missing from the MT version, known because this is an acrostic psalm. Although there are 22 letters in this alphabet, in the MT Psalm 145 contains only 21 verses, because a verse beginning with *nun* should come between verses 13 (the *mem* verse) and 14 (the *samek* verse). The MT's shorter verse 13 is translated in the Authorized (King James) Version: "Thy kingdom is an everlasting kingdom, and thy dominion endureth throughout all generations." The Septuagint supplies, in Greek of course, the additional *nun* verse (which we may call 13b) following verse 13 (13a):

> (13a) Your Kingdom is a kingdom of all the ages, and your dominion is in every generation and generation.

> (13b) The Lord is faithful in all his words, and devout in all his deeds.

This suggests that the Hebrew text used by the Greek translator had the missing *nun* verse. This is now confirmed by 11QPs^a, in which Psalm 145 contains both the *mem* verse and the missing *nun* verse in Hebrew. However, there is one difference against the LXX: "*God* (*The Lord*) is faithful in his words, and gracious in all his deeds."

Proverbs

This book is a collection of moral and religious teachings important for training in wisdom, prudence, and moral character. Fragments of only three Proverbs scrolls were found in Cave 4 at Qumran (both late first century B.C.E. or early first century C.E.). Only six of the 31 chapters in this major wisdom book (1, 2, 7, 13, 14, and 15) are represented.

The MT version and the Septuagint of Proverbs represent two different editions of the book, but the fragments from Qumran seem to agree with the traditional Hebrew one. Several variant readings are preserved, often involving only single letters but with noticeable differences in meaning. One example is in Proverbs 14:32, where 4QProv^a agrees with the MT: "but the right]eous [have refug]e *in their death* (Hebrew *bmwtw*)," in contrast to the Septuagint, which reads "*in their piety* (translating the Hebrew *btwmw*)."

Another variant reading is in Proverbs 14:34, where 4QProv^a and the Septuagint read "Righteousness] exalts a nation, but [sin *di*]*minishes* peoples," in contrast to the MT's "*is the loyalty of* peoples."

Ecclesiastes (Qohelet)

This book contains the words of the "Teacher" or "Philosopher," traditionally Solomon, who reflected deeply on the transitory nature of life and its contradictions. Only two Ecclesiastes scrolls were discovered, both in Cave 4 at Qumran. The oldest is 4QQoh^a (about 175–150 B.C.E.), which is among the very earliest scrolls, and is housed at the Amman Museum in Jordan. Between them, 4QQoh^a and 4QQoh^h preserve text from four chapters (1, 5, 6, and 7) of the 11 in the biblical book.

The two Ecclesiastes scrolls—like the MT and the Septuagint—exhibit a single edition of this book, although 4QQoh^a in particular preserves several variant readings.

One example is in Ecclesiastes 7:2, where 4QQoh^a reads "It is better to go to the house [of mourning than to go to the house of *j*]*oy*," in contrast to the MT's and the Septuagint's "house of *feasting*." A second is in Ecclesiastes 7:5, where the MT and the Septuagint read

"It is better to hear the *rebuke* of the wise *than a man hearing* the song of fools." Here 4QQoh[a] has "the *rebukes* of the wise" and "*than*] *to hear* the song of fools."

Song of Songs (Canticles)

The Song of Songs (which means "The Greatest of All Songs") is a collection of love poems, several of which are erotic and romantic. Some early rabbis and early church fathers tried to prevent inclusion of this book in the Hebrew Bible or Christian Old Testament, in view of its celebration of sexual love. Others, however, recognized the Song as Scripture and interpreted it in different ways. For the Jewish sages, the Song depicts the relationship between God (the Bridegroom) and Israel (the Beloved or Bride), while many church fathers saw it as portraying the relationship between Christ and his church. In more recent times, both Jews and Christians have increasingly come to recognize and appreciate the sexual and romantic nature of the Song of Songs.

Four manuscripts of the Song were found at Qumran. All were copied in the Herodian period (30 B.C.E.–68/70 C.E.), the latest being 6QCant (about 50 C.E.). Between them, these scrolls preserve text from seven of the Song's eight chapters.

One important manuscript is 4Cant[b], which is missing two large segments (3:6–8 and 4:4–7), and possibly ended at 5:1. Another that is significant is 4QCant[a], in which a large block of text between Canticles 4:7 and 6:11 (about 30 percent of the book) is missing. This is noteworthy because in the traditional MT, Canticles 4:7 forms the *end* of a content unit, and Canticles 6:11 is the *beginning* of another unit. Thus the absence of 4:8–6:10 was no mere accident, but rather the section seems to have been deliberately omitted (or was not part of the text being copied by the scribe). One explanation for this omission is that the sensual language and erotic imagery found in much of Canticles 4:8–6:10 made some readers nervous, which led to the removal of the large block from the book.

It is interesting to note, then, that 4QCant[a] and 4QCant[b] each lack a section at exactly the same point (Cant 4:7)—but whereas 4QCant[a] omits a large piece of text *starting* after 4:7, 4QCant[b] omits the three verses *preceding* the end of 4:7.

When these two scrolls were copied, the Song may have contained all eight chapters, with 4QCant[a] and 4QCant[b] deliberately omitting large blocks of text. Two alternative explanations are that the text of the Song was not settled by the late first century B.C.E. or that these two scrolls represent different editions of this little book.

4. The Prophets

Books of the Prophets are represented in 68 scrolls, of which 65 were found at Qumran and three at other sites in the Judean Desert.

Isaiah

With its message of judgment and comfort and visions of the end times and the coming kingdom of God, Isaiah is an important book for both Jews and Christians. The Isaiah scrolls are of special interest, in view of their contents and the fact that the *Great Isaiah Scroll* is the best known of all the Dead Sea Scrolls.

Isaiah was one of the four most popular books at Qumran, with 22 manuscripts recovered in the caves. One more was found farther south at Wadi Murabba'at (MurIsa). The Qumran Isaiah scrolls were copied over the course of nearly two centuries, from about 125 B.C.E. (1QIsa^a) to about 60 C.E. (4QIsa^c).

The *Great Isaiah Scroll* (1QIsa^a) is the only scroll to emerge virtually intact from the Qumran caves. In 54 columns it preserves all 66 chapters of Isaiah, except for small gaps resulting from leather damage. A few other Isaiah scrolls are quite substantial (notably 1QIsa^b and 4QIsa^b and 4QIsa^c), and between them also preserve generous portions of the book.

Many scholars believe that chapters 1–36 (or 1–39) are the work of "First Isaiah" (who lived in Jerusalem the second half of the eighth century B.C.E.), and that chapters 40–55 record the prophecies of "Second Isaiah" (after the fall of Jerusalem in 587 B.C.E. and during the exile). It is interesting to note that 1QIsa^a is carefully divided into two halves, each containing exactly 27 columns and 33 chapters of the book, which leads some scholars to believe that the most ancient dividing point between First and Second Isaiah was the end of chapter 33.

For the "book of Isaiah," the scrolls and other ancient witnesses preserve apparently only one general edition, with no consistent patterns of variant readings or large rearrangements. Some manuscripts are close to the MT: 1QIsa^b, 4QIsa^a, 4QIsa^b, 4QIsa^d, 4QIsa^e, 4QIsa^f, and 4QIsa^g. Other scrolls, most notably 1QIsa^a and 4QIsa^c, contain hundreds of variant readings from the traditional form of the Hebrew text.

Many variant readings are unimportant for understanding the meaning of the scriptural book, but are significant in other ways. For example, differences in spelling and grammar and changes in word order provide rich evidence for the ancient use of Hebrew; and errors by various scribes tell us much about individual copyists (some were careless!) and scribal habits during the late Second Temple period.

Of greater interest to most readers are variant readings that provide insights on the late stages of the book's composition. Many involve one or more verses that are present in some texts but absent from others. For example, in Isaiah's call narrative (Isa 40:6–8), the original scribe of 1QIsa^a has a shorter text. A later scribe inserted above the line a long addition that is also found in the MT. In this longer version, verse 7 now has three parts (with one in the original 1QIsa^a) and verse 8 has two (with only one by the original scribe) (see **Table 4**).

Some would argue that the longer text in the MT is the correct one, with the original omission in 1QIsa^a due to error (the scribe's eye skipping from "The grass withers, the flowers fade" in v. 7 to v. 8, thus losing the intervening text). However, it is more likely that 1QIsa^a originally copied a text with the earlier, shorter form. First, the shorter text makes better sense than the expansionistic form found in the MT, toward which the later scribe of 1QIsa^a "corrected" the manuscript. Second, the Septuagint has the identical short form, which shows that for verses 7–8 the Greek translator was using a Hebrew text like 1QIsa^a, not one like the MT.

Table 4.	
Isaiah 40:6–8 in 1QIsaᵃ LXX	**Isaiah 40:6–8 in MT**
(6) A voice says: "Proclaim!" So I said, "What am I to proclaim?" All flesh is grass, and all its beauty is like the flowers of the field. (7) The grass withers, the flowers fade,	(6) A voice says: "Proclaim!" So I said, "What am I to proclaim?" All flesh is grass, and all its beauty is like the flowers of the field. (7) *The grass withers, the flowers fade, when the breath of the LORD blows on it; surely the people are the grass.* (8) The grass withers, the flowers fade;
(8) but the word of our God stands forever.	but the word of our God stands forever.

Many other variants provide preferable readings to the MT of Isaiah, several of which could be viewed as correct and belonging to the original text of the book. One example is at Isaiah 1:15, which concludes with "your hands are filled with blood" in 4QIsaᶠ, the MT and the Septuagint, but 1QIsaᵃ completes the parallelism with "your fingers with iniquity."

An important variant is found in the Fourth Servant Song at Isaiah 53:11. Here the reading in the traditional text is difficult or obscure: "*He* (i.e., the Servant) *shall see* of the travail of his soul" (King James Version), or "Out of the suffering of his soul *he shall see.*" A different meaning is found in 1QIsaᵃ with the additional word *light*, with its implications of hope and life. This reading is supported by the only two other Isaiah scrolls that preserve this verse (1QIsaᵇ and 4QIsaᵈ) as well as the Septuagint.

Table 5.	
Isaiah 53:11 as in MT (King James Version)	**1QIsaᵃ, 1QIsaᵇ, 4QIsaᵈ (cf. LXX)**
He shall see of the travail of his soul, and shall be satisfied: by his knowledge shall my righteous servant justify many; for he shall bear their iniquities.	Out of the suffering of his soul *he will see light*, and find satisfaction. And through his knowledge my servant, the righteous one, will make many righteous, and he will bear their iniquities.

Isaiah is one of the most influential and oft-quoted books among the nonbiblical scrolls, both in Jewish writings imported to Qumran and in works specifically composed by the *Yahad* Essenes. The latter include the *Pesharim on Isaiah*, of which five were found at Qumran. By quoting a base text and commenting on it as addressing the *Yahad*'s life and beliefs, these commentaries underscore the importance and scriptural status of the book of Isaiah at Qumran.

Jeremiah

Jeremiah preached during the closing years of the Kingdom of Judah and survived the destruction of Jerusalem and the Temple by the Babylonians in 587/586 B.C.E. When many Jews were exiled to Babylon, the prophet remained in Jerusalem to help those still there to start anew but was then forced to flee to Egypt. Nine Jeremiah scrolls were found at Qumran, preserving text from only 31 of the book's 52 chapters (4, 7–15, 17–22, 25–27, 30–33, 42–44, and 46–50). The oldest is 4QJer^a (about 200 B.C.E.), and the latest is 4QJer^c (late first century B.C.E.).

As to the form of Jeremiah, two scrolls (4QJer^a and 4QJer^c) are close to the consonantal MT, but the contents of two others (4QJer^b and 4QJer^d) are strikingly similar to the Hebrew text from which the Greek Scriptures were translated. Most notably, the version of Jeremiah in these scrolls and the Septuagint is about 13 percent shorter than the longer one found in the MT. This similarity extends to small details as well. Thus were two ancient literary editions of Jeremiah: an earlier, shorter edition (4QJer^b, 4QJer^d, and the Septuagint), and a later, longer edition (4QJer^a, 4QJer^c, and the MT).

The contrast is clear in Jeremiah 10:3–11, which presents a satire on idols. While 4QJer^a (before it was damaged) and the MT have all nine verses, 4QJer^b (when fully extant) and the Septuagint never had verses 6–8 and 10. A short extract is given:

Table 6.	
Jeremiah 10:9–10 in 4QJer^a MT	**In 4QJer^b LXX**
(9) [Hammered silver is brought from Tarshish and gold from Uphaz, the work of the craftsman and of the hands of the goldsmith with blue and pur]ple [for their clothing; they are all the product of skilled workers]. (10) [But the Lord is the true God; he is the living God and] the everlasting King; at [his a]nger [the earth quakes, and the nations cannot endure his wrath].	(9) [Hammered silver is brought from Tarshish and gold from Uphaz, the work of the craftsman and of the hands of the goldsmith] with blue and purple [for their clothing; they are all the product of skilled workers].

Lamentations

The five poems in this book are a reaction to ancient Israel's greatest disaster: the destruction of Jerusalem and the Temple in 587/586 B.C.E. In moving and heartfelt poetry, the cry of people who survived this traumatic event rings out: *Why?*—which is the Hebrew title for the book and the first word in three of the five laments.

Four Lamentations scrolls were found at Qumran, which between them preserve text from all five chapters of the book. The oldest is 4QLam from the early Herodian period (30 B.C.E. to 1 C.E.). These manuscripts contain a form of Lamentations similar to the one in the traditional MT, but 4QLam and 5QLam[a] preserve several distinctive readings that do not agree with either the MT or the Septuagint. Several such variant readings are evident in the following excerpt from Lamentations 1 in 4QLam and the MT and the Septuagint:

Table 7.	
Lam 1:17 (4QLam)	**Lam 1:17 (MT LXX)**
(17) Zion spreads forth [her] h[ands; there is none] to comfort her *among all her lovers; you, O* Lord, *are righteous.* The Lord *has kept watch* concerning Jacob, so that his neighbors should be his adversaries. *Zion has been banished* among them.	(17) Zion spreads forth her hands; there is none to comfort her. The Lord *has commanded* concerning Jacob, so that his neighbors should be his adversaries. *Jerusalem has become a filthy thing* among them.

The several different readings are denoted by italics, including: the longer text ("among all her lovers") in 4QLam; the form of God's name ("LORD" [*Adonay*] in 4QLam versus "LORD" [*Yahweh*] in the MT), and the different endings following "adversaries." The final variant in 4QLam ("has been banished") is also supported by the Septuagint. One more feature (not included in the example) is that in 4QLam, verse 17 is followed by verse 16.

This book is a fine example of Hebrew poetry, with chapters 1–4 each containing an acrostic poem. Modern scholars and translations lay out this book in poetic format, rather than in prose style. It is interesting to note that scribe of 3QLam also laid out his text in poetic units; however, the scribes of 4QLam, 5QLam[a], and 5QLam[b] did not do so, giving the appearance of prose. The question of when poetic layout came about is not just an ancient one; compare for example, the prose layout of Lamentations in the King James Bible (1611) and the poetic layout in modern Bibles such as the New Revised Standard Version, the New American Bible, the New International Version, and the Jewish Publication Society's *Tanakh*.

Ezekiel

Ezekiel was a priest and prophet who lived mostly in exile in Babylon following Jerusalem's fall in 587/586 B.C.E. His prophecies—to both the people of Jerusalem and the Babylonian exiles—feature judgment, hope, consolation, a restored nation, and a future Temple.

Six Ezekiel were found at Qumran and one more atop Masada (MasEzek). The oldest is 4QEzek[c] (early to mid-first century B.C.E.). These scrolls preserve portions of 18 chapters (1, 4, 5, 7, 10, 11, 13, 16, 23, 24, 31–37, and 41) of the 48 chapters that make up the biblical book.

The textual form (especially in 11QEzek) is very similar to Ezekiel in the consonantal MT. However, 4QEzek[b], which preserves material from the prophet's inaugural vision in chapter 1, may have contained only this part of the book. Also, while 4QEzek[a] is very fragmentary, it preserves text from verses 15 and 17 of Ezekiel 23, but has no space for verse 16, which must have been missing from the undamaged text.

Daniel

The book of Daniel was written (or finalized) during a time of persecution for the Jewish people under a pagan king. Set in Babylon during the exile, the stories of Daniel and his friends encouraged readers to remain faithful to God, to refuse compromise, and to expect triumph over wickedness and idolatry. A book like this must have brought encouragement to the Yahad, who at times felt persecuted by other Jews and threatened by Hellenism.

A total of 11 Daniel scrolls were discovered at Qumran, which between them preserve text from the first 11 of the book's 12 chapters. This does not point to a shorter version of Daniel, since Daniel 12:10 is quoted in the *Florilegium* (4Q174), which tells us that it is "written in the book of Daniel the Prophet." All ten scrolls were copied in the space of 175 years, from about 125 B.C.E. (4QDan[c]) to about 50 C.E. (4QDan[b]). Of all the biblical scrolls, 4QDan[c] is closest in date to when the book itself was composed (about 165 B.C.E.), and shows that it was being read by the *Yahad* only 40 years after being written.

There are two ancient forms of Daniel: the 12-chapter version preserved in the MT and the longer version found in the Greek Bible (which includes the *Additions to Daniel*). Seven of the Daniel scrolls originally contained the entire book in the shorter form, not the longer one preserved in the Septuagint. The eighth manuscript, 4QDan[e], preserves text only from chapter 9 and may have contained only the Prayer of Daniel (Dan 9:4b–19). In that case, it would not strictly qualify as a copy of the book itself.

With respect to the text of Daniel, all ten scrolls reveal no major disagreements against the consonantal MT, although 1QDan[a] is closest to it. Several variant readings are noteworthy. One is in Daniel 2:20, after the meaning of King Nebuchadnezzar's dream was revealed to Daniel. 4QDan[a] reads: "Daniel sa[id]: "Blessed be the name of *the great God* [from a]ge to age, for wisdom and power a[re] his," whereas the MT has only *God* for the divine name. The scroll's text is supported by the Septuagint, which reads *the Great Lord*.

Another significant variant appears in Daniel 7:1, where the traditional MT reads: "In the first year of King Belshazzar of Babylon Daniel had a dream and visions of his head upon his bed. Then he *wrote down the dream, he related the sum of the words*." The king's last actions seem awkward, causing scholars to suspect even before the discovery of the scrolls that "he related the sum of the words" may be a later addition to the original text. This is now confirmed by 4QDan[b], which reads only "[then] he wrote down the [dream]," with no space for more text. The shorter reading is accepted and translated by the New Revised Standard Version.

A final question concerns the bilingual nature of Daniel, which in the Hebrew Bible opens in Hebrew, switches to Aramaic at chapter 2:4b, and then reverts to Hebrew at

8:1. The four scrolls that preserve material from the relevant sections (1QDan[a], 4QDan[a], 4QDan[b], and 4QDan[d]) support the same transitions from Hebrew to Aramaic and back again, which confirms that Daniel existed in this form very early on and was most likely compiled in Hebrew and Aramaic.

The Twelve Minor Prophets

The Minor Prophets make up 12 books in the Septuagint and Christian Bibles, but the single Book of the Twelve in the Hebrew Bible. This is a collection of warnings of judgment and words of comfort from many prophets, some in the northern kingdom (Hosea, Amos), others in the southern kingdom (Joel, Micah, Nahum, Habakkuk, Zephaniah), and others during or after the exile (Obadiah, Jonah, Haggai, Zechariah, Malachi).

Fifteen scrolls of the Minor Prophets were found in the Judean Desert. Thirteen are from the caves at Qumran, and are dated from 150 B.C.E. (4QXII[a], perhaps 4QXII[b]) to 25 B.C.E. (4QXII[g]). Two more were found farther south at Murabba'at (MurXII), and Nahal Hever (8HevXII gr). These scrolls preserve text from 63 of the 67 chapters in the Minor Prophets, with only four (Zechariah 7 and 13, and Malachi 1 and 4) not represented.

Table 8. Order of the Minor Prophets	
Hebrew Bible	**Septuagint**
Hosea	Hosea
Joel	*Amos*
Amos	*Micah*
Obadiah	*Joel*
Jonah	*Obadiah*
Micah	*Jonah*
Nahum	Nahum
Habakkuk	Habakkuk
Zephaniah	Zephaniah
Haggai	Haggai
Zechariah	Zechariah
Malachi	Malachi

But were the 12 prophetic books grouped into one book in ancient times? Seven scrolls confirm this to be so; the other three (4QXII[d], 4QXII[f], 5QAmos) contain parts of only one book, only because most of their text has been lost. And what about the order of component books in the Minor Prophets scrolls: do they support the traditional Hebrew order found in the MT or the one in the Septuagint? As the table shows, the difference involves five books, which appear in bold italics.

The Minor Prophets scrolls generally follow the traditional Hebrew order—even the one from Cave 8 at Nahal Hever (8HevXII gr), which is written in Greek. However, in the oldest manuscript, 4QXII[a] (150 B.C.E.), Jonah follows Malachi as the last book, which suggests some fluidity in the earliest collections of the Minor Prophets.

The textual form in these scrolls is generally close to the traditional MT, including 8HevXII gr, which contains a Septuagint text that has been corrected to agree more closely with the consonantal MT. However, many variant readings exist in 8HevXII gr, and especially in 4QXII^a, 4QXII^c, 4QXII^e, and 4QXII^g. All these texts may be described as "slightly mixed": usually in agreement with the traditional MT, but sometimes with the Septuagint, and sometimes with neither ("independent readings").

In the first example (Hosea 11:8), a Minor Prophets scroll from Cave 4 (4QXII^g) preserves an ancient reading, *He has turned back upon my heart,* which differs from the MT ("*My heart is turned over within me*") and the Septuagint ("*My heart is turned over*"). Both Hebrew texts are difficult; the Greek may be an attempt to make sense of the translator's Hebrew source.

Second, in an oracle against Nineveh (Nahum 3:8–10), the ending of verse 8 is difficult, but is fortunately preserved in two scrolls. 4QXII^g at Qumran reads: "(8) Are you better than [N]o-amo[n, that was] situated by the Nile, [that had waters around her; *whose*] *wall was a rampart of the sea?*" This ending differs from the Greek Minor Prophets scroll at Nahal Hever (8HevXII gr), which reads "*whose*] *strength is the sea, wate[r her wall,*" as well as the Septuagint ("*whose dominion is the sea, and whose wall is water*") and the MT ("*whose rampart was the sea, and whose wall was of the sea*").

In addition to the ten Minor Prophets scrolls discussed above, seven or eight *Pesharim* were written on several Minor Prophets: two on Hosea (4QpHos^a, 4QpHos^b), two on Zephaniah (1QpZep, 4QpZeph^a), one or two on Micah (1QpMic, 4QpMic?), and one each on Nahum (4QpNah) and Habakkuk (1QpHab).

6

The Dead Sea Scrolls
and the Biblical Text

This chapter discusses the significance of the biblical scrolls. The first section considers six aspects of these manuscripts (early collections, the number of scrolls for each book, abbreviated or excerpted texts, scrolls on papyrus, the paleo-Hebrew scrolls, and scrolls in Greek and Aramaic). The second section examines the implications of the biblical scrolls for our understanding of the text of the Hebrew Bible/Old Testament, including several theories of textual development.

1. Observations on the Biblical Scrolls

1.1 Early Collections of Scriptural Books

Eleven scrolls found at Qumran and one from Murabbaʿat contain the remains of more than one book. Most are from the Pentateuch, with the represented books in the titles: 4QGen-Exod^a, 4QpaleoGen-Exod^l, 4QExod-Lev^f, and 4QLev-Num^a. Several others also contain more than one book, although this is not evident from their titles: four *Reworked Pentateuch* scrolls: 4QRP^a (Genesis, Exodus, and Deuteronomy), 4QRP^b (Exodus, Numbers, and Deuteronomy), 4QRP^c (all five books), and 4QRP^d (Exodus, Leviticus, Numbers, and Deuteronomy). Also: 4QExod^b (Genesis and Exodus); 1QpaleoLev (Leviticus and Numbers); and most likely Mur 1 (Genesis, Exodus, and Numbers). Yet more scrolls most likely contained two or more books, on the basis of their large parameters: 4QGen^b, 4QGen^e, 4QExod^e, SdeirGen (from Wadi Sdeir), and MasDeut (from Masada).

All this evidence confirms the traditional order of the Pentateuch (Genesis to Deuteronomy) and that it was viewed as a collection by the *Yahad*. A few scrolls (notably 4QReworked Pentateuch^b and 4QRP^c) may have contained all five books before they were damaged, in which case they must have been very long (up to almost 100 feet).

According to the Babylonian Talmud (*Baba Batra* 13b), the 12 books of the Minor Prophets are to be combined in a single collection. Seven scrolls confirm that they were copied together in ancient times and follow the traditional Hebrew order, not the order found in the Septuagint. However, in the oldest manuscript, 4QXII^a (150 B.C.E.), Malachi is followed by Jonah as the final book, which suggests some fluidity in the earliest groupings.

In Jewish tradition, five of the Writings are grouped together as the Five Scrolls or Five Megillot: Song of Songs, Ruth, Lamentations, Ecclesiastes, and Esther. In Christian Bibles, these are arranged differently, with Ruth and Esther among the Historical Books, Ecclesiastes and the Song among the Poetic Books, and Lamentations among the Prophets. Do the scrolls offer clues on whether the Five Megillot were grouped together? Esther was excluded from the *Yahad*'s Scriptures, and in one scroll from Qumran (4QLam), Lamentations was preceded by another book, which is now lost, but was most likely Jeremiah. Thus the Qumran fragments do not affirm the Five Megillot as a single collection.

1.2 The Number of Manuscripts for Biblical Books

The number of biblical **scrolls available to scholars** is 270, comprising 252 from Qumran and 18 from other sites. The Qumran numbers include ten Greek scrolls, three Aramaic *targums*, the five *Reworked Pentateuch* scrolls, and about 30 more (presumably from Qumran) acquired by universities, seminaries, and other institutions since 2000. (The 270 total has been adjusted down from 303, since 11 scrolls from Qumran and one from Muraba'at preserve parts of more than one book in 33 cases. These can only be counted once.)

The **grand total of biblical scrolls** is 318, of which about 300 were most likely found at Qumran. About 48 (perhaps a few less) scrolls are held by private parties and will most likely be "on the market" in future years. Not much is known about these, except that almost all are fragments of biblical books.

In the **Table**, the books represented by most manuscripts are Deuteronomy (42 scrolls, with 39 at Qumran), Psalms (42, with 39 at Qumran), Genesis (34, with 30 at Qumran), Exodus (31, with 30 at Qumran), Isaiah (23, with 1 at Qumran), and Leviticus (24, with 22 at Qumran). Only Esther is absent, and Chronicles and Ezra are represented by one scroll each.

These figures are as accurate as possible, but any final count is elusive: (a) Some "biblical" texts were most likely shorter compositions (for example, 4QPs^g, 4QPs^h, 5QPs, 4QCant^a, 4QCant^b, 4QDan^e). (b) Some may constitute more than one scroll (4QGen^{h1}, 4QGen^{h2}, 4QDeut^j, Mur 1). (c) Some may be part of the same scroll, not separate ones (4QJer^b, 4QJer^d, and 4QJer^e).

1.3 Abbreviated or Excerpted Biblical Texts

A few "biblical" scrolls contain only excerpted or abbreviated texts, often for liturgical use. Some examples are: 4QDeut^j and 4QDeut^n (Deuteronomy 31, on the covenant),

Table 1.			
Book	**Qumran**	**Other**	**Total**
Deuteronomy	39	3	42
Psalms	39	3	42
Genesis	30	4	34
Exodus	30	1	31
Isaiah	22	1	23
Leviticus	22	2	24
Numbers	15	3	18
Daniel	11	0	11
12 Minor Prophets	13	2	15
Jeremiah	9	0	9
Ezekiel	6	0	6
1 and 2 Samuel	7	0	7
Job	6	0	6
Ruth	5	0	5
Song of Songs	4	0	4
Lamentations	4	0	4
Judges	5	0	5
1 and 2 Kings	5	0	5
Joshua	3	0	3
Proverbs	3	0	3
Ecclesiastes	2	0	2
Nehemiah	2	0	2
1 and 2 Chronicles	1	0	1
Ezra	1	0	1
Esther	0	0	0
(Total	284	19	303)
Adjusted Total	**252**	**18**	**270**
"On the Market"	48	0	48
Grand Total	**300**	**18**	**318**

4QDeut^q (the Song of Moses in Deut 32:1–44), 1QPs^a, 4QPs^g, 4QPs^h, and 5QPs (Psalm 119), and 4QDan^e (perhaps only Daniel's Prayer in Dan 9:4b–19).

1.4 Biblical Scrolls Written on Papyrus

The scrolls, especially the biblical ones, were almost always written on leather parchment, which was prepared from ritually pure animals and thus preferred by the Qumran scribes for copying biblical texts. In contrast, papyrus, apparently made by non-Jews in Egypt, was considered by many to be impure. About 100 papyri were found at Qumran, mostly letters and bills, but nine contain text from biblical books: four of the Pentateuch (pap4QGen, pap7QLXXExod, pap4QLXXLev^b, pap6QDeut?), one of Kings (pap6QKings), one of the Psalms (pap6QPs), two of the Prophets (pap4QIsa^p and pap6QDan), and a possible tenth one from Cave 7, written in Greek (pap Biblical Text gr).

1.5 The Paleo-Hebrew Biblical Scrolls

Twelve biblical scrolls are written in paleo-Hebrew, rather than the square script in which the vast majority of the scrolls were copied. Eleven are from the Pentateuch (4QpaleoGen^m, 6QpaleoGen, 4QpaleoGen-Exod^l, 4QpaleoExod^m, 1QpaleoLev, 2QpaleoLev, 6QpaleoLev, 11QpaleoLev^a, 1QpaleoNum, 4QpaleoDeut^r, and 4QpaleoDeut^s), and the twelfth is of Job (4QpaleoJob^c). This script was most likely used for books that were considered especially important, of great antiquity, and attributed to Moses. The inclusion of Job may anticipate the rabbinic tradition in the Babylonian Talmud that it was written by Moses (*Baba Batra* 14b, 15a). Another relevant text in this script is 4QpaleoParaJoshua (with portions of Joshua 21). These paleo-Hebrew texts may derive from the Sadducees, since writing in this script was forbidden by the Pharisees (Mishna, Tractate *Yadayim* 4.5; Babylonian Talmud, *Sanhedrin* 21b).

1.6 Biblical Scrolls in Greek and Aramaic

Several scrolls were written in Greek, and date from the second century B.C.E. to the early first century C.E. Most are biblical (or, rather, scriptural) manuscripts with material from pentateuchal books: Exodus (pap7QLXXExod), Leviticus (4QLXXLev^a and pap4QLXXLev^b), Numbers (4QLXXNum), and Deuteronomy (4QLXXDeut). Also noteworthy are: an extensive Greek scroll of the Minor Prophets found in Cave 8 at Nahal Hever (8HevXII gr), a Greek paraphrase of Exodus (4Q127), the Letter of Jeremiah (pap7QEpJer gr), and possibly *1 Enoch* (pap7QEn gr).

Several Hebrew scrolls contain a textual form similar to the Septuagint and are close to its Hebrew source. For example, 4QJer^b and 4QJer^d contain a Hebrew text akin to the one from which the Septuagint was translated and present a version of Jeremiah about 13 percent shorter than the longer one found in modern Bibles. Besides these striking examples, many more scrolls preserve individual readings that are found in the Septuagint but not in the MT.

Three targums (translations into Aramaic) were found at Qumran: 4QtgLev, 4Qtg-Job, and 11QtgJob. In light of the rabbinic tradition in the Babylonian Talmud that Moses wrote Job (*Baba Batra* 14b, 15a), it appears that only books of Moses were eligible for translation into Aramaic.

2. The Scrolls and the Text of the Hebrew Bible/Old Testament

Several forms or editions of the Old Testament have existed since early times, most notably the pre-Masoretic Text, the Samaritan Pentateuch, and the Septuagint (Greek Bible). In the survey of the biblical scrolls, several were placed in one of four textual categories: (a) like the Masoretic Text; (b) like the Samaritan Pentateuch; (c) like the presumed Hebrew text translated by the Septuagint; and (d) mixed or nonaligned. As the biblical manuscripts from Qumran and other locations near the Dead Sea were studied, theories of textual development took shape and were developed by several scholars.

2.1 The Theory of Local Texts

Frank Moore Cross (1921–2012) of Harvard University, building on the earlier work of William F. Albright, developed a theory of development for the first five books of the Bible. He identified three main text-types, which he termed *local texts*, all of which are represented among the biblical scrolls from Qumran and other ancient manuscripts.

(a) The Palestinian Text

The Hebrew Bible, or most of it, was written in Palestine, where it continued to be studied and copied for many centuries. The main representative of this text is the Samaritan Pentateuch, which remains the Bible of Samaritan Jews to this day. The SP preserves the ancient Palestinian text, but with the later addition of vowels and sectarian passages. Among the scrolls, examples of this form include 4QpaleoExod^m, 4QExod-Lev^f, and 4QNum^b.

(b) The Babylonian Text

Jews carried the Palestinian text to other places, notably Babylonia when they went into exile in 587/586 B.C.E. As it was copied over the centuries, variations arose, some due to decisions made by scribes and others due to error. Cross concluded that the consonantal form of the Masoretic Text is the result of copying and finalization that took place among Babylonian Jews. Examples include 4QGen-Exod^a, 4QSam^b, 1QIsa^b, 4QJer^a, and 4QPs^c.

(c) The Egyptian Text

Following the conquests of Alexander the Great, many Jews moved to Egypt, with their descendants speaking Greek fluently or even as their first language. Because many of these Jews knew little Hebrew and had assimilated Greek culture, the need arose for a Greek translation of the Hebrew Bible. Beginning with the Pentateuch in the third century B.C.E., a group of Jewish scholars in Egypt translated a Hebrew text from Palestine into Greek (the Septuagint). Examples include 4QLev^d, 4QJer^b, and 4QJer^d.

2.2 Multiple Texts, Creative Authors, and Copyists

Shemaryahu Talmon of the Hebrew University (1920–2010) proposed that rather than text-types or families, the biblical text was known from the beginning in a variety of forms. Talmon also focused on the textual and sociological aspects of the biblical scrolls and eliminated the distinction between authors and copyists. He pointed out that the MT, SP, and Septuagint were salvaged from a larger pool of text forms, only because the rabbis, Samaritans, and Christians each preserved their own particular collection of texts. Other forms also existed but perished together with the groups that once held them sacred.

2.3 Textual Variety, but the Pre-Masoretic Text as Dominant

Emanuel Tov (editor in chief of the Dead Sea Scrolls Publication Project, 1990–2009) finds greater textual diversity than Cross among the Qumran biblical scrolls. They do not neatly fall, Tov observes, into one of just three categories, but represent a larger number of textual forms. Nevertheless, most texts can be placed in one of four broad groups, according to the degree of closeness to the MT, the SP, or the Septuagint; Tov adds a fifth group using different criteria. He recognizes the problem of grouping texts according to the degree of closeness to later textual witnesses, but he regards it as necessary because three early forms already existed in the last centuries before the Common Era. His calculation of the percentages for the various groups is based upon 130 biblical texts from Qumran, since the remaining 90 texts are too fragmentary for textual analysis.

(a) Pre-Samaritan (or Harmonistic) Texts

The textual form (Cross: Palestinian) in the SP, although the Samaritan Bible itself is later and contains additional material. The Qumran witnesses are characterized by orthographic (spelling) corrections and harmonizations with parallel texts found elsewhere in the Pentateuch. Tov estimates these at no more than 5 percent of the Qumran biblical texts; they are restricted to the Pentateuch, and comprise 21 percent of the Torah scrolls.

(b) Proto-Masoretic (or Proto-Rabbinic) Texts

A form (Cross: Babylonian) characterized by a stable text with the consonants and distinctive readings found in the MT. For Tov, 48 (37 percent) of the Qumran biblical scrolls fall into this category, with 20 (15 percent) strictly close to the MT, 18 (14 percent) equally close to the MT and the SP, and ten (7.5 percent) equally close to the MT and the Hebrew source of the LXX.

(c) Texts Close to the Presumed Hebrew Source of the Septuagint

A form (Cross: Egyptian) close to the Hebrew source from which the LXX was translated. Many other scrolls also share distinctive readings with the Septuagint, but do not fall in this category. According to Tov, these make up no more than 5 percent of the Qumran biblical texts.

(d) Nonaligned Texts

Many Qumran texts show no consistent closeness to the MT, the SP, or the Septuagint, since they agree with more than one ancient version in different places. Examples include 2QExod^a, 4QExod^b, 11QpaleoLev^a, 4QDeut^b, 1QIsa^a, 4QIsa^c, 4QPs^a, 11QPs^a, 4QCant^a, and 4QDan^a. Some also contain readings not known elsewhere (for example, 4QJosh^a, 4QJudg^a, and 4QSam^a). Tov estimates this group at 28 (37 percent) of the Qumran biblical scrolls.

(e) Scrolls Written in the "Qumran Practice"

(These are not included in Tov's statistics since most are counted among the other four groups.) According to Tov, these were copied by scribes from the Qumran community and feature long orthography and morphology (such as word endings), frequent errors and corrections, and a free approach to the text. He identifies 18 examples, including 4QExod^b, 4QDeut^j, 1QIsa^a, 4QIsa^c, and 11QPs^a. Most are characterized as textually independent, and so are nonaligned.

2.4 Successive Literary Editions

Eugene Ulrich (chief editor of the Biblical Scrolls, 1990–2009) proposes a model of successive literary editions for the development of the text of various biblical books. These editions occurred later in the compositional process of the Scriptures, which took place in several stages that were different for each book. Each new edition resulted from the creative efforts of an author or scribe, who intentionally revised the edition (or passages) before him in the light of new religious or national challenges. Usually, the newer edition replaced the older one(s), but this was not always the case. Examples are 4QpaleoExod^m and 4QNum^b, which share common features with the SP, the 11QPs^a-Psalter, and the book of *Jubilees* (with its 364-day calendar instead of the 354-day one practiced by the rabbis).

Ulrich provides two steps to help discern these variant literary editions: (a) Ignoring spelling differences, since a manuscript's orthography is seldom related to any particular edition. (b) Ignoring variant readings not related to the pattern of variants, by which an author or scribe reworked an existing edition into a revised edition.

One obvious example of different literary editions is Jeremiah, with the MT's longer version in 4QJer^a and 4QJer^c, and the Septuagint's shorter version in 4QJer^b and 4QJer^d. Of the 24 books in the traditional Hebrew Bible (the MT), Ulrich identifies variant literary editions for at least 12, and as many as 16, during the closing centuries of the Second Temple period:

- Six among the Qumran biblical scrolls (Exodus, Numbers, Joshua, Jeremiah, Psalms, Song of Songs).

- Possibly four more from Qumran (Judges, Samuel, the Minor Prophets, Lamentations).

- When the SP and LXX are also taken into consideration, six or seven more (Gen 5 and 11, Kings, Ezekiel, the Minor Prophets, Job [?], Proverbs, Daniel).

2.5 The Biblical Scrolls and the Development of the Biblical Text

On the positive side:

- The identification of Local Texts by Cross was a leap forward in our understanding of the development of the text of the Hebrew Bible.

- Talmon showed that the MT, SP, and LXX are only three forms of the biblical text, and that many other forms once existed.

- Tov's grouping of biblical scrolls is more nuanced than the Local Texts theory and identifies more categories among the biblical scrolls from Qumran. His four categories are broad, especially the Nonaligned Texts, which include numerous forms of the biblical text. Tov's case that the pre-Masoretic Text was the dominant form among the Qumran scrolls is a very strong one.

- Ulrich's Successive Literary Editions is a clear advance forward, with variant editions among the Qumran biblical scrolls for 12 (and up to 16) books of the Hebrew Bible.

Some constructive criticism:

- Cross' division of the biblical scrolls from Qumran into three textual categories—a very early proposal—is too restrictive, since further different forms are evident.

- Talmon's approach downplays the existence of distinct groupings or families of texts that can be readily identified.

- Tov's term *proto-Masoretic* implies too close a relationship with the medieval Masoretic Text; *pre-Masoretic* is preferable. Also, his decision to place texts that are equally close to the MT and the SP, or to the MT and the LXX, among the pre-Masoretic group is problematic. Tov justifies this as "in accord with statistical probability," thus decreeing that Qumran biblical texts close to two ancient textual forms must be pre-Masoretic unless otherwise proven.

In fact, of the 48 (37 percent) Qumran biblical scrolls in this category, only 20 (15 percent) are strictly close to the MT, while the other 28 (22 percent) are just as close to the SP or the Hebrew source of the LXX. Tov's percentages for the pre-Masoretic group may need adjustment downward, and those for the pre-Samaritan group and (less so) the Hebrew source of the Septuagint may have to be increased.

- Ulrich's identification of variant editions for up to 16 of the 24 books of the traditional Hebrew Bible has its challenges. Some scholars question whether every book he lists containing variant readings, or patterns of variants, qualifies as a different literary edition. All readily agree that there are two editions of Jeremiah, for instance, but the evidence for some books in Ulrich's list is not as clear (for example, Judges and Job).

Concluding Comments

For scholars and laypeople who read and research the biblical scrolls, it seems most profitable to keep three questions in mind:

(1) Into which textual category should each scroll be placed: pre-Samaritan, pre-Masoretic, close to the Hebrew source of the Septuagint, or nonaligned?

(2) What methods and criteria should be used for placing a scroll in one of these categories?

(3) Can we identify a distinct literary edition of a particular biblical book (or part of it) in the scroll being studied?

7

The Scrolls, the Apocrypha, and the *Pseudepigrapha*

Of the almost 1,250 Dead Sea Scrolls, about 1,050 were found at Qumran: the Biblical Scrolls (almost 300 at Qumran), the Nonbiblical Scrolls (about 600 at Qumran), and Apocrypha and *Pseudepigrapha* (including the New *Pseudepigrapha*) total about 150.

Most Apocrypha and *Pseudepigrapha* are found in Christian Bibles with longer Old Testaments, such as Roman Catholic and Greek Orthodox Bibles, and so it could be argued that they belong among the Biblical Scrolls. These writings are very significant for understanding early Judaism, since they were written or describe events in the Second Temple period (516 B.C.E. to 70 C.E.), especially between the return from exile (Ezra-Nehemiah) and the earliest Pauline writings (1 Thessalonians) and Gospels (Mark).

1. The Apocrypha and *Pseudepigrapha*

The terms Apocrypha and *Pseudepigrapha* are not easy to understand, since each has more than one meaning.

Apocrypha is a plural word (singular: *Apocryphon*) that means "hidden or secret writings," originally to be read only by initiates into a Christian group. The term was eventually used for works similar to biblical books in content, form, or title, although not accepted by all Christians as Scripture. The most common use is "books or parts of books that appear in Roman Catholic Bibles but not in Jewish or Protestant ones." Almost all these books derive from the Septuagint, but were not accepted by the rabbis who finalized the Jewish canon or by the church leaders who fixed the Protestant canon during the Reformation. For Catholics and Orthodox Christians, these writings qualify as Scripture and are known as the Deuterocanonicals.

There are ten Apocrypha altogether. Eight are complete books: Tobit, Judith, 1 and 2 Maccabees, the Wisdom of Solomon, Sirach (also known as Ecclesiasticus or the Wisdom of Jesus ben Sira), Baruch, and the Letter of Jeremiah. Two Apocrypha are supplements to other books: the Additions to Esther (in eight sections) and the Additions to Daniel (the Prayer of Azariah and Song of the Three Young Men; Susanna; and Bel and the Dragon). All were written during the Second Temple period, the oldest being Tobit (fourth or third century B.C.E.), and the latest the Wisdom of Solomon (about 40 C.E. or earlier).

The term *Pseudepigrapha* (singular: *Pseudepigraphon*) means "writings falsely attributed to ancient authors." In a more general sense, it refers to virtually all ancient Jewish works—outside of the Old Testament, the Apocrypha, and a few other major writings (notably Philo and Josephus)—that were known to us prior to the discovery of the Dead Sea Scrolls. Unlike the Apocrypha, the term *Pseudepigrapha* and the writings it contains are normally written in italics. There are two groups of *Pseudepigrapha:*

The first group contains eight writings—in addition to the Apocrypha—that are recognized as Scripture by various Orthodox churches. One (*Psalm 151*) forms the conclusion to the book of Psalms. The other seven are books, some of which have more than one name: the *Prayer of Manasseh, 1 Esdras* (or *3 Ezra*), *2 Esdras* (or *4 Ezra*), *3 Maccabees, 4 Maccabees, 1 Enoch,* and *Jubilees.* Most were written during the Second Temple period, the oldest being *Jubilees* and *1 Esdras* (second century B.C.E.), and the latest *2 Esdras* (late first to third centuries C.E.). Because these books form part of various Orthodox church Bibles, an argument could be made that the term *Apocrypha* applies to them as well. In that case, *Apocrypha* could be more broadly defined as "books or parts of books that appear in Roman Catholic or Orthodox Bibles, but not in Jewish or Protestant ones."

The second group of *Pseudepigrapha* contains scores of compositions that were known to scholars before the discovery of the Dead Sea Scrolls. The vast majority are Jewish writings from the Second Temple period, but a few are later and of Christian origin, such as *2 Esdras* 1–2 (= *5 Ezra*) and *2 Esdras* 15–16 (= 6 Ezra). Prominent *Pseudepigrapha* are: the *Assumption of Moses,* the *Letter of Aristeas,* the *Life of Adam and Eve,* the *Martyrdom and Ascension of Isaiah, Psalms 152–155,* the *Psalms of Solomon,* the *Sibylline Oracles,* and the *Testaments of the Twelve Patriarchs.*

2. Apocrypha and *Pseudepigrapha* in the Dead Sea Scrolls

Text from at least nine Apocrypha and *Pseudepigrapha* are found among the scrolls. For convenience, these will be discussed in one section, and in alphabetical order.

2.1 1 Enoch *(or Ethiopic Enoch)*

This important composition survives in full only in Ethiopic (with 108 chapters), and some Greek sections are cited by ancient authors or known from early manuscripts. As preserved in the Ethiopic tradition, the complete work consists of five "booklets": the Book of the Watchers (chs. 1–36), the Similitudes or Parables (37–71), the Astronomical Book (72–82), the Book of Dreams (83–90), and the Epistle of Enoch (91–108). These include the earliest Jewish examples of apocalypses, in which human history is surveyed from beginning to end.

Each booklet contains revelations supposedly given to Enoch, son of Jared and the seventh generation from Adam (Gen 5:21–24), who "walked with God; then he was no more, for God took him away" into heaven (Gen 5:24). This explains why the author assumes the identity of Enoch rather than another biblical character; because he is now in heaven, Enoch becomes the ideal recipient of the revelations described in the booklets.

A prominent theme is the story of disobedient angels who came down from heaven, married earthly women, and produced gigantic offspring. According to *1 Enoch*, these giants were the cause of the great evil that made God send the flood to punish them and destroy the world. Such ideas are based on the key text of Genesis 6:1–4, which describes the *sons of God* who married the daughters of men; *1 Enoch* takes these *sons of God* to mean angels (compare Job 8:37). Since Genesis 6:1–4 comes just before the flood story, for the authors of *1 Enoch* it was the evil resulting from the angels' gigantic offspring—far more than Adam, Eve, and their descendants—that explains the explosion of human sin that caused God to send the devastating flood.

A second major theme in *1 Enoch* is judgment. The flood story (the "first judgment") highlights the divine response to great evil and serves as a warning of judgment to come. In his exhortations, Enoch himself refers to this example several times; it is interesting to note that some New Testament writers do so as well (for example, 2 Pet 3:5). It is also worthy of note that the fourth booklet (chs. 72–82) presents the earliest Jewish text on astronomical matters.

Material from *1 Enoch* is preserved in 11 scrolls from Qumran, all in Aramaic. The two oldest are 4QEn^a ar and 4QEnastr^a (early second century B.C.E.), and the latest is 4QEnastr^a (early first century C.E.). A possible Greek scroll of *1 Enoch*, written on papyrus, was found in Cave 7 (abbreviated pap7QEn gr), but some scholars dispute that any of the Cave 7 Greek fragments contain text from *1 Enoch*. The Qumran evidence suggests that the book was written in Aramaic, later translated into Greek, and from the Greek rendered into Ethiopic and other languages.

The Enoch scrolls found at Qumran also suggest that the earliest form of *1 Enoch* made up a "pentateuch" of five booklets modeled after the five books of Moses, to which the compiler added chapters 106 and 107. This early form lacked the Similitudes (Parables) of Enoch (chs. 37–71), which feature *the son of man*, who will play a role in the final judgment, and is of interest to New Testament scholars: Were the Similitudes an early source on which the Gospel writers drew for their descriptions of Jesus as the Son of Man? Many scholars believe that in place of the Similitudes the version of *1 Enoch* found at Qumran contained a separate composition known as the *Book of Giants* (represented in 9 or 10 scrolls), which concerns the wicked offspring of disobedient angels. It appears that this booklet was later replaced by the Similitudes.

To judge from their distinctive writings found at Qumran, the Essene movement were enormously influenced by *1 Enoch*. For example, the Astronomical Book (chs. 72–82), which describes a solar calendar of 364 days (but also a lunar calendar of 354 days), reinforced the *Yahad*'s interest in the correct calendar and divinely appointed festival days. One scholar, Gabriele Boccaccini, proposed that the Essenes were an off-spring of Enochic Judaism, specifically as a radical group, which then split from the main Enochic heritage just before the composition of the sectarian texts found at Qumran. The Enochic literature may have been more influential in the earlier period of the *Yahad* Essenes' history than in the latter part, since most of the Enochic scrolls are relatively early, which suggests that *1 Enoch* was not extensively used at Qumran in the first century C.E.

The *Yahad* viewed *1 Enoch* as Scripture, at least in the earlier part of their history. Although the book is not included in the Bibles of modern Jews, Protestants, or Roman Catholics, it is regarded as Scripture by one Christian tradition, the Ethiopian Orthodox Church.

2.2 Jubilees

This book survives in full only in Ethiopic (with 50 chapters) and partly in a Latin translation, both of which were translated from the Greek, which is now lost. *Jubilees* presents itself as a revelation from God, delivered through an angel of his presence to Moses on Mount Sinai (Exod 24:18). The angel presents an overview of the history of humankind and of God's chosen people, beginning with creation and ending with the exodus from Egypt, the Passover, and the Sabbath.

Written about 160 B.C.E., *Jubilees* gets its name by dividing the history it covers into 50 units of 49 years each. The author took the term *jubilee* to mean not the fiftieth year (as in Lev 25), but rather the 49-year period marked off by the fiftieth year.

Table 1. Outline of the Book of *Jubilees*	
1:1–29	Apostasy of God's people and their future restoration
2:1–4:33	Primeval History: The creation and Adam
5:1–10:26	Stories about Noah
11:1–23:8	Stories about Abraham
23:9–34	Thoughts on Abraham's death
24:1–45:16	Stories about Jacob and his family
46:1–50:13	Stories about Moses

Since it retells many events described in Genesis and Exodus, *Jubilees* is often categorized as "rewritten Bible." The author follows the general outline of the biblical accounts, but at times omits, condenses, expands, or alters them. In this way he presents his own views on historical, theological, and legal matters. For example, the long account of the plagues in Exodus 7–10 receives only a few verses in *Jubilees* 48:4–11, while Reuben's apparent incest with Bilhah (Gen 35:22) is extensively explained in *Jubilees* 33:2–20.

About 15 fragmentary copies of *Jubilees* were found at Qumran (the precise number is uncertain), all written in Hebrew, with at least one on papyrus. The oldest is 4QJub^a (125–100 B.C.E.), and the latest is 11QJub (about 50 C.E.). Comparison with the

Ethiopic and Latin versions shows that the ancient translators carried out their task with great care and literalness, with some exceptions of course. At least six more scrolls are related in some way to it: 4QPseudo-Jubilees[a, b, c] (4Q225–27), 4QText with a *Citation of Jubilees* (4Q228), possibly pap4QJubilees? (4Q482), and a *Work Similar to Jubilees from Masada* (Mas 1j).

The large number of copies and several related works show that *Jubilees* was much used by the Essene movement and very popular at Qumran; only Deuteronomy, Psalms, Genesis, and Isaiah are represented by more scrolls. In contrast to *1 Enoch*, which seems to have been more influential in the earlier period of the *Yahad*'s history, the sort of exegesis and biblical interpretation represented in *Jubilees* became increasingly important to the Qumran community during their later history. None of the *Jubilees* manuscripts is as early as two of *1 Enoch* (4QEn[a] ar and 4QEnastr[a] ar), and those that are preserved date from about 125 B.C.E. to 50 C.E.

The influence of *Jubilees* is evident in several texts composed by the Yahad, and in several of its distinctive traditions. These include: (a) the division of history into 49-year jubilee periods; (b) dating covenants to the third month (especially the fifteenth day), which may have inspired the community's practice of renewing the covenant annually on the Festival of Weeks; and (c) the 364-day solar calendar as the true annual calendar (which also features in the Astronomical Book of *1 Enoch*).

Jubilees was most likely viewed as Scripture by the *Yahad*. Like *1 Enoch*, this book is not included in the Bibles of modern Jews, Protestants, or Roman Catholics, but also like *1 Enoch*, it is regarded as Scripture by one Christian confession, the Ethiopian Orthodox Church.

2.3 The Letter (or Epistle) of Jeremiah

This small book (73 verses in one chapter) is addressed to Jews deported to Babylon by King Nebuchadnezzar (probably in 597 B.C.E.). It contains warnings on the helplessness of idols and condemns idolatry. Most likely written in Greek in the fourth or third century B.C.E., the letter is part of the Apocrypha, appearing as chapter 6 of Baruch in the Latin Vulgate, but separated from Baruch by Lamentations in the Septuagint.

It is represented by a single scroll from Cave 7 in Qumran that was copied about 100 B.C.E., inscribed on papyrus, and written in Greek—hence the abbreviation pap7QEpJer gr. The scroll is very damaged (with text from vv. 43–44 in just a small fragment), but probably contained only the letter and not the first five chapters of Baruch.

2.4 Psalms 151A and 151B

In the Septuagint, the Psalter ends not with Psalm 150 but with *Psalm 151*, which also concludes the Psalter used by Orthodox Christians today. Before the discovery of the Dead Sea Scrolls, no Hebrew text survived of this psalm, which is also found in Latin and Syriac translations based on the Greek. However, an earlier Hebrew form of *Psalm 151* is preserved in column 28 of 11QPs[a] (30–50 C.E.).

While this psalm is a single composition in the Septuagint, 11QPs^a contains two distinct psalms (*151A* and *151B*), each with its own superscription (heading) and which represent the original Hebrew. *Psalm 151A* is a poetic interpretation of the events surrounding David's anointing (1 Sam 16:1–13), and *Psalm 151B* covers his encounter with Goliath (1 Sam 17:17–54). The Greek translator reworked and synthesized all this material into a single composition, with a different order of verses, and with *Psalm 151A* condensed into verses 1–5 and *Psalm 151B* into verses 7–8.

Psalms 151A and *151B* are the only truly "autobiographical" psalms, in that they without any doubt relate to actual events in David's life. For example:

> He made me shepherd of his flock and ruler over his kids. (*Psalm 151A:1*)

> He sent his prophet to anoint me, Samuel to make me great; my brothers went out to meet him. (*151A:6*)

> Then I [s]aw a Philistine uttering defiances from the r[anks of the enemy]. (*Psalm 151B:2*)

As in the Septuagint, the 11QPs^a-Psalter ends with *Psalm 151*. Thus, in the first century C.E. at least two Jewish groups were using a book of Psalms that ended with *Psalm 151* (although the order of psalms in the two collections is very different). *Psalm 151* is more Davidic in the 11QPs^a-Psalter than in the Septuagint. The Greek title seems to downplay its status, perhaps reflecting the concerns of later editors about the place of *Psalm 151* in the Greek Psalter at a time when the collection now found in the MT (which ends with Psalm 150) was becoming increasingly influential:

- A Hallelujah of David, Son of Jesse. *Psalm 151A* (11QPs^a)

- At the beginning of [Da]vid's po[wer], after God's prophet had anointed him. *Psalm 151B* (11QPs^a)

- This Psalm is truly written by David, although it is outside the number, after he had fought with Goliath in single combat. *Psalm 151:1* (LXX)

2.5 Psalms 154 and 155 (Syriac Psalms II and III)

These compositions are found in medieval copies of the Syriac, most notably the Book of Discipline (tenth century) and Mosul manuscript 1113 (twelfth century). Both are mostly preserved in 11QPs^a (30–50 C.E.), but in unconnected columns (18 and 24). Verses 17–20 of *Psalm 154* also feature in a composition discovered in Cave 4, *A Prayer for King Jonathan* (4Q448). The Qumran evidence shows that the Mosul copy is the most faithful Syriac version of *Psalms 154* and *155* and contains significant variant readings against later manuscripts. 11QPs^a represents the Hebrew text used by the translator, with an almost identical correspondence in wording.

Psalm 154 is written in excellent biblical-style poetry and may be classified as a call to worship. One notable feature is the personification of Wisdom as a woman, which also occurs in the Hebrew Bible (notably Prov 8:34) and in the Apocrypha (Sirach 1:15):

> [155:5] For it is to make known the glory of the LORD that Wisdom has been given,
>
> [6] and it is for recounting his many deeds she has been revealed to humanity:
>
> [7] to make known to simple ones his power, to explain his greatness to those lacking sense,
>
> [8] those who are far from her gates, those who stray from her portals. (*The Dead Sea Scrolls Bible*, 573)

Psalm 155 is a psalm of thanksgiving that incorporates a plea for deliverance, and abounds with biblical vocabulary (reminiscent of Pss 22 and 51). It is made up of three strophes, the first of which (vv. 1–7) presents the psalmist's desperate cries for deliverance. In the second strophe (vv. 8–14), the psalmist asks for his suffering to lead to him learning God's law, and requests God's justice and protection from overwhelming situations and the "evil plague":

> [11] Remember me and do not forget me, and do not lead me into what is too difficult for me. [12] Cast far from me the sin of my youth, and may my transgressions not be remembered against me. [13] Purify me, O LORD, from the evil plague, and let it not again turn back on me. (*The Dead Sea Scrolls Bible*, 580)

In the final strophe (vv. 15–21), the psalmist confidently affirms God's positive response to his pleas and God's ability to save him.

2.6 Tobit

This book features Tobit, a Jewish exile from the northern kingdom of Israel, who rose to prominence in Nineveh, capital of ancient Assyria. However, he suffered several reverses, which included poverty and culminated in blindness. His son Tobias eventually rescued and married a relative named Sarah, found a cure for his father's blindness, and secured his fortune. The book of Tobit (written in the fourth or third century B.C.E.) emphasizes the virtues of faithfulness in times of distress, caring for the poor and hungry, and honoring one's parents.

Five copies were discovered in Cave 4 at Qumran, four written in Aramaic (one on papyrus), and the other in Hebrew. The oldest is 4QTobit^d ar (about 100 B.C.E.), and the latest is 4QTobit^e (30 B.C.E.–20 C.E.). None of these scrolls is fully preserved, but between them all 14 chapters of Tobit are represented. The best-preserved manuscript is 4QpapTobit^a ar, which contains portions of chapters 1–7 and 12–14.

The four Aramaic scrolls indicate that Tobit was originally written in Aramaic, since there was a tendency at Qumran—as part of a literary and nationalist renaissance—to translate works composed in Aramaic into Hebrew, but not vice versa. Another indication that the Aramaic text of Tobit was earlier, and that the Hebrew was translated from it, is that the only Hebrew copy is dated 30 B.C.E. We thus have in Cave 4 one of the earliest examples of a book in its original language (Aramaic), used alongside a translation into another language (Hebrew).

The form of Tobit in both the Aramaic and the Hebrew scrolls generally agrees with the longer edition preserved in later Greek and Latin manuscripts. However, neither the Greek nor the Latin is directly translated from an Aramaic form such as the one in the Qumran texts, since these later versions contain words and phrases that were misunderstood by the translators.

2.7 The Wisdom of Ben Sira (also known as Sirach or Ecclesiasticus)

Jesus ben Sira was a Jewish teacher who compiled a book of wise sayings and instructions in Hebrew somewhere between 190 and 180 B.C.E. We know this because the author's grandson later translated it into Greek and added a preface of his own. The traditional form is based on this Greek translation, which is found in the Septuagint, and is titled Sirach or Ecclesiasticus. Another title, the Wisdom of Jesus Ben Sira (or simply Ben Sira) is preferred by many scholars, who recognize the Hebrew origins of the book. It should be noted, however, that the original Hebrew form is substantially different from the traditional Greek one.

Sirach is found in ancient Greek, Latin, and Syriac versions, but the quest for the original Hebrew text has presented problems. Ben Sira/Sirach was excluded by the rabbis from their list of scriptural books, but the Hebrew text was known during the early centuries of the Common Era. Early in the twentieth century, several Hebrew copies, copied in the eleventh and twelfth centuries, were discovered in the Cairo Genizah. None of the Cairo copies is complete, but between them about two-thirds of the book's 51 chapters are preserved.

Only three copies containing text from Ben Sira were found among the scrolls, two at Qumran and one at Masada, where over 900 Jewish defenders took their lives in 73 or 74 C.E.

The *Masada* scroll (MasSir) is the most extensive, preserving text from chapters 39–44. Copied in 100–75 B.C.E., only about 100 years later than the original, it confirms that the medieval copies in the Cairo Genizah basically represent the original Hebrew version, but with numerous corruptions and later changes. One example is Sirach 42:1–5, which instructs readers to stand up for principles, ensure that God's law be observed, promote honesty and integrity, and not allow themselves to be exploited in commercial transactions:

> [1b] [B]ut do not be ashamed of the following things, and do not show partiality to people and commit sin: [2] Of the law of the Most High and his covenant, and of rendering judgment to acquit the wicked; [3] of keeping accounts with a partner or with a traveling companion, and of dividing an inheritance and property; [4a] of accuracy with scales and weights, of polishing measures and weights; [4b] of buying much or lit[tle; [5a] and of] profit in dealing with merchants. (*The Dead Sea Scrolls Bible*, 603)

The two scrolls found at Qumran (preserving portions of only three chapters) are important. The Cave 2 copy (2QSir) apparently contained a text of Sirach similar to the one found in later Greek manuscripts (but in Hebrew). The Cave 11 text is not from a Ben Sira manuscript, but part of the *Great Psalms Scroll* (11QPs^a), which was copied in 30–50 C.E. Columns 21–22 originally contained the concluding autographical poem on Wisdom (Sir 51:13–30). Its inclusion in a collection of psalms shows that this poem was still being used as a "floating piece" in the first century C.E., long after its incorporation into the book of Ben Sira.

The original text in 11QPs^a presents an acrostic Wisdom poem, which curiously ends with an additional twenty-third verse. Comparison with the later Greek version and the medieval Cairo Genizah Hebrew text reveals interesting differences. For example, the later texts have blurred the acrostic nature of the poem and have replaced many erotic images in the original Hebrew with pious ideas, in line with his overall purpose of pursuing wisdom in a more spiritual or philosophical sense. This is illustrated in verses 21–22 (using the traditional verse numbering from the Septuagint):

> **Original Hebrew** (11QPs^a): ^{21}I stirred up my desire for her, and on her heights I do not waver. ^{22}I opened my hand . . . and I perceive her unseen parts.

> **Revised Version** (Septuagint): ^{21} I directed my soul towards her, and in my deeds I was exact. ^{22} I stretched my hands on high, and perceived her secrets.

The text in 11QPs^a is highly erotic with its sexual imagery: most notably, the Hebrew word *hand* can also mean "penis," and *unseen parts* can also be translated "nakedness."

2.8 New Pseudepigrapha

About 150 scrolls preserve *Pseudepigrapha* that were previously unknown to scholars. Very few are sectarian writings, since they were not composed by the Essene movement, but were used by them. Most present biblical characters in transformed settings, and almost all are written in Aramaic. Scholars therefore use *ar* in the official names for these texts (for example, *Testament of Judah* ar). The main New *Pseudipigrapha* are:

(1) *Genesis Apocryphon* (1QapGen). This badly damaged document was among the first seven scrolls to be discovered in Cave 1. It tells the angelic marriage story that results in Noah's birth, then presents his wondrous childhood, the flood, the division of the earth among Noah's descendants, and the story of Abraham as far as Genesis 15 (the covenant).

(2) Texts featuring Noah: 1Q19 (Noah) and possibly 4Q534–36 (Noah).

(3) A text featuring Jacob: 4Q537 (Testament of Jacob?).

(4) Texts featuring Levi: 1Q21 and 4Q213–14 (Aramaic Levi) and 4Q540–41 (Apocryphal Levi).

(5)   Texts featuring Joseph: 4Q371–73 (*Apocryphon of Joseph*); 4Q474 (*Text Concerning Rachel and Joseph*); and 4Q539 (*Testament of Joseph*).

(6)   A text featuring Judah or Benjamin: 4Q538 (*Testament of Judah*).

(7)   A text featuring Qahat (the Aramaic form of Hebrew *Kohath*): 4Q542 (*Testament of Qahat*).

(8)   Texts featuring Amram: 4Q543–48, 4Q549? (*Visions of Amram*).

(9)   Texts featuring Moses: 1Q22 (*Apocryphon of Moses*); 1Q29, 4Q375–76 (*Three Tongues of Fire*); 2Q21 (*Apocryphon of Moses?*); 4Q249 (*Midrash Sefer Moshe*); 4Q374 (*Exodus/Conquest Traditions*); and 4Q408 (*Apocryphon of Moses?*).

(10) Texts featuring Joshua: 4Q123 (*Paraphrase of Joshua*); 4Q378–79 (*Apocryphon of Joshua*); and 4Q522 (*Prophecy of Joshua*).

(11) Texts featuring Samuel: 4Q160 (*Vision of Samuel*) and 6Q9 (*Apocryphon of Samuel-Kings*).

(12) Texts featuring David: 2Q22 (*Apocryphon of David?*) and 4Q479 (*Descendants of David*)

(13) A text featuring Elijah: 4Q382 (*Paraphrase of Kings*).

(14) A text featuring Elisha: 4Q481a (*Apocryphon of Elisha*).

(15) Texts featuring Jeremiah and Ezekiel: 4Q383–91.

(16) A text featuring Malachi: 5Q10–11 (*Apocryphon of Malachi*).

(17) Texts featuring Daniel: 4Q242 (*Prayer of Nabonidus*) and 4Q243–45 (*Pseudo-Daniel A* and *B*).

Concluding Comments

Three of the Apocrypha are represented among the Dead Sea Scrolls: the Letter of Jeremiah, Tobit, and the Wisdom of Ben Sira (Sirach or Ecclesiasticus). Six previously known *Pseudepigrapha* are also found: *1 Enoch, Jubilees,* and *Psalms 151A, 151B, 154,* and *155.* Several of these were regarded as Scripture or as very authoritative by the *Yahad* at Qumran, especially *1 Enoch, Jubilees,* and *Psalms 151A* and *151B.* The New *Pseudepigrapha* affirm the *Yahad* Essenes' interest in, and use of, texts that present biblical characters.

Pictures and Illustrations

Figure 1. Overview of Khirbet Qumran and Surrounding Area: Several caves where Dead Sea Scrolls were found are on the left side of the ravine *(Werner Braun)*. (From Eugene Ulrich, "Dead Sea Scrolls," *Eerdmans Dictionary of the Bible* (2000), 32. Reproduced by permission of publisher; all rights reserved.)

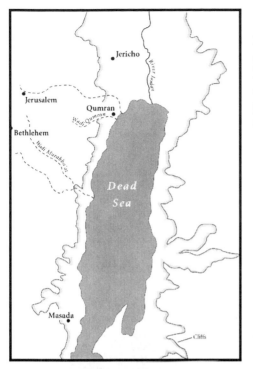

Figure 2. Location of Qumran and Other Sites Near the Dead Sea. (From Jodi Magness, *The Archaeology of Qumran and the Dead Sea Scrolls* (2002), 11. Reproduced by permission of publisher; all rights reserved.)

Figure 3. Cave 1 at Qumran: Muhammed edh-Dhib crawled through the upper opening to find the first Scrolls. The lower opening was made later. (Courtesy Catherine Murphy.)

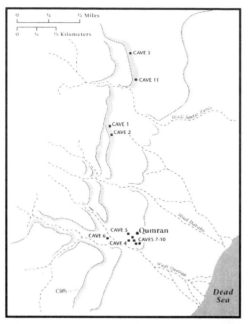

Figure 4. Location of the Qumran Caves, with Part of the Dead Sea in the Bottom Right Corner. (From Jodi Magness, "Qumran," *Eerdmans Dictionary of Early Judaism* (2010), 1130. Reproduced by permission of publisher; all rights reserved.)

Figure 5. Caves 10 (left), 4 (right), and the Upper Plateau. (Courtesy Catherine Murphy.)

Figure 6. Meeting Hall and Adjoining "Pantry," Facing Southeast. (Courtesy Catherine Murphy.)

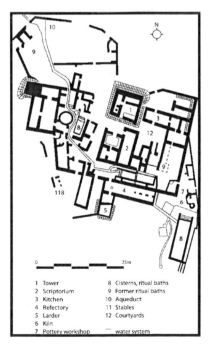

1 Tower	8 Cisterns, ritual baths
2 Scriptorium	9 Former ritual baths
3 Kitchen	10 Aqueduct
4 Refectory	11 Stables
5 Larder	12 Courtyards
6 Kiln	
7 Pottery workshop	— water system

Figure 7. Site Plan of the Settlement at Qumran. (From Jodi Magness, "Qumran," *Eerdmans Dictionary of Early Judaism* (2010), 1128. Reproduced by permission of publisher; all rights reserved.)

Figure 8. Graves in the Main Cemetery, Facing Northwest. (Courtesy Catherine Murphy.)

Figure 9. John Trever, Mar (Metropolitan) Samuel, and Father Butrus Sowmy. (© John Trever, Ph.D., Digital Image by James E. Trever.)

Figure 10. Exterior of the Shrine of the Book, Jerusalem: The white domed roof contrasts with the tall black pillar, providing a fitting home to the scroll titled *War of the Sons of Light against the Sons of Darkness.* (Photograph © and Courtesy the Israel Museum, Jerusalem).

Figure 11. Scroll Jar from Cave 1 at Qumran. (© John Trever, Ph.D., Digital Image by James E. Trever.)

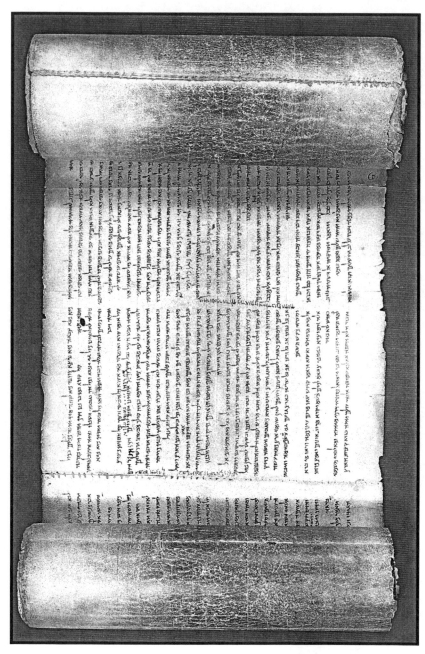

Figure 12. The *Great Isaiah Scroll* (1QIsaᵃ) with Rolls, Opened at Columns 32–33, containing Isaiah 38:8–40:28. (© John Trever, Ph.D., Digital Image by James E. Trever.)

Figure 13. The Author in the Vault of the Shrine of the Book (2005): Working on the Great Isaiah Scroll. (Courtesy C. J. Davis.)

Figure 14. A Daniel Scroll from Cave 1 (1QDanᵃ), with Text from Daniel 1:1-17 and 2:2-6. (© John Trever, Ph.D., Digital Image by James E. Trever.)

Figure 15. The Hebrew University Isaiah Scroll (1QIsaᵇ), Columns 25–26, with Text from Isaiah 57:17–61:2 (*Ardon Bar Harma*). (Photograph © and Courtesy the Israel Museum, Jerusalem.)

Figure 16. The *Habakkuk Pesher* (1QpHab), Column 7. (© John Trever, Ph.D., Digital Image by James E. Trever).

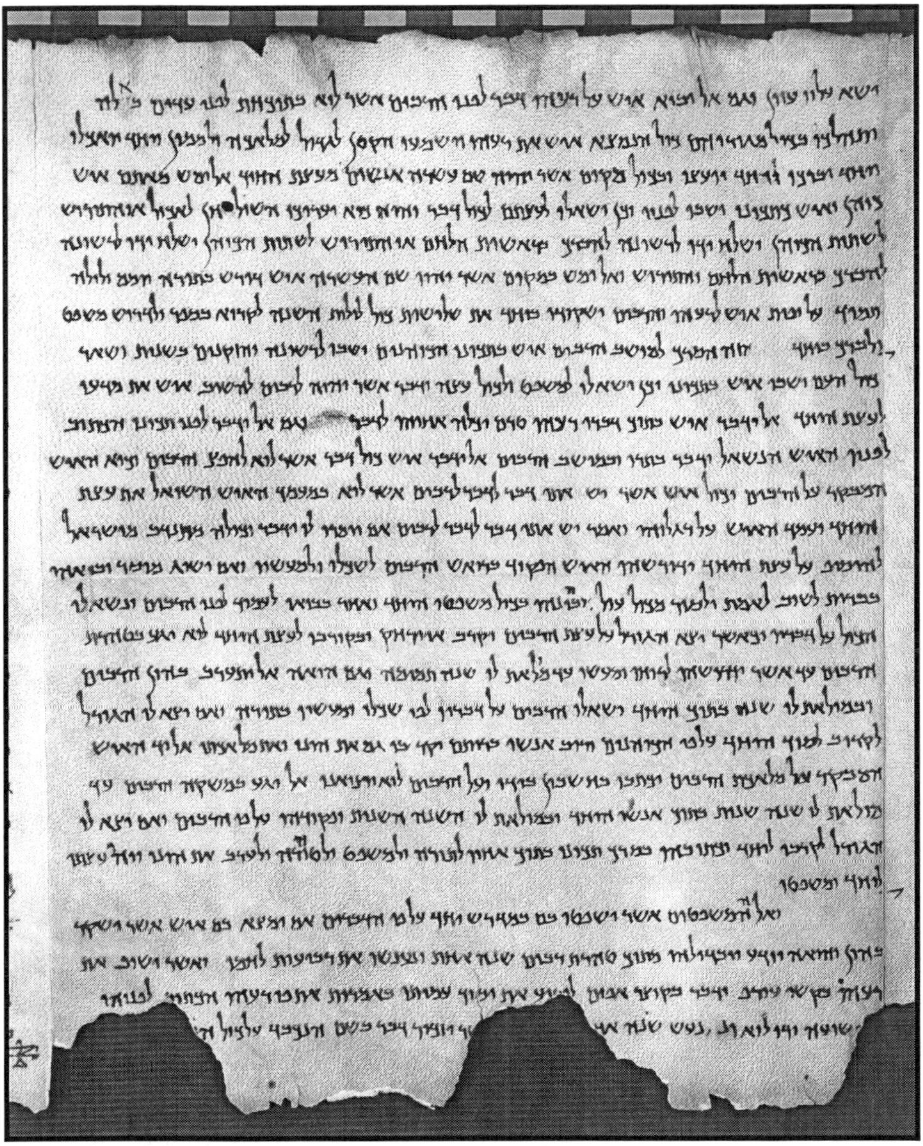

Figure 17. The *Rule of the Community* (1QS), Column 6. (© John Trever, Ph.D., Digital Image by James E. Trever.)

8

The Shape and Contents of the Scriptures Used at Qumran

1. Hebrew Bible or Old Testament?

1.1 Jewish, Protestant, Roman Catholic, and Orthodox Bibles

This chapter considers what constitutes the Bible, or the issue of canon, which is not easily understood. This is because different groups have different Bibles—most notably the Hebrew Bible in Judaism, and the Old and the New Testaments used by the church.

It will be helpful to deal with one important question right away: Do any of the scrolls contain New Testament writings? Almost all scholars agree that these ancient writings were written too early to contain New Testament texts. Thus the New Testament can be excluded here; the books in that part of Christian Bibles were written after the Qumran period.

With respect to the Hebrew Bible or Old Testament, differences are to be found between Jewish, Protestant, Roman Catholic, and Orthodox Bibles. A listing of books is given below. Most readers are aware that for all Jewish and Christian groups, the first five books are the same: Genesis, Exodus, Leviticus, Numbers, and Deuteronomy. In the Hebrew Bible, this group is known as the *Torah*, and in Christian Bibles as the Pentateuch.

The number and order of the other books differ sharply between the Hebrew Bible and Christian Bibles. The Hebrew Bible places Joshua through the Book of the Twelve Prophets in the *Nebi'im* ("Prophets"), and Psalms through Chronicles in the *Kethubim*

("Writings"). This Bible is often called the *Tanakh* (featuring the first letters of *Torah*, *Nebi'im*, and *Kethubim*). In contrast, the Old Testament—found in Christian Bibles— groups the books after the Pentateuch into the Historical Books, Poetry or Wisdom, and the Prophets.

Table 1. The Hebrew Bible and the Old Testament	
JEWISH *TANAKH* (Total: 24 Books)	**PROTESTANT, CATHOLIC, AND ORTHODOX OLD TESTAMENTS** (Totals: Protestant 39, Catholic 46, Orthodox 49)
***Torah* [Law]** (5 Books) Genesis—Deuteronomy	**Pentateuch** (5 Books) Genesis—Deuteronomy
***Nebi'im* [Prophets]** (8 Books) Joshua Judges Samuel (1 book) Kings (1 book) Isaiah Jeremiah Ezekiel Minor Prophets (1 book) Hosea to Malachi	**Historical Books** (12 Books, Catholic Bible 16, Orthodox 18) Joshua Judges Ruth 1–2 Samuel 1–2 Kings 1–2 Chronicles 1 Esdras (Orthodox Bibles) Ezra (in Orthodox Bible, 2 Esdras = Ezra and Nehemiah) Nehemiah Tobit (Catholic and Orthodox Bibles) Judith (Catholic and Orthodox Bibles) Esther (+ Additions in Catholic and Orthodox Bibles) 1 and 2 Maccabees (Catholic and Orthodox Bibles) 3 Maccabees (Orthodox Bibles)
***Kethubim* [Writings]** (11 Books) Psalms Proverbs Job Song of Songs Ruth Lamentations Ecclesiastes Esther Daniel Ezra-Nehemiah (1 book) Chronicles (1 book)	**Poetry/Wisdom** (5 Books, Catholic Bible 7, Orthodox 8) Job Psalms (+ Psalm 151 in Orthodox Bibles) Prayer of Manasseh (Orthodox Bibles) Proverbs Ecclesiastes Song of Songs Wisdom of Solomon (Catholic and Orthodox Bibles) Sirach (Catholic and Orthodox Bibles)
	Prophets (17 Books, Catholic andt Orthodox 18 + Additions) Isaiah Jeremiah Lamentations Baruch + Letter of Jeremiah (Catholic and Orthodox Bibles) Ezekiel Daniel (+ Additions in Catholic and Orthodox Bibles) Minor Prophets (12 books) Hosea through Malachi

In the MT of the Tanakh, the order for some books in the Writings varies between manuscripts; for example, the Aleppo and Leningrad codices end with Ezra-Nehemiah rather than Chronicles. Whether it ends with either of these books, the Hebrew Bible culminates with a clear theological message: the return to the land of Israel after the exile, in fulfillment of God's covenant promises to Abraham and later Israelite leaders. The religion, city walls, and Temple are being rebuilt by Ezra, Nehemiah, and Zerubbabel, and Israel's history is being retold to the returned exiles by the Chronicler.

In contrast, the Old Testament of Christian Bibles ends with prophecies of judgment and the promise of the messianic age. The theological message is also clear: Jews and the nations must forsake wickedness, be aware of coming judgment, and prepare for the coming of the Messiah. For Christian readers, the coming of Jesus and the reference to John the Baptist as preparing the way of the Lord flow from the expectations and future orientation of the final books of the Old Testament.

Differences between these Bibles are also found with respect to content, including entire books. The Hebrew Bible (with 24 books) and the Protestant Old Testament (with 39) contain the same texts. The total in Jewish Bibles is far lower because the following groups are each counted as single books: 1–2 Samuel, 1–2 Kings, the Twelve Minor Prophets, Ezra-Nehemiah, and 1–2 Chronicles.

Roman Catholic Bibles contain an additional seven books, for a total of 46: Tobit, Judith, 1–2 Maccabees, the Wisdom of Solomon, Sirach (or Ecclesiasticus), and Baruch (with the Letter of Jeremiah). Catholic Bibles also contain the Additions to Esther (in eight sections) and the three Additions to Daniel.

Orthodox Bibles include all the writings found in the Catholic Old Testament plus a further three, for a total of 49: 1 Esdras, 3 Maccabees, and the Prayer of Manasseh. These Bibles also have a longer ending to the Psalter (Psalm 151). In Orthodox tradition the books designated 1–2 Samuel are known as 1–2 Kingdoms, 1–2 Kings as 3–4 Kingdoms, 1–2 Chronicles as 1–2 Paralipomena, and Ezra-Nehemiah together as 2 Esdras. The Old Testaments of some other Orthodox churches contain even more books (for example, *1 Enoch* and *Jubilees* in the Ethiopian Bible). Because of these differences, the Jewish Hebrew Bible and the Christian Old Testament are quite different. These two terms are not interchangeable.

1.2 Canon, Bible, and Scripture

The differences between the Hebrew Bible and the various Christian Old Testaments are due to the different canons of Scripture accepted by these communities. A *canon* is the closed list of books that was officially accepted by a community (whether Jewish or Christian) as authoritative and binding for religious practice and doctrine.

The term belongs to the post-biblical period, and should not be used for collections of sacred books, whether Jewish or Christian, before the third century C.E.; thus there was no canon of books used by the *Yahad* Essenes at Qumran. The same applies to the word *Bible*, which usually denotes a book consisting of writings accepted by Jews or Christians as inspired by God and thus of divine authority. The problem with using this term for writings prior to the third century is that it implies the completion of the Jewish Scriptures and their existence in one book or collection at that time. This assumption, however, is valid only later, since there was no completed Hebrew Bible or Greek Old Testament during the Qumran period or the period of the New Testament writers.

For most scholars, the term *Scripture* (adjective *scriptural*) seems most fitting for uniquely sacred or authoritative writings in the Second Temple period, well before canons were formed and complete Bibles were used.

2. Ancient Evidence Outside the Scrolls Found at Qumran

Passages and references in several groups of early Jewish writings (from about 200 B.C.E. to 100 C.E.) show that most or all Jews considered certain books as Scripture (divinely revealed and uniquely authoritative). There was widespread agreement on the scriptural status of many books, but less agreement on others.

2.1 Passages from the Apocrypha and the Pseudepigrapha

Several texts among the Apocrypha and the *Pseudepigrapha* contain important evidence on books or groups of books that the writers regarded as Scripture.

(a) Sirach 38:34–39:1; 44–50; and the Prologue

Sirach (also known as Ecclesiasticus or the Wisdom of Jesus ben Sira) was written in Hebrew about 190 or 180 B.C.E. One passage (38:34–39:1) refers to "the law of the Most High, the wisdom of all the ancients, prophecies, and sayings, parables and proverbs." The poem in praise of famous men from biblical times (chs. 44–50) refers to events in the five books of Moses, Joshua, Judges, 1–2 Samuel, 1–2 Kings (with parallels from Chronicles and Isaiah), Jeremiah, Ezekiel, possibly Job, and the Twelve Minor Prophets. If Chronicles and Job are removed, this poem confirms the order of books in the first two divisions of the Hebrew Bible (the Law and the Prophets). Half a century later, the author's grandson translated the book into Greek, adding his own prologue. The prologue mentions three series of books that were apparently considered as Scripture by himself and his audience. (The third series is vaguely defined, and was possibly not as authoritative.)

> Many great teachings have been given to us through **the Law** and **the Prophets** and **the others that followed them**, and for these we should praise Israel for instruction and wisdom. . . . So my grandfather Jesus, who had devoted himself especially to the reading of **the Law** and **the Prophets** and **the other books of our ancestors**, . . . Not only this book, but even **the Law** itself, **the Prophecies**, and **the rest of the books** differ not a little when read in the original. (New Revised Standard Version)

(b) 2 Maccabees 2:2–3, 13–14

This book, which deals with the events leading up to and following the Jewish Revolt under Judas the Maccabee, was completed in 124 B.C.E. After the Law is mentioned in 2:2–3, verse 13 tells us that Nehemiah founded a library and "collected the books about the kings and prophets, and the writings of David and letters of kings about votive offerings." Here the books about the kings and the prophets may mean the Historical Books (1–2 Samuel, 1–2 Kings, possibly 1–2 Chronicles) and the Prophetic Books, the writings of David may denote Psalms, and letters of kings about votive offerings may denote Ezra (which contains royal letters concerning offerings in the Temple). This identification is not certain, since our author does not state which books he is describing.

(c) *4 Ezra* 14:23–48

This book, often included as chapters 3–14 of 2 Esdras, was written after 70 C.E. (the year that the Romans destroyed the Temple), and finalized in about 100. The author meditates on the destruction of the Temple and adds that the Scriptures were lost in this terrible event. Ezra prays that God's Holy Spirit will inspire him to write down all that had been recorded in God's Law (here meaning all the Scriptures). By divine inspiration he dictates 94 books, in two groups: "Make public *the twenty-four books* that you wrote first, and let the worthy and the unworthy read them; but keep *the seventy* that were written last" (14:45–46).

The passage seems to suggest that by about 100 C.E., the 24 books making up the Hebrew Bible had been assembled and were accepted by many Jews as a distinct collection of scriptural writings. The collection was apparently near to being closed, since it could not be expanded to include the other 70 inspired writings (various Pseudepigrapha). Yet it still falls short of being a Bible or a canon, since the passage does not confirm that the 24 books were accepted by all Jews as supremely authoritative.

(d) *4 Maccabees* 18:10

Composed sometime in the first century B.C.E. or the first century C.E., this book includes the following passage: "While he was still with you, he taught you *the Law* and *the Prophets*" (18:10). References follow to the narratives in the Pentateuch and the books of Daniel, Isaiah, "the psalmist David," Proverbs, and Ezekiel. It is possible, but not certain, that here *the Prophets* includes the book of Daniel, Psalms, and the book of Proverbs.

2.2 Passages from Hellenistic Jewish Writings

(a) Philo, *On the Contemplative Life*, 25

Philo was a Jewish philosopher who lived in Alexandria, Egypt, from about 20 B.C.E. to about 50 C.E. In one treatise he describes a Jewish group called the Therapeutae, who shared much in common with the Essenes living at Qumran. For example: each house contained a consecrated room or sanctuary, in which the Therapeutae were initiated into the mysteries of the sacred life. "They take nothing into it, . . . except *laws* and *oracles delivered through the mouth of prophets*, and *psalms and anything else which fosters and perfects knowledge and piety*" (*On the Contemplative Life*, 25).

Philo's language is reminiscent of the three series of books mentioned earlier by Ben Sira's grandson: (1) *laws* (= the grandson's *Law*); (2) *and oracles . . . of prophets* (= *Prophets*); (3) *psalms and anything else which fosters and perfects knowledge and piety* (= *the others, the other books of our ancestors*, or *the rest of the books*). Unlike the grandson, however, Philo's wording suggests that the Psalms is the most prominent book in the third series.

(b) Josephus, *Against Apion* 1.37–41 and *Antiquities* 10.35

In *Against Apion*, which he wrote in the 90s C.E., the Jewish historian Josephus defends the veracity of the ancient books that record the history of the Jewish people:

> We do not possess myriads of inconsistent books, conflicting with each other. Our books, those which are justly accredited, are but *two and twenty*, and contain the record of all time.

> Of these, *five are the books of Moses*, comprising the laws and the traditional history from the birth of man down to the death of the lawgiver. This period falls only a little short of three thousand years. From the death of Moses until Artaxerxes, who succeeded Xerxes as king of Persia, *the prophets* subsequent to Moses wrote the history of the events of their own times in *thirteen books*. *The remaining four books contain hymns to God and precepts* for the conduct of human life. (Trans. H. St. John Thackeray, *Against Apion* 1.38–40)

Most scholars agree that Josephus' listing of 22 books is one way of counting the books in the Hebrew Bible and is based on the Hebrew alphabet with its 22 letters; and his five books of Moses are the Pentateuch (Genesis to Deuteronomy). But Josephus' other two categories are more difficult to explain. The second contains the 13 books written by the prophets, whereas in the Jewish *Tanakh* the *Nebi'im* (Prophets) only has eight. The mention of the Artaxerxes as the endpoint of prophetic succession indicates that Ezra, Nehemiah, and Esther were included in this prophetic group since he is the latest Persian king mentioned in these books.

Several groupings for Josephus' 13 prophets have been proposed, although scholars generally agree on 11: Joshua, Judges, Samuel, Kings, Ezra-Nehemiah (one book), Esther, Isaiah, Jeremiah, Ezekiel, Daniel and the Twelve Minor Prophets (in one book).

- The remaining two books are identified as Chronicles and Job by H. St. John Thackeray (1926), who also combines Ruth with Judges and Lamentations with Jeremiah.

- Roger Beckwith (1985) also includes Chronicles and Job, with Ruth possibly combined with Judges and Lamentations with Jeremiah.

- VanderKam and Flint (2002) and VanderKam (2010) are more exclusive, counting 1 and 2 Samuel and 1 and 2 Kings as four books (not two), and so omitting Chronicles and Job.

- In *Antiquities* 10.35, Josephus mentions Isaiah and "also others, twelve in number." This could correspond with the 13 books of the prophets referred to in *Against Apion*, but may instead refer to the books of Isaiah and the Twelve Minor Prophets. As for Josephus' third series in *Against Apion*, the remaining four books that contain hymns to God and precepts, there is disagreement among scholars about which books belong. All four must be among the books now termed the *Kethubim* (Writings). For St. John Thackeray and Beckwith, they are Psalms, Proverbs, Ecclesiastes, and the Song of Songs. VanderKam and Flint also propose Psalms, Proverbs, and Ecclesiastes, but Job rather than the Song of Songs.

2.3 Passages from the New Testament

(a) Luke 24:44 and Similar Passages

The expression *the law (of Moses) and the prophets*, is found several times in the New Testament (for example: Matt 5:17; 7:12; 22:40; Luke 16:16, 29, 31); (*Moses and the prophets*): John 1:45; Acts 13:15; 28:23; and Rom 3:21).

Luke's Gospel also mentions *Moses and all the prophets* in 24:27, but a longer expression follows later. The resurrected Jesus says to his followers: "These are my words that I spoke to you while I was still with you—so that everything written about me in *the law of Moses, the prophets, and the psalms* must be fulfilled" (Luke 24:44). Here "the psalms" most likely is a reference to the book of Psalms. Some scholars suggest that it encompasses other books now found in the Writings, but the evidence seems insufficient.

(b) Matthew 23:34–35 (= Luke 11:49–51)

In this key passage, Jesus speaks of "prophets, sages, and scribes" who are martyred in various ways, "from the blood of righteous Abel to the blood of Zechariah son of Barachiah, whom you murdered between the sanctuary and the altar." Since the reference is to "*all* the righteous blood shed on earth" (v. 34), the passage may signify that by Jesus' day the Scriptures began with Genesis (the murder of Abel, Gen 4:8) and ended with the book of Chronicles (Zechariah slain by Joash, 2 Chron 24:20–22).

The Gospel passage refers to the prophet Zechariah *son of Barachiah*, whose message is recorded in the book of Zechariah. There, however, the Zechariah slain by Joash is called *son of Jehoiada*, who served as high priest when the kings Ahaziah and Joash ruled. One explanation is that Jesus is referring to Zechariah son of Baris (or Baruch), who was in Jerusalem during the First Jewish Revolt (Josephus, *Jewish War* 4.334–44). Even if Jesus is referring to the first and last books in a list of Scriptures, Luke gives no indication of which and how many other books came between them.

2.4 Summary of the Ancient Evidence Outside the Scrolls Found at Qumran

These passages from the Apocrypha and *Pseudepigrapha,* Hellenistic Jewish Writings, and the New Testament provide valuable insights into Jewish perceptions of Scripture outside of Qumran from about 200 B.C.E. to about 100 C.E.

Most or all Jews were familiar with two series of Scriptures: (1) the law, the laws, Moses, the law of Moses, or the books of Moses; (2) the Prophets, (the) prophecies, or oracles delivered through the mouths of prophets.

Additional books were also regarded as Scripture, but it is not clear if an actual third series was familiar to most authors. Some refer to these additional books in general terms (*the others that followed them, the other books of our ancestors,* or *the rest of the books*), others speak of poetic or wisdom books (*psalms and anything else which fosters and perfects knowledge and piety; the remaining four books* [*which*] *contain hymns to God and precepts*; and *sayings, parables, and proverbs*), and one source mentions narratives (*the books about the kings and prophets,* and *the letters of kings about votive offerings,* 2 Maccabees 2:13).

2.5 So Which Books Were Included Among These Scriptures?

- The Law or Torah. The many references to the *law of Moses, the books of Moses,* and so forth, show that well before the second century B.C.E., Genesis to Deuteronomy made up the first part of what was to become the Jewish Bible.

- The Prophets or *Nebi'im.* There is no firm evidence that this section contained the same list of prophets found in the Jewish canon (Joshua through the Twelve Minor Prophets), although Isaiah, Jeremiah, Ezekiel, Daniel, and the Minor Prophets were included.

- The Other Books. It is difficult to decide whether a distinct third series containing the Psalms and other books was emerging. In one source (4 Maccabees 18:15; cf. v. 10), *the psalmist David* seems to be among the prophets, but in two others *the writings of David* (2 Maccabees 2:13) or *the psalms* (Luke 24:44) are mentioned separately from the prophets. If there was such a series, it must have contained many of the books now preserved in the Writings (Psalms to Chronicles), but not all of them, and others besides.

By the end of this period (about 200 B.C.E. to about 100 C.E.), there was, as yet, no canon or closed list of books accepted by all Jewish people as supremely authoritative. But the ancient sources bear witness to the canonical process at work.

3. Evidence from the Scrolls Found at Qumran

3.1 Two Important Questions

What light do the Dead Sea Scrolls shed on the Scriptures and the canonical process? Like most previous books that explore this issue, I will focus on the sectarian scrolls found at Qumran. These contain compositions by the Essene movement, whose best-known center was at Qumran. The sectarian scrolls help answer two questions: (1) What do the sectarian scrolls from Qumran reveal about the structure of the Hebrew Bible/Old Testament? (2) What do they reveal about the contents of the Hebrew Bible/Old Testament? The sectarian scrolls are the ones containing the *Yahad*'s ideology or distinctive language; the vast majority were written by them or the movement's founders.

3.2 What Do the Sectarian Scrolls Reveal About the Structure of the Hebrew Bible/Old Testament?

Is there any evidence in the scrolls for the threefold division of Scripture as found in the Jewish Bible, or the fourfold arrangement found in Christian Old Testaments?

The *Rule of the Community* speaks of God's commands through *Moses and all his servants the prophets* (1QS 1:3), while the *Damascus Document* mentions *the books of the Law and the books of the prophets* (CD 7:15, 17). *Some of the Works of the Law* outlines several of the *Yahad*'s rules of observance, refers to the *b[ook of Mo]ses* (4QMMT C, line 21), and mentions *the [book of] Moses* and *the [books of the prophet]s* (C 17).

Two groupings of Scripture thus seem clear:

(1) *The book of Moses*, which is equivalent to *the Law* or *the law of Moses* (note 2 Kgs 14:6: *the book of the law of Moses*).

(2) *The prophets* or *the books of the prophets*.

The published edition of *Some of the Works of the Law* (Qimron and Strugnell, 1994) contains another passage that is most intriguing:

> [And] we have [also [10]written] to you so that you may have understanding in *the book of Moses* [and] in *the book[s of the Pr]ophets* and in *Davi[d* and [11]in *the events]* of *ages past*. . . . (C 9–11, author translation)

Two texts mentioned earlier come to mind: 2 Maccabees 2:13 ("the books about the kings and prophets, and the writings of David and letters of kings about votive offerings") and Luke 24:44 ("the law of Moses, the prophets, and the psalms must be fulfilled"). So if the editors' placement of fragments is correct, this portion of MMT would indicate three divisions of biblical books.

However, *in the book[s of* is preserved on the isolated frg. 17, while *[the Pr]ophets and in Davi[d]* is on frg. 15, which does not join directly with frg. 17. The reconstructed text is thus not certain, and does not provide firm evidence for a threefold division of biblical books at Qumran. A threefold division remains possible, but is not confirmed.

The words that follow in the MMT passage are also of interest: *[and in the events] of ages past*, which possibly denotes writings of a narrative nature such as annals. Such language (also in 2 Macc 2:13) may refer to Joshua and to Kings, perhaps also Chronicles, Ezra, and Nehemiah. This suggests that, for some Jews at least, what are now the Former Prophets in modern Hebrew Bibles were grouped together as Historical Books (as in the

Septuagint). Unfortunately, here the text of 4QMMT is also broken and fragmentary, so this grouping is possible, but not confirmed.

3.3 What Do the Sectarian Scrolls Reveal About Contents of the Hebrew Bible/Old Testament?

We cannot simply assume that the Yahad Essenes accepted as Scripture all the books now found in traditional Hebrew Bibles or Christian Old Testaments. So how do we tell whether they regarded a book as especially authoritative? No single approach is sufficient for deciding this, so nine criteria may be used:

(1) Statements Indicating Scriptural Status. For example, the *Florilegium* quotes Daniel 12:3 and states: "As it is written in the Book of Daniel the Prophet" (4Q174 2:3).

(2) The Appeal to Prophecy. For example: *David's Compositions* in the *Great Psalms Scroll* (11QPs[a]) says David composed [5]3,600 psalms; and 364 songs to sing before the altar . . . [6]for all the days of the year, 364; . . . [11]*through prophecy* which was given him from before the Most High (col. 27:5–6, 11).

(3) Claims of Divine Authority. Three examples are *1 Enoch* (1:2; 10:1–11:2), *Jubilees* (1:5–18, 22–28, 26–29; 2:1), and the *Temple Scroll* that presents itself as a new Deuteronomy directly from God.

(4) Davidic Titles. Two examples are from the *Great Psalms Scroll: Psalm 151A* (beginning with "Hallelujah! A Psalm of David Son of Jesse") and *Psalm 151B* (at the start of David's power after the prophet of God had anointed him).

(5) *Pesharim* and Other Commentaries. Books on which commentaries were written were viewed as Scripture by the commentators and their audiences. At least 17 copies of *Pesharim* were found at Qumran: six on Isaiah (3QpIsa and 4QpIsa[a–e]); two each on Hosea, Micah, and Zephaniah; one each on Nahum and Habakkuk; and three on the Psalms. Other types of commentary were also found, such as *A Commentary on Genesis and Exodus* (4Q422), which may be classified as "rewritten Bible."

(6) Quantity of Manuscripts Preserved. Although most Qumran scrolls are fragmentary and others have been lost altogether, the number of manuscripts for a particular book indicates how extensively it was used at Qumran, and most likely its authoritative status for the *Yahad* Essenes. Books represented by the greatest number are: Deuteronomy (39 scrolls), Psalms (39), Genesis (30), Exodus (30), Isaiah (22), Leviticus (22), *Jubilees* (about 15), and *1 Enoch* (at least 12).

(7) Translation into Greek or Aramaic. Translation of a Hebrew work into Greek may indicate its authoritative status for its scribe or users. Several Greek scrolls were found at Qumran, mainly of books from the Pentateuch, such as Exodus (pap7QLXXExod) and the Letter of Jeremiah (pap7QEpJer gr).

A few books were translated into Aramaic, resulting in the Targums of Leviticus and Job (4QtgLev, 4QtgJob, 11QtgJob).

(8) Dependence on Earlier Books. Several sectarian texts show a general dependence on earlier works, which suggests those writings were authoritative to the later writers. For example, the *Genesis Apocryphon* is an Aramaic work that rehearses the lives of Enoch, Lamech, Noah and his sons, and Abraham.

(9) Books Quoted or Alluded to as Authorities. The final criterion is presented in greater detail. Ways in which a book was used in later writings often point to its special authority or scriptural status. The sectarian scrolls from Qumran feature several types of quotations of or allusions to scriptural books. One type is quotations with introductory formulae, for example, "As God said" in the *Damascus Document* (CD) 6:13–14, referring to Malachi 1:10. Another is quotations or allusions without introductory formulae, such as the "precious corner-stone" of Isaiah 28:16 in the *Community Rule* (1QS) 8:7. A third type is Midrashic Texts, for example, Psalm 1:1 and Psalm 2:1 used as base texts in the *Florilegium* (4Q174).

The list below features in one column the number of scrolls preserved (criterion 6) and in the next column quotations of or allusions in key or otherwise important sectarian scrolls (criterion 9). The biblical books are grouped as found in the traditional Hebrew Bible (Law, Prophets, Writings), but this does not mean the *Yahad* movement at Qumran placed them in these three divisions. Books not in the traditional Hebrew Bible are listed in a fourth group (Other Books). The sectarian scrolls that are referenced using their abbreviations are:

CD: the *Damascus Document* (CD, 4Q266–73, 5Q12, 6Q15)

1QS: the *Rule of the Community* (1QS)

1QM: the *War Scroll* (1QM, 1Q33, 4Q491–96)

1QH^a: the *Hodayot* or *Thanksgiving Psalms* (1QH^a)

4QFlor: the *Florilegium* (4Q174)

4QTestim: the *Testimonia* (4Q175)

4QMMT: *Some of the Works of the Law*

11QMelch: the *Melchizedek Text* (11Q13)

PesherIsa, etc.: *Pesharim* on Isaiah, Hosea, Micah, Nahum, Habakkuk, Zephaniah, Psalms

PesherApocWeeks: *Pesher on the Apocalypse of Weeks* (4Q247)

ApocrMal: *Apocryphal Malachi* (5Q10)

Table 2.		
(Law):		
Book	***No. of Scrolls***	***Used in Distinctive Sectarian Works***
Genesis	25	CD (3x)
Exodus	22	1QS, CD (2x), 4QFlor, 4QTestim
Leviticus	18	1QS, CD (20x), 11QMelch (2x)
Numbers	11	1QS, CD (18x), 1QM, 4QFlor (3x), 4QTestim (3x), 11QMelch
Deuteronomy	38	1QS, CD (12x), 1QM (2x), 4QTestim
Reworked Pentateuch	5	
(Prophets):		
Book	***No. of Scrolls***	***Used in Distinctive Sectarian Works***
Joshua	2	4QTestim
Judges	3	
1 & 2 Samuel	4	CD?, 1QM, 4QFlor (3x)
1 & 2 Kings	3	
Isaiah	22	CD (16x), 1QS (4x), 1QM, 4QFlor (2x), 11QMelch (6x), PesherIsa (101x)
Jeremiah	7	11QMelch (6x)
Ezekiel	6	CD (4x), 4QFlor
12 Minor Prophets	8	
Hosea		CD (6x), PesherHos (22x)
Joel		CD (2x)
Amos		CD (2x), 4QFlor
Obadiah		
Jonah		
Micah		CD (8x), PesherMic (13x)
Nahum		CD (2x), PesherNah (24x)
Habakkuk		PesherHab (35x)
Zephaniah		1QS, PesherZeph (6x)
Haggai		
Zechariah		CD (2x), PesherIsa
Malachi		CD (3x), 4QFlor, 11QMelch (3x), ApocrMal
(Writings):		
Book	***No. of Scrolls***	***Used in Distinctive Sectarian Works***
Psalms	37	CD (2x), 1QH^a, 4QFlor (3x), 11QMelch (3x), PesherPs (43x)
Job	6	CD (2x)
Proverbs	2	CD (2x)
Ruth	4	
Song of Songs	4	
Ecclesiastes	2	
Lamentations	4	
Esther	0	
Daniel	10	4QFlor, 11QMelch
Ezra	1	(the name *yahad*, cf. Ezra 4:3)
Nehemiah	2	CD (2)
1 & 2 Chronicles	1	
(Other Books):		
Book	***No. of Scrolls***	***Used in Distinctive Sectarian Works***
1 Enoch	at least 12	PesherApocWeeks(?)
Jubilees	about 15	CD (see also 4Q228, 4Q265)
The Temple Scroll	about 15	
Letter of Jeremiah	1	
Ben Sira (= Sirach)	2	
Tobit	4	

Concluding Comments

The wealth of information in section 3 above gives a profile of which books were viewed as authoritative Scripture by the Yahad Essenes at Qumran.

- The Books of Moses/the Law. It comes as no surprise that Genesis, Numbers, Exodus, Leviticus, and (especially) Deuteronomy were held in great esteem, with multiple copies and numerous citations and allusions. *Reworked Pentateuch* is included here because it contained several of or all the books of the Pentateuch.

- The Prophets. For the Essene movement, this group most likely differed from the traditional list in the Hebrew Bible. Isaiah, Jeremiah, Ezekiel, and the Twelve Minor Prophets certainly featured, but probably also Daniel and perhaps the Psalms.

- Books found today in the Writings. A third series of Scriptures *may* have been emerging among the Yahad movement. However, the key passage in 4QMMT is reconstructed and by no means certain, so the evidence is insufficient. Nevertheless, some books that do not sit well among the books of Moses or the Prophets were also viewed or used as authoritative Scripture.

Some contained narratives, but are represented by few manuscripts and are seldom quoted, if at all (Joshua, Judges, Samuel, Kings, Chronicles, Ezra and Nehemiah). Second Maccabees 2:13 and a section of MMT—again, partly reconstructed—may refer to a series of Historical Books, in which case these books *could* be grouped together. In view of their great size, Samuel, Kings, and Chronicles are not well represented (four, three and one scroll, respectively), although Samuel is referenced several times. Joshua, Judges, and Ruth fare better (especially Ruth in view of its size), but Esther was not accepted as Scripture by the *Yahad*.

Several books among the traditional Writings feature poetic or wisdom teaching (Psalms, Proverbs, Job, Lamentations, Song of Songs, and Ecclesiastes). The Psalms were regarded as Scripture, and (as already mentioned) may have been considered among the Prophets. Job was also viewed as Scripture, being found in several copies (six), quoted twice, and probably believed to be written by Moses. Proverbs is represented (in two scrolls) and quoted quite seldom in view of its size, while the Song of Songs (Canticles) fares better at four copies, but Ecclesiastes less so at two.

- Additional Books. Several more books feature in the list above. *1 Enoch* was most likely viewed as Scripture by the *Yahad* at Qumran, as were *Jubilees* and most likely the *Temple Scroll*. Ben Sira is a long book (51 chapters) but is hardly represented and had little impact. However, to judge by its four scrolls, the far shorter Tobit was more significant.

9

The Nonbiblical Scrolls

Introduction: The Categories Used

At least half of the nonbiblical scrolls, probably more, represent texts composed by the Essene (*Yahad*) movement. Containing the movement's ideology or distinctive language, these are known as the *sectarian scrolls*. The remaining (nonsectarian) scrolls contain ideas and language not easily distinguished from writings by other parties in Palestinian Jewish society and thus seem not limited to the movement. It is tempting to neatly divide the nonbiblical scrolls into sectarian and nonsectarian groupings, but in many cases this proves unworkable since identifying sectarian content and language is often not possible. The nonbiblical scrolls will be explored here in seven sections: (1) Rules. (2) Legal Texts. (3) Commentaries on Authoritative Texts. (4) Poetic Texts, Calendars, Prayers, and Liturgies. (5) Wisdom (Sapiential) Texts. (6) Eschatological Texts. (7) The Copper Scroll, Other Documentary Texts, and Nonsectarian Texts.

1. Rules

Some of the most distinctive sectarian scrolls contain text from various Rules. This term means "Collections of Regulations or Precepts" (for example, the much later Rule of St. Benedict). The Rules found at Qumran contain legislation for community life by explaining regulations on how to join the group, meetings of members, meals, even the conduct of war. Prominent Rules include: the *Damascus Document,* the *Rule of the Community*, the *Rule of the Congregation*, the *Rule of Blessings*, and the *War Rule.*

1.1 The Damascus Document

This work was known well before the discovery of the Dead Sea Scrolls. In 1896, Solomon Schechter of Cambridge University found among the texts from Cairo Genizah a full medieval copy and a smaller one of a lost composition he called *Fragments of a Zadokite Work*. Scholars were surprised to find at least ten fragmentary copies at Qumran: eight in Cave 4 (4Q266–73), one in Cave 5 (5Q12), and one in Cave 6 (6Q15). It was preserved by the Karaites, a medieval Jewish group who, like the *Yahad* Essenes, opposed the pharisaic-rabbinic approach to law. The genizah was part of the Karaites' Ben Ezra Synagogue in Old Cairo.

The high number of copies found in the Qumran caves (ten) indicates that the *Damascus Document* (scholarly abbreviation of CD) was important to the group associated with the nearby site. It is fully preserved only in the Cairo Genizah texts, according to which the contents are divided by column. CD falls into two main sections:

- The Admonition (cols. 1–8 and 19–20) urges separation from the wicked, places the group's origin 390 years after Jerusalem's destruction (587/6 B.C.E.), draws lessons from biblical history, contains warnings, and threatens punishments.

- A list of rules or statutes (cols. 15–16 and 9–14) is drawn from biblical law. For example: concerning transgressors, skin diseases, membership of the New Covenant (Essene) community, the Sabbath, sacrifices, the Temple, and the temple city. Some rules are for the community (the roles of priests and the Guardian, punishments for offenses). Also featured is a ritual for expelling unfaithful members, apparently at the annual Covenant Renewal Ceremony in the third month.

The *Damascus Document* was addressed to a community whose members lived in camps (CD 7:6; 10:23), which were communal groups in various towns in Israel. These men had families, earned wages, and owned property. Yet they were also a remnant, for whom God raised the Teacher of Righteousness—the movement's early and most prominent leader—to lead them in the proper way (1:10–11) so as to enter the (new) covenant (2:2, cf. 6:12). The qualifications of those desiring membership were assessed by the Guardian (Hebrew *Mabeqqer* or *Paqid*, possibly another name for the Instructor), who also taught members about the works of God.

The mention of Damascus (6:19) has proved puzzling: Did they migrate to the Syrian city of Damascus, or is this name symbolic for a place of exile (see Amos 5:26–27)? The conclusion states these regulations are to be followed during the present "era of wickedness" and are in agreement with "the most recent interpretation of the Law" (4Q266, frg. 11 lines 19–20).

1.2 The Rule of the Community

One of the most important scrolls discovered in Cave 1 was an almost complete copy (11 columns) of a constitution for the *Yahad* community at Qumran. Most scholars name this work the *Rule of the Community*, although some prefer its Hebrew name, *Serekh ha-Yahad* (hence the abbreviation 1QS—Cave 1/Qumran/*Serekh* or *Rule*). Ten more copies (all fragmentary) were found in Cave 4 (4Q255–64a) and another in Cave 5 (5Q11).

Two Cave 4 copies (4Q256 and 4Q258) preserve shorter versions of columns 5–7; 4Q258 may well have lacked columns 1–4 altogether and begun with column 5. Both preserve additional material at the end, and a third copy from Cave 4 (4Q259) has a calendrical text called *Otot* (Signs). When all these are compared, understanding the development of this Rule becomes difficult, since the latest form of the text is in the earliest copy (1QS, 100–75 B.C.E.). It likely grew as follows: The lost original consisted of a shorter form of columns 5–9 and the *Otot*, and was later lengthened with scriptural justifications for the regulations. Later, it was prefaced with columns 1–4 and the *Otot* section was replaced with columns 10–11.

This *Rule of the Community* contains legislation for a group of men who have withdrawn from society—presumably the Yahad at Qumran, and perhaps others like it. It calls this community a *yahad*, and provides precepts for admission into the Covenant of Grace (1:7), for understanding the fellowship, and how to live as a member. Led by the *Maskil* (Instructor, probably a priest) and examined by the Guardian—possibly the same man— the membership consisted of priests, Levites, and Israelites. Obedience to the Torah was paramount—everyone was ranked annually according to his observance of it. Humanity is divided into two overall groups, the Sons of Light and the Sons of Darkness (1:9–10). The community portrayed here is in many ways akin to a monastic order; most scholars identify it with the *Yahad* at Qumran, and as part of the wider Essene movement.

Table 1. An Outline of the *Rule of the Community*	
(1QS, 4Q255–64a, 5Q11)	
1:1–15	The Covenant and the Role of the Teacher
1:16–3:12	New Members, Annual Review of Membership, Exclusion of Some
3:13–4:26	The Two Spirits and the Problem of Good and Evil
5:1–20	General Rules for Conduct of the Community
5:20–7:25	Specific Rules for Conduct of the Community
8:1–9:2	An Inner Council or an Early Manifesto
9:3–11	Purpose, Prophet, Two Messiahs
9:12–10:5	Rules for the *Maskil* (Instructor)
10:5–11:22	A Sample Prayer to Be Delivered by the *Maskil*

1.3 The Rule of the Congregation *and the* Rule of Blessings

These two works are found as appendixes to the Cave 1 copy of the *Rule of the Community* (1QS). For many years this appeared to be the only copy of either, but nine scrolls published in 2000 (4Q249a–i, all in a cryptic script) may be copies of the *Rule of the Congregation*.

The *Rule of the Congregation* (1QSa or 1Q28a) declares: "This is the rule for all the congregation of Israel in the Last Days" (col. 1:1), and provides instructions for the last days, assemblies, and members of the community, who are to live according to the law of the Sons of Zadok, the priests, and keep God's covenant (1:1–3). In contrast to the *Rule of the Community*, this end-times *Yahad* includes women and children (1:5), and is led by priests and organized in military fashion (1:22–25). People with impurities or physical blemishes are forbidden membership because "the holy angels are [part of] their congregation" (2:8–9; cf. 1:25–2:10). The final section (2:11–22) describes a messianic banquet (or rather banquets, line 22), and reminds many readers of the Lord's Supper in the New Testament:

> [When] they gather [at the] communal [tab]le, [having set out bread and w]ine so the communal table is set [18][for eating] and [the] wine (poured) for drinking, none [may re]ach for the first portion [19]of the bread or [the wine] before the Priest. For [he] shall [bl]ess the first portion of the bread [20]and the wine, [reac]hing for the bread first. Afterw[ard] the Messiah of Israel [shall re]ach [21]for the bread. [Finally], ea[ch] member of the whole congregation of the *Yahad* [shall give a bl]essing, [in descending order of] rank. This procedure shall govern [22]every me[al], provided at least ten me[n are ga]thered together (2:17–22). (*The Dead Sea Scrolls: A New Translation*, 140)

The *Rule of Blessings* (1QSb or IQ28b) is the second appendix to the *Rule of the Community*. Like the *Rule of the Congregation*, it also seems for the last days and expresses important features of the *Yahad's* ideology. Many blessings are presented, all to be recited by the *Yahad's* leader, the Instructor. The final blessing is for the Davidic Messiah, the Prince (or Leader) of the Congregation (5:20–29), whose rule will bring justice for all: "[With righteousness he will judge the poor], and decide with equity for [the me]ek of the earth" (4:21, quoting Isa 11:2).

1.4 The War Rule (or War Scroll)

The *War Rule* provides instructions on how the community is to array itself during an eschatological battle, and will be discussed below in Eschatological Texts.

2. Legal Texts

Many compositions found in the Qumran caves are legal in character. Some contain regulations for community life, even the conduct of war. Other legal texts explain laws found in the Pentateuch (especially Exodus through Deuteronomy) and apply them to the Yahad as a community. Several of these are now discussed, bearing in mind that many works listed in other groups also feature laws and legal material.

2.1 Some of the Works of the Law (MMT)

This important work is abbreviated here as MMT because it contains the key Hebrew phrase *miqsat ma'ase ha-torah* (*Some of the Works of the Law*). The text has been reconstructed by scholars from six partial copies (sections A–F = 4Q327, 4Q394–99).

Also called the *Halakhic Letter* or *A Sectarian Manifesto*, MMT is a key text for understanding the Essene (*Yahad*) movement. Many scholars regard it as a letter (although the senders and recipients are not identified), but others view it as a public treatise, or a treaty with another community, or a collection of laws. It contains calendrical material (section

A), about 24 laws mainly from the Torah and their correct interpretation (section B), and an epilogue (section C). The epilogue is very illuminating:

> Now, we have written to you *some of the works of the Law*, those which we determined would be beneficial for you and your people, because we have seen [that] you possess insight and knowledge of the Law. Understand all these things and beseech Him to set your counsel straight and so keep you away from evil thoughts and the counsel of Belial. Then you shall rejoice at the end of time when you find the essence of our words to be true. And it will be reckoned to you as righteousness, in that you have done what is right and good before Him, to your own benefit and to that of Israel (C, lines 26–32). (*The Dead Sea Scrolls: A New Translation*, 462)

One party is clearly writing to another, giving what they believe is the correct interpretation of the calendar and many points of biblical law.

Section A: The Calendrical Section (4Q327). Presented here is the 364-day *solar* calendar (measured by the sun) as opposed to the 354-day *lunar* calendar (by the moon). This point of dispute is familiar to students of early Judaism and rabbinical Judaism, since having the correct calendar is crucial for fixing the festivals that all Jews were required to observe. For the Essene movement, the 364-day calendar was the correct one, while for the Pharisees it was the 354-day one.

Section B: The Legal Section. The 24 (or so) laws in dispute concern what must be done to avoid mixing the holy with the sacred with respect to sacrifices, priestly gifts, purity, forbidden marriages, and persons prohibited from entering the sanctuary. Such matters also took central stage in debates among the early rabbis and in their great compilations of Jewish law, the Mishnah and the two (Palestinian and Babylonian) Talmuds. The expertise of many Jewish scholars has been central in analyzing texts such as MMT, and in showing that law was one of the main concerns of the Essene movement.

To explain each ruling is beyond the scope of this book, but one example will suffice. A major issue for most Jewish groups of the late Second Temple period, and the rabbinic period that followed, was ritual purity: What must I do to become clean and remain undefiled? What must I avoid because it will defile me or my community? These are also major concerns in the book of Leviticus. In a section on unclean creatures that swarm upon the earth (such as the mouse and the chameleon), the Israelites are told:

> (33) And if any of [these unclean creatures] falls into any earthen vessel, all that is in it will be unclean, and you shall break the vessel. (34) Any food that could be eaten shall be unclean if water from any such vessel comes upon it; and any liquid that could be drunk shall be unclean if it was in any such vessel. (Lev 11:33–34)

Passages such as this may have given rise to later speculation on whether contact between vessels extends even to streams of liquid: Does impurity pass through a stream of liquid from an impure container to a pure one? We know from the Mishnah (*Yadayim* 4.7) that the Pharisees taught that impurity does not pass through (the more lenient view), but the Sadducees taught that it does (the stricter view). The ruling in 4QMMT reads:

[Co]ncerning Streams of Liquid: We have determined that they are not intrinsically [p]ure. Indeed, streams of liquid do not form a barrier between the impure and the pure. For the liquid of the stream and that in its receptacle become as one liquid (B, lines 55–58). (*The Dead Sea Scrolls: A New Translation*, 458–59)

Analyses of all 24 rulings in Section B suggest the group represented by MMT (the Essenes) and the Sadducees shared the stricter, more demanding approach to the law, while the Pharisees' approach was more moderate.

Section C: The Epilogue. The group has separated itself, does not share in the practices rejected in *MMT*, and the recipients must accept these correct understandings of the Law. Although some scholars believe the writer is trying to persuade certain Sadducees, he is most likely appealing to wavering members of his own group. They are to stand firm and not follow the Man of Mockery (or Man of the Lie), who has rejected the Teacher's claims and allied himself with the Pharisees by compromising on biblical law.

2.2 The Temple Scroll

The *Temple Scroll* (11Q19) is the longest (about 28 feet) and one of the best preserved scrolls found at Qumran. Four more fragmentary copies were also found (11Q20, 11Q21?, 4Q365a?, and 4Q524).

The author of the *Temple Scroll* has compiled a "new Deuteronomy" intended to guide Israel in the period leading up to God's creation of a new heaven and new earth. Although he quotes many times from the Pentateuch (especially Deuteronomy), he deliberately omits the name of Moses. Laws are almost always presented as spoken by God in the first person to Moses, who must be inferred from the phrase "your brother Aaron" (col. 44:5). Where the Pentateuch has God speaking in the third person ("the LORD said"), this text has him speaking in the first person ("I say to you").

An outline of the *Temple Scroll* suggests that it moves from the center (the Temple) outward to include laws about festivals, the Temple courts, Jerusalem, and other towns.

Table 2. An Outline of the *Temple Scroll*	
(1Q19–21, 4Q365a?, 4Q524)	
Cols. 1?–2	The Covenant, Moses at Mount Sinai (cf. Exod 34). *God gives instructions on:*
3–13	Building the Temple and altar
13–29	The festivals and their sacrifices
30–45	The courtyards of the Temple complex and various buildings in them
45–51	Protecting the Temple's sanctuary, and several purity laws
22–66	The judicial system (cf. the law code in Deut 12–23), including duties of priests, levites, judges, and the king; and rules for going to war

This ideal Temple will be constructed by humans in the future and is enormous: a complex measuring 2,860 feet (1,700 cubits) per side, with a total perimeter of 11,450 feet (6,800 cubits). This was the size of the entire city of Jerusalem in the Hasmonean period (about 150–30 B.C.E.)!

Exactly who compiled the *Temple Scroll* is not clear, but it reflects the ideology of the *Yahad* Essenes. For example, the list of festivals and their dates presupposes the 364-day year found in *Jubilees* and sectarian texts such as the Qumran calendars. For some scholars, the *Temple Scroll* was written by the Teacher of Righteousness and presents the true understanding of the Mosaic Torah that God revealed to him. There is little hard evidence for this, although one of the *Psalms Pesharim* (4Q171, see 3.1 below) mentions a law that the Teacher sent (frgs. 1–2, col. 4.8–9). Since the 4Q524 copy is dated 150–125 B.C.E., the *Temple Scroll* must have been composed no later, before the *Yahad* group moved to Qumran in the late second century.

(Another important and related composition is the *New Jerusalem* text, which will be discussed under Eschatological Texts below.)

2.3 Other Legal Texts

(Note: *Reworked Pentateuch* is placed by some scholars in this group but is an edition of the Torah.) Sections of more legal texts were found at Qumran, with most dealing with issues of purity, which were very important for the *Yahad:*

- *Halakha A* (4Q251). For example: On types of marriages that were forbidden

- *Halakha B* (4Q264a). Example: On what could be said and not be said on the Sabbath

- *Miscellaneous Rules* (4Q265). Example: A woman's time of impurity after giving birth

- *Purification Liturgy* (4Q284). On periods of purification

- *Harvesting* (4Q414). On purity of liquids from crops such as figs and olives

- *Ordinances* (4Q159, 513, 514). Example: Not dressing like the opposite sex (cf. Deut 22:5)

3. Commentaries on Authoritative Texts

The Scriptures played center stage for the *Yahad* Essenes at Qumran, with the books of Deuteronomy, the Psalms, Genesis, Exodus, and Isaiah represented by the largest number of scrolls. Most of the sectarian scrolls found in the Qumran caves use "biblical" language or deal with scriptural passages and characters. Two groups in particular interpret the Scriptures in a systematic way.

3.1 Pesharim (Continuous Commentaries)

Many prophetic books in the Hebrew Bible have two time frames, often for the writers themselves: present realities and future events. Many of the Prophetic Books reflect the circumstances of the prophet's time—usually difficult ones—and look forward to future judgment, vindication, restoration, or salvation. Thus it is not surprising that some writers among the Essenes chose sections from certain Prophetic Books as authoritative Scripture for which they provided authoritative commentary. The *Pesharim* quote and explain consecutive stretches of text from one scriptural book. Believing he was living in the last days, each commentator sought to interpret, or unlock, a prophet's words for his own time. Since some *Pesharim* refer to specific events, and in a few cases even mention specific names, they are very important for understanding the *Yahad* at Qumran and the history of the times in which they lived. Seventeen or 18 *Pesharim* have been identified, with commentary on passages from seven scriptural books (Isaiah, Hosea, Micah, Nahum, Habakkuk, Zephaniah, Psalms, and one unidentified text). Two are discussed in more detail.

(a) Pesher Habakkuk

One of the first seven scrolls discovered in Cave 1, this pesher (1QpHab) comments on chapters 1–2 of Habakkuk, introducing the interpretations with the Hebrew word *pesher*. Since it is well preserved and contains important material, 1QpHab has dominated discussion of the continuous commentaries.

The *Yahad* were confident their interpretation of Scripture was true because God had revealed the mysteries of the Prophets to their early leader, the Teacher of Righteousness. The writer of *Pesher Habakkuk* believed that the biblical prophet, who was active in the late 600s B.C.E., was writing about the Teacher and his opponent the Wicked Priest. The approach of all the pesher writers to Scripture and its interpretation is illustrated in a famous passage from 1QpHab often quoted by scholars. We are told that Habakkuk did not know when the period was referring to would be complete, that the prophet was in fact referring to the Teacher of Righteousness, and that God had revealed to the Teacher the true meaning of the words spoken by the Prophets:

> So I will stand on watch and station myself on my watchtower and wait for what he will say to me, and [what I will reply to] His rebuke. Then the LORD answered me [and said, "***Write down the vision plainly***] ***on tablets, so that with ease*** [*someone can read it*]." (Hab 2:1–2)

> [This refers to . . .] then God told Habakkuk to write down what is going to happen to the generation to come; but when that period would be complete he did not make known to him. When it says, "***so that with ease someone can read it***," this refers to the Teacher of Righteousness to whom God made known all the mysterious revelations of his servants the prophets. (1QpHab 6:12–7:5) (*The Dead Sea Scrolls: A New Translation*, 84)

Another compelling quotation interprets Habakkuk's prophecy that the nations will be amazed about Judah:

> ["***Look, traitors, and see,*** [17]***and be shocked—and amazed—for*** (*the LORD*) ***is doing something in your time that you would not believe it if***][2:1] ***told***" (Hab 1:5).

[This passage refers to] the traitors with the Man of the [2] Lie, because they have not [obeyed the words of] the Teacher of Righteousness from the mouth of [3] God. It also refers to the trai[tors to the] New [Covenant], because they did not [4] believe in God's covenant [and desecrated] his holy name [5] and finally, it refers [to the trai]tors in the Last [6] Days. They are the cru[el Israel]ites who will not believe [7] when they hear everything that [is to come upon] the latter generation that will be spoken by [8] the Priest in whose [heart] God has put [the ability] to explain all [9] the words of his servants the prophets, through [whom] God has foretold [10] everything that is to come upon his people and [his land]. (1QpHab 1:16–2:10) (*The Dead Sea Scrolls: A New Translation*, 81)

For the commentator, Habakkuk had predicted long ago what was to take place in the *Yahad's* history. Two key individuals are named: the Teacher of Righteousness (also called the Priest) and the Man of the Lie, an important opponent in a community who had refused to accept the Teacher's authority and claims. Three groups of traitors are specified: the followers of the Man of the Lie, those who had rejected the group's new covenant, and those who did not believe the Teacher's inspired interpretations of prophecy.

(b) The *Psalms Pesharim*

Three *Psalms Pesharim* were found in the Qumran caves: 1QpPs (1Q16), 4QpPs^a (4Q171), and 4QpPs^b (4Q173). The fact that there *are Psalms Pesharim* is surprising, since it seems that the continuous commentaries were written only on Prophetic Books—although another scroll, 4QpUnidentified (4Q172), is also a challenge. The commentators most likely regarded the Psalms as prophecy and David as a prophet (in the *Great Psalms Scroll, David's Compositions* says David composed a total of 4,050 psalms and songs "through prophecy which was given him from before the Most High" [col. 27:2–11]).

The best preserved *Psalms Pesher* is 4QpPs^a on Psalm 37. This psalm encourages the righteous (whom God will reward) to keep faith despite the apparent successes of the wicked (whom he will punish). In the Pesher, the righteous are the members of the Yahad and their leader the Teacher of Righteousness, while the wicked denote their enemies, the Wicked Priest and the Man of the Lie.

3.2 Thematic Commentaries

Unlike the *Pesharim*, which quote and explain consecutive stretches of text from one scriptural book, the Thematic Commentaries gather and interpret passages from several scriptural works, in the belief that a common theme or group of themes can be traced. For these authors, scriptural books were interrelated and so a passage in one book could be clarified by passages found later in that book or in others.

(a) The *Melchizedek Text* (11Q13)

Some texts mention Melchizedek, king of Salem and a priest of the Most High God, who met Abram after he defeated the kings and rescued Lot (Gen 14:17–20). The *Melchizedek Text* (11Q13) is based on Leviticus 25 (which deals with the Year of Jubilee) and interprets verse 13 in light of Deuteronomy 15:2 and Isaiah 61:1. While the two scriptural passages focus on returning property to original owners and remitting debts, the author of 11Q13 uncovers an eschatological meaning. Column 2:4 gives the interpretation: "[Leviticus 25:13] applies [to the L]ast Days and concerns the captives, just as [Isaiah said, '*To proclaim liberty to the captive*s]' (Isaiah 61:1)." The members of the community are then called the "inheritance of Melchizedek," who "will return them to what is rightfully theirs. He will proclaim to them the jubilee, thereby releasing th[em from the debt of a]ll their sins" (col. 2:6).

Melchizedek will release those who have been captive to Belial, and will act as the judge of the eschatological age. The writer then interprets Psalms 82:1 and 7:7–8 in "the year of Melchizedek's favor" (col. 2:9–11). Psalm 82:1–2 is interpreted (line 12) to mean Melchizedek's judgment of Belial and the spirits predestined to him (the fallen angels).

As the eschatological liberator of the righteous, Melchizedek comes as a divine being or angel (lines 10–11). Here he is equivalent to the archangel Michael (the *War Scroll* 17:6–8), the Prince of Light (the *Rule of the Community* 3:20), and the Angel of Truth (the *Rule of the Community* 3:24).

> "*A godlike being* (Hebrew, *Elohim*) *has taken his place in the* [*divine*] *coun*[*cil*]; *in the midst of the divine beings* (Hebrew, *Elohim*) *he holds judgment*" (Psalm 82:1). David also s[ays] concerning him, "*Over* [*him*] [11] *take your seat in the highest heaven; a divine being* (Hebrew, *El*) *will judge the peoples*" (Psalm 7:7–8). [col. 2:10–11] (*The Dead Sea Scrolls: A New Translation*, 592)

(b) Other Thematic Commentaries

The most important are the *Florilegium* (4Q174), the *Testimonia* (4Q175), and *Catena A* (4Q177). Others have a similar approach but focus on one book—the *Commentary on Genesis* (4Q252), which explains selected passages from Genesis in order but skips large parts of the text; and one *Pesher on Isaiah* (4Q163), which also uses verses from Jeremiah, Hosea, and Zechariah.

4. Poetic Texts, Calendars, Prayers, and Liturgies

4.1 Poetic Texts

The book of Psalms is one of the two most represented among the biblical scrolls, so it is not surprising to find similar texts among the sectarian scrolls—though adapted to new times and new situations. Poems appear in many scrolls that are best placed in other categories (for example, the *Rule of the Community*). Some, however, are completely poetic.

(a) The *Hodayot* (*Thanksgiving Hymns*)

The most prominent collection is the *Hodayot*, in the well-preserved *Thanksgiving Scroll* from Cave 1 (1QH[a]) and seven more fragmentary copies (1Q35 and 4Q427–32).

There are about 35 hymns, which are introduced by *"I give thanks to You, O Lord"* or some-times *"Blessed are You, O Lord."* They do not share the same content as biblical psalms, but reflect the ideology of the Essene movement in forms that often flow free of biblical style.

Most of the *Hodayot* use the first person "I," and express powerful feelings, cries, or beliefs. Scholars divide them into two types: the Community Hymns and the Teacher Hymns. Some *Hodayot* are difficult to place, but there are about 14 Community Hymns and 14 Teacher Hymns.

The Community Hymns present the prayers and thoughts of ordinary members of the *Yahad,* usually praise, obedience, or God's judgment of evil. For example, Hymn 26 opens with:

> [16] Blessed are You, O Lord, God of compassion [and rich] in mercy, for You have made [th]e[se things] known that I might declare [17] Your wondrous works, and not keep silent day and n[ight]. All power is Yours [. . .] [18] by Your mercy, in Your great goodness and abun[dance of compassion. I] shall delight in [Your] fo[rgiveness . . .] (col. 8:16–18) (*The Dead Sea Scrolls: A New Translation*, 195)

In the Teacher Hymns (concentrated in cols. 10–17), the speaker is the movement's early charismatic leader, the Teacher of Righteousness. He tells of his suffering and trials, the plots of Belial and the wicked, God's grace in saving him, and the knowledge that has been revealed to him. One foremost example is Hymn 15, in which the Teacher tells of Belial's plots and, a bit later, how God has revealed to him knowledge for illuminating the members of the community (who are called *the many*):

> [13] You, O God, reject every plan [14] of Belial, and Your counsel alone shall stand, and the plan of Your heart shall remain for ever. They are pretenders; they hatch the plots of Belial, [15] they seek You with a double heart, and are not founded in Your truth. . . .

> [28] But by me You have illumined the face of many (or, *the general membership*) and have strengthened them uncountable times, for You have given me understanding of the mysteries of [29] Your wonder. In Your wondrous council You have confirmed me, doing wonders before many (or, *the general membership*) for the sake of Your glory and making known [30] Your mighty deeds to all living. What is mortal man in comparison with this? (12:13–15, 28–30) (*The Dead Sea Scrolls: A New Translation*, 184–85)

(b) Noncanonical Psalms

This collection, which is found in four scrolls (4Q380–81), is written in the style of biblical psalms. Some suggest they were composed by David, for example: "A Psalm of the man of God" (4Q381 frg. 24.4). In one scroll (4Q381), the word *selah* appears twice (for example, frg. 31.3). As in the biblical psalms, praise of God is a prominent theme, as well as pleas for God's help and destruction of wicked enemies.

One psalm is identified as "the Prayer of Manasseh, king of Judah, when the king of Assyria imprisoned him" (4Q381 frg. 33.8). Manasseh was an idolatrous king whose wicked acts were sufficient to bring destruction on Judah (2 Kgs 21:1–18). He was then captured and imprisoned by the conquering Assyrians. We are told in 2 Chronicles

33:10–13 that Manasseh prayed to God from his prison and that God accepted his pleas and restored him. Since the words of this prayer are not given in 2 Chronicles, later Jews sought to supply them. One attempt is found in our Noncanonical Psalm; another is the *Prayer of Manasseh* among the *Pseudepigrapha*.

4.2 Calendars (Calendrical Texts)

(a) Exploring Calendars and Festivals

Calendars and the calendrical texts in the sectarian scrolls do not make for easy reading. Here I will identify the Jewish festivals, highlight the two different calendars used by the Essene (*Yahad*) movement and other Jews, and introduce the main calendrical texts.

(b) Jewish Festivals and Calendars

Most readers are familiar with several Jewish holidays observed today. Many are special days and festivals that originate in the Hebrew Bible. The Sabbath is on the seventh day of the week; Leviticus 23 mentions more festivals and (mostly) the days they were to be observed.

The best known festival is Passover, which falls on the fourteenth day of the first month (thus **1/14**). Eight more, as the year progresses, are: Unleavened Bread (**1/15–21**), Firstfruits or Waving of the *Omer* (in the first month), Second Passover (**2/14**, see Num 9:6–13), Weeks (in the third month, 50 days after the waving of the *omer*), the Day of Remembrance, or Trumpets (**7/1**), the Day of Atonement (**7/10**), Booths or Tabernacles (**7/15–21**). Another festival, which is connected with the book of Esther, is Purim (**12/14**).

Like all devout Jews of their day, the *Yahad* Essenes observed the religious festivals, except for Purim from the book of Esther. They did so according to a calendar that differed from the one used by the other main Jewish groups. The Pharisees, Sadducees, and Temple establishment observed festivals according to the moon (a lunar calendar), but the Essenes observed them according to the sun (a solar calendar). This meant that their festivals fell on different days from those of the Pharisees and Sadducees.

Two early books had enormous influence on the Essene movement, not least with respect to calendars. In *1 Enoch*, the Astronomical Book (chs. 72–82) describes a solar calendar of 364 days (and also a lunar one of 354 days). While *1 Enoch* does not connect the solar calendar with the festivals, the book of *Jubilees* does. For its author, the 364-day solar calendar was the true annual calendar, and festival days had been divinely appointed according to it. Moreover, the Pharisees, Sadducees, and Temple establishment, with the 354-day lunar calendar, were observing the wrong festival days and so were out of tandem with God's unchanging order for the luminaries in the heavens and humans on earth.

(c) Calendrical Texts

More than 20 calendrical texts were found at Qumran, which regulate or synchronize festivals, schedules, and liturgies. Most take into account solar calendars (364 days) and lunar ones (354 days); several do not advocate for one calendar over the other, but concentrate on the days and numbers.

Schedules for Festivals. Because it was so important to observe festivals on the correct days, some texts specify days, weeks, months, seasons, festivals, or Sabbaths in the 364-day system. One is the *Calendrical Document* (4Q327), which gives the dates of Sabbaths and festivals, most likely for a whole year.

Other texts provide schedules for a lunar month. *Phases of the Moon* (4Q317) specifies the amount of the moon's surface that is illuminated on successive nights. While the moon is waxing (rising), every night another one-fourteenth of its surface is lit; then when the moon is waning (going down), every night another one-fourteenth is darkened.

Priestly Courses (or Shifts). In 1 Chronicles 24:7–18, King David divided the priestly families into 24 courses or shifts. As the practice developed, these groups rotated in their Temple duties, one serving for a week (from Sabbath to Sabbath) and being relieved by the next in the list. Knowing the names of which groups were on duty, and when, became a method for naming weeks—and so in some Qumran calendars the 24 names are used to denote weeks. With 52 weeks in a year, each shift would serve for two weeks (and provide the name for them), but four shifts would serve for three weeks (providing the name for them); thus 48 shifts (24 x 2) + 4 shifts (4 x 1) = 52. Over six years, each of the 24 groups would get its turn to serve for three weeks in one year.

A series of texts arose, known loosely as the *Mishmarot* (4Q320–29), which means "Watches" or "Priestly Courses." *Calendrical Document A* (4Q320) gives a sequence of festivals and the priestly group in whose course each fell. *Mishmarot A–C* (4Q322–24) list the dates when the courses would begin their week of duty. *Calendrical Document D* (4Q325) correlates priestly shifts with events such as Sabbaths and festivals. Finally, *Mishmarot F and G* (4Q328–29) list the priestly courses and when they served over a six-year rotation. The last two texts depict the hierarchy of time, and may belong to a later stage in the development of the 364-day calendar (see J. Ben-Dov, *Head of All Years* [2008], 28).

Synchronizing Texts. Some texts even synchronize dates in the solar and lunar calendars. These equivalences are at times also supplemented with the names of the priestly course on duty at the time. In *Calendrical Document A* (4Q320), the final two days of the first year and the first two of the second year are given below (frg. 1 i, lines 6–9). *Note:* Jedaiah, etc., are the names of the priests and thus their courses. Also, "of the lunar month" and "solar month" are not in the text, but are clearly implied.

[6] [On the 5th day of Jeda]iah is the 29th day (of the lunar month), on the 13th day of the (1st solar) month.

[7] [On the Sabbath of Ha]kkoz is the 30th day (of the lunar month), on the 30th day of the 2nd (solar month).

[8] [On the 1st day of Elia]shib is the 29th day (of the lunar month), on the 29th day of the 3rd (solar month).

[9] [On the 3rd day of Bilga]h is the 30th day (of the lunar month), on the 28th day of the 4th (solar month). (4Q320 frg. 1 col. i, lines 6–9) (*The Dead Sea Scrolls: A New Translation*, 394).

Otot (4Q319) is even more complicated. It synchronizes four dates: jubilees (49-year units); days both the lunar month and the solar year began together (once every 23 years); the priestly course on duty on that date (only *Gamul* and *Shecaniah* are possible); and sabbatical years. *Otot* presents the datings for periods of six jubilee years, which is (6 x 49 =) 294 years.

Other Texts Related to the Calendar. Some texts contain divinatory, astronomical, or astrological information. The quasi-scientific *Zodiacal Physiognomy* (4Q186) tries to correlate a person's physical characteristics with the parts of his spirit that are in light or in darkness. (See also *Physiognomy*, 4Q561.) *Zodiology and Brontology* (4Q318) is an astrological work that gives the dates of the month and the zodiacal sign in which the moon has appeared and predicts events that will take place if thunder occurs in a particular sign of the zodiac.

4.3 Prayers and Liturgies

Part of the *Yahad*'s resistance to the lunar calendar was their reliance upon prayers and liturgy instead of Temple worship. The movement's own prayers and actions compensated for the liturgical vacuum created by lack of access to the Jerusalem Temple. Several texts present the words or acts of worship for days, Sabbaths, and festivals.

(a) Daily Prayers

Daily Prayers (4Q503) contains distinct blessings of God, which are to be recited each day of the month, evening and morning. There is an astronomical aspect: the time of each blessing is based on the proportions of daylight and darkness according to laws governing the motion of the luminaries (*1 Enoch* 73–75, 77–79). There is also a historical aspect: These blessings are to be recited only during Nisan, the month in which the Passover took place. The preserved part of the scroll seems to be from the first month.

Words of the Luminaries (4Q504–6) presents communal blessings to be recited each day of the week. In these prayers, a theme that clearly stands out is God's covenant with Israel. One prayer asks for forgiveness and recalls God's past faithfulness: "May your anger and fury at all [their] sin[s] turn back from your people Israel. Remember [12] the wonders that you performed while the nations looked on—surely we have been called by your name" (504 frgs. 1–2 ii.11–12). Another prayer celebrates God's choice of Israel (frgs. 1–2 iii.2–14), while the Sabbath Prayer offers praise and reaches its crescendo with the double Amen!

> [4] *Praises for the Sabbath Day.* Give thanks to [the Lord, bless] [5] His holy name forever with a [holy] so[ng. Praise him], [6] all the angels of the holy firmament, and [all the Holy Ones above] [7] the heavens, the earth and all its handiwork; [. . . the great] [8] Abyss, Abaddon, the waters and all that is in [them. [9] Let] all his creatures [bless him] continuously, forever and [ever. Amen! Amen]! (504 frgs. 1–2 frg. vii.4–9). (*The Dead Sea Scrolls: A New Translation*, 525)

(b) Sabbath Prayers

The *Songs of the Sabbath Sacrifice* are for worship in the "celestial temple" of heaven, not the Jerusalem Temple. These rituals were for Sabbath days when—through participation in the angelic liturgy—the earthly and heavenly communities joined in worship. The angels' praises took place according to the 364-day calendar followed by the *Yahad,* and so on earth they, too, were worshiping God on the appointed days.

Nine fragmentary copies were found in the Qumran caves (4Q400–407, 11Q17), and one more at Masada (Mas1k). The collection was probably written in the early first century B.C.E. Although some scholars believe the *Songs of the Sabbath Sacrifice* was not a sectarian text (one composed by the Essene movement), most believe it was, but also that it had broader appeal and was quite widely circulated (hence the copy found at Masada).

Imagery from Ezekiel 40–48 is used in particular, but also from Isaiah, Exodus, and *1 Enoch.* The 13 Songs describe worship around God's throne in the heavenly realms, the angels' prayer service in the temple on high, and the inner throne room where God's presence and the other godlike beings reside. Like most of the Rules, these Songs are for the Instructor. The seventh (and central) Sabbath Song opens:

> [30] *A Text belonging to the Instructor. The Song accompanying the sacrifice on the seventh Sabbath, sung on the sixteenth of the (second) month.*
>
> Praise the most high God, you who are exalted among all [31] the wise divine beings. Let those who are holy among the godlike sanctify the glorious King, he who sanctifies by his holiness each of his holy ones.
>
> You princes of praise [32] among all the godlike, praise the God of majestic [pr]aise. Surely the glory of his kingdom resides in praiseworthy splendor; therein are held the praises of all [33] the godlike, together with the splendor of [his] entire rea[lm]. (4Q403 frg. 1i.20–33) (*The Dead Sea Scrolls: A New Translation,* 469)

The Sabbaths mentioned are the first 13 of a year, making 91 days—exactly one-quarter of the year in the 364-day calendar that underlies the text.

(c) Other Prayers and Liturgies

Berakhot or Blessings (4Q286–90) apparently contains the liturgy for the annual "Covenant Renewal Ceremony" that is mentioned in the *Rule of the Community.* There are blessings for God, and curses for Belial, his lot, and Malki-resha. The term *yahad* is preserved (for example, 4286 frg. 7ii:1, 4Q288 frg. 1.1). Some prayers and liturgies are for festivals. *Festival Prayers* (1Q34 [both versions] and 4Q507–509) emphasizes the Day of Atonement and the Festivals of Wine and Oil, which feature in the sectarian calendar. *Times for Praising God* (4Q409) mentions the Festivals of Wood and the Firstfruits and the Day of Remembrance, which are also in this calendar. The mention of "tree branches" (frg. 1.11) may refer to the Feast of Booths (Tabernacles).

Several more scrolls, all of them fragmentary, preserve prayers for various occasions. Two examples are *Grace After Meals* (4Q434a) and *Purification Liturgies* (4Q414; 4Q512).

5. Wisdom (Sapiential) Texts

Few Wisdom texts were found near Qumran: two each of Proverbs and Ecclesiastes, and six of Job (which fares better). Among the Apocrypha, two copies containing text from Ben Sira were found at Qumran and one at Masada. The Nonbiblical Scrolls include several other Sapiential texts.

Wiles of the Wicked Woman

The *Wiles of the Wicked Woman* (4Q184) presents a vivid picture of Lady Folly. In the book of Proverbs, wisdom is personified as a wise woman, Lady Wisdom, who invites all to come to her house and learn from her (Prov 8:1–9:6). She is contrasted with the seductress who allures simple (naïve) men with the prostitute's charms (Prov 7:1–27). In *Wiles of the Wicked Woman*, this loose woman is more dramatically portrayed as Lady Folly:

> [11] She lies secretly in wait [12] . . . She hides in the city streets, she plants herself in the city gates, [13] . . . Her eyes dart to and fro, she flutters her eyelids seductively, looking for a [14] righteous man to catch, for a strong man to trip up, for someone honest to lead astray, for innocent youths, [15] to keep them from keeping the commandments, . . . [17] She seeks to make people go wrong in the ways of Hell, seducing the human race by flattery. (4Q184 frg. 1.11–13, 17) (*The Dead Sea Scrolls: A New Translation*, 273)

Instruction

The largest text is *Instruction*, which survives in seven scrolls (1Q26; 4Q415–18a, 423), perhaps eight (4Q418c). It is laid out in traditional wisdom fashion (a sage instructing a younger person called "one who understands"). The sage gives advice on expected topics, such as finances, relations in society, and family issues. For example: "Do not pride yourself on your need when you are poor, lest [21] you despise your life, and moreover, do not disdain your wife, your closest companion" (4Q416 frg. 2ii:17–21). Here the mention of *your wife* means that if this is a sectarian scroll, its instructions are directed to Essenes who were allowed to marry (as in the *Damascus Document*). Another section reads:

> [8] Yes, you are needy. Do not crave anything except your inheritance, and do not be consumed by it, lest you cross [9] the boundaries of the Law. If (God) should return you to an honorable position, conduct yourself accordingly, and, knowing **the secret of the way things are**, seek its causes; then you will know [10] his true inheritance, and you will live righteously, for God will make his face shine in all your ways. (4Q416 frg.2iii, lines 8–10) (*The Dead Sea Scrolls: A New Translation*, 488)

Some ideas in *Instruction* are not found in the biblical Wisdom books. The above quotation includes a phrase used many times (and only) in this work: "*the secret of the way things are*" or "*the/mystery that is/will be.*" This knowledge comes only through special insight:

> [8] and then you will know the difference between [goo]d [and [evil according to their] deeds. For the God of knowledge is the counsel of Truth, and in ***the secret of the way things*** are [9] he has made plain its basis [and its actions [11] . . . and with the faculty of understanding [the sec]rets of his purpose [are made known], [12] with blameless conduct [in all] his deeds. (4Q417 frg. 2 i.8–9, 1–12) (*The Dead Sea Scrolls: A New Translation*, 483)

So there is an eschatological dimension, with special knowledge revealed only by God (4Q416 frg.2 iii.17–18; 4Q418 frg. 123 ii.2–4; 1Q26 frg. 1.4). The *one who understands* knows God's times and where history is moving. By living accordingly, he will find purpose and contentment—but God will judge the wicked (416 frg. 1.10–16). Since it contains eschatological motifs alongside sapiential ones, *Instruction* raises important questions about the relationship between wisdom and end-times writings in Judaism during the late Second Temple period.

Other Texts

There are a few more Wisdom texts, all of them fragmentary. One, 4Q185 (*Sapiential Work*), calls on people to seek Wisdom, remember God's deeds in the past, and know more about his ways. Here Wisdom (possibly the Torah) does not seek out human beings, but is given to them by God as a possession. Some scholars feel 4Q185 may not be a sectarian text, but aspects such as the role of angels in the judgment of human beings suggest that it is. An excerpt:

> [13] Happy is the man who puts (Wisdom) into practice [. . . by means of] [14] cunning one cannot find her, nor can one hold on to her by flattery. As she is given to his ancestors, so he will obtain her [and hold on to her] [15] with all his might and with all his [. . .] without limit. Then he can bestow her on his offspring, and true knowledge to [his] people. (4Q185 frg. 1–2ii.13–15) (*The Dead Sea Scrolls: A New Translation*, 275)

Mysteries (1Q27; 4Q299–301) speaks of the reward of the good and punishment of the wicked who did not live in accord with "*the secret of the way things are*" or "*the/mystery that is/will be*" (a term found in the text called *Instruction* above). *Ways of Righteousness* (4Q420–21) was originally a Wisdom text, then expanded with material as found in the Rules. It offers instructions about prudent, humble, faithful, and righteous living, and mentions the Instructor. *Instruction-like Work* (4Q424) gives the types of people to be sought out, and warns against associating with others (such as cheats, complainers, and stingy people). The *Sage to the Children of Dawn* (4Q298) involves the acquisition of wisdom, but also with an eschatological perspective. Here the Instructor, who speaks in the first person, enjoins initiates or the Sons of Light—here called the *Children of Dawn* or *men of understanding*—to increase learning, do justice, and walk humbly.

The *Songs of the Sage* (4Q510–11) and *Apocryphal Psalms* (11QapocPs or 11Q11) contain incantations for driving away evil spirits, with the biblical Psalm 91 included in the latter. The *Songs of the Sage* contains incantations for the Instructor, and in other sections he thanks God and proclaims his power and wonders. Here is a sample:

> [4]And I, the Instructor, proclaim [God's] glorious splendor so as to frighten and to te[rrify] [5] all the spirits of the destroying angels, spirits of the bastards, demons, Lilith, howlers, and [desert dwellers . . .] [6] and those which fall upon men without warning to lead them astray from a spirit of understanding and to make their heart and their [. . .] desolate during the present dominion of [7] wickedness and predetermined time of humiliations for the Sons of Lig[ht], . . . [8] [bu]t for an era of humiliation for transgression. (5Q510 frg. 1.4–8) (*The Dead Sea Scrolls: A New Translation*, 527)

6. Eschatological Texts

The term *eschatology* means the "study of the last things or end times." The Essenes, especially those who lived or met at Qumran, believed they were living at the end of days, in the final age of world history. So it is no surprise that eschatology features in many of the nonbiblical texts at Qumran, both sectarian and nonsectarian. Several have been discussed in other sections (such as the *Temple Scroll* and the *Pesharim*). Some texts, however, are characterized by a strong eschatological perspective and fit best in their own category. Two are discussed here in detail.

6.1 The War Rule (or War Scroll)

This work is a Rule since it provides instructions on how the community is to array itself during an eschatological war. Yet because of its subject matter, the *War Rule* is markedly more eschatological than the other Rules and so is covered in this section.

The best-preserved copy is from Cave 1, with 19 columns, and abbreviated 1QM (from *Milhamah*, Hebrew for "War"). Fragments from eight related scrolls were found in Cave 4. Six (4Q491–96) may be copies of, or sources for, the *War Rule*, while the others are now called *War Scroll-like Text A* (4Q497) and *War Scroll-like Text B* (4Q471).

The *War Rule* lays out the eschatological war in which the attackers are the Sons of Light, the "sons of Levi, the sons of Judah, and the sons of Benjamin, those exiled to the wilderness" (1:2), who belong on the side of God. They are opposed by the Sons of Darkness, whose leader is Belial (Satan), and who at first are Israel's neighbors (Edom, Moab, Ammon, possibly Amalek, and Philistia) together with the Kittim of Assyria (1:1–2). The war then spreads to include the Kittim of Egypt and the kings of the north (1:1–4).

The focus is on the final war (seven battles lasting 40 years) between the forces of God and Belial, in which God and his angels fight on the side of the Sons of Light, and Belial and his spirits fight on the side of the Sons of Darkness. After six battles, the two armies are tied, the Sons of Light having won the first three and the Sons of Darkness the next three. In the seventh and final battle, the hand of God prevails and the Sons of Darkness are destroyed (1:13–16).

Table 3. Outline of the *War Rule* (1QM, 4Q491–96)
1. Description of the Eschatological War (col. 1:1–15)
2. Annihilation of Sons of Darkness and Service to God During the 40 War Years (1:16–2:15)
3. The Trumpets, Banners, and Shields (2:16–5:2)
4. Arming and Deployment of Divisions and Deployment of the Cavalry (5:3–6:17)
5. Recruitment and Age of the Soldiers (7:1–7)
6. Ministry of the Priests and Levites (7:9–9:8)
7. Maneuvers of the Battle Divisions (9:10–18)
8. Addresses, Prayers, and Blessings by the Chief Priest and the Leaders (10:1–15:3)
9. The Final Battle in Seven Engagements (15:4–18:9)
10. Thanksgiving for Final Victory (18:10–19:8)
11. Ceremony After the Final Battle (19:9–14)

Several interesting features emerge. First, service of the Temple was expected to continue during the war (2:1–6). Second, the war would last 40 years, including five sabbatical years in which no fighting would take place, six in which the entire congregation would do battle, and 29 during which a "war of divisions" would be fought against specific enemies who are named (2:6–10).

Finally, this is a holy war, and so the priests and Levites are prominent, as in Joshua's conquest of Jericho. The chief priest and other priests offer prayers reciting God's victories for Israel in the past, and the leaders of the battle pronounce blessings (7:9–15:3). No blemished or ritually unclean man is permitted to fight, "for holy angels are present with their army" (7:6). Prayers of thanksgiving are offered for the final victory (18:10–19:8), and the chief priest, other priests, and Levites are prominent in the ceremony after the final battle (19:9–14).

6.2 The New Jerusalem Text

Written in Aramaic, the *New Jerusalem Text* was extensively used at Qumran (seven fragmentary copies survive: 1Q32; 2Q24; 4Q554; 4Q554a; 4Q55; 5Q15; and 11Q18). It was likely not composed by the *Yahad*, but by Jews opposed to the desecration of the Temple by the Syrian king Antiochus Epiphanes in 167/66 B.C.E., or to Judean kings in the Hasmonean period (about 150 to 63 B.C.E.), who also took the role of high priest.

Although the words *New Jerusalem* (and *Temple*) are not found, this text clearly deals with the eschatological Jerusalem and its Temple. The document takes the form of a guided tour of heaven and ends in a final battle with the nations. It is said to originate with a book or writing, which is shown to the visionary and read by his guide, most likely an angel (11Q18 frg. 19.5).

The author is shown features of the future city and Temple, together with several details and measurements. The most striking aspect of these architectural features is their huge proportions.

The tour begins outside the New Jerusalem. The visionary sees the measurements of the wall enclosing the city, which has 12 gates (see the *Temple Scroll* 39:12–13). Each gate is named for one of Jacob's 12 sons—and so the New Jerusalem's gates signify the reunification of the 12 tribes of Israel (cf. Ezek 48:30–35 and Rev 21:12–13).

The author is also shown the city blocks, houses, avenues, streets, dining halls, stairs, and towers of the New Jerusalem. The sizes of these structures suggest that the city is organized to house large groups of pilgrims. Thus this heavenly model serves to fulfill the prophets' visions of the eschatological Jerusalem to which all nations will come in the last days.

A similar pattern most likely followed in the description of the eschatological Temple. Unfortunately, hardly anything survives of the passages depicting its architecture, measurements, the precious metals used for its construction, or utensils, or furniture. Better preserved are details of the priests' rotating courses, the high priest's vestments, the priestly activities, and rituals practiced in the Temple, including the slaughtering of animals used for sacrifices and the celebration of Passover and other festivals. Such passages remind us that the Yahad Essenes were not opposed to the Temple or the priesthood—only to the Jerusalem Temple and its leadership in their day.

While the *New Jerusalem Text* has affinities with Ezekiel's description (48:15–35) of the future Jerusalem and the heavenly Jerusalem in Revelation, there is one important difference. The damaged final column (in 4Q554) contains a prophecy of the kingdoms to come, leading up to the final battle between the Gentile nations and Israel, with Israel at last being triumphant. (Together with the *Temple Scroll*, this text is part of a tradition linking the description of the eschatological Temple and city in Ezekiel 40–48 [on which it is partly modeled] with that of the New Jerusalem in the book of Revelation 21:9–22:7):

> [14][. . . will rise up] [15]in place of it, and the kingdom of P[ersia . . . and then will rise up] [16]the Kittim in place of it. All these kingdoms will appear one after another [. . .] [17]others numerous and lordly with them [. . .] [18]with them Edom and Moab and the Ammonites [. . .] [19]of the whole land of Babylon, not [. . .] [20]and they will do evil to your descendants until the time of [. . .] [21]in all the peoples the kingdom of (4Q554 frg. 2 iii.14-21) (*The Dead Sea Scrolls: A New Translation*, 562–63)

Thus the New Jerusalem comes in the context of the final battle with the nations, which emphasizes the eschatological character of the entire composition. But if this section is correctly placed, the *New Jerusalem Text* differs from both the *Temple Scroll's* future Jerusalem and Revelation's heavenly Jerusalem: while they describe an ideal future city, this text places the New Jerusalem and its Temple before the final battle (and so, in the last days).

6.3 The Messianic Apocalypse

The *Messianic Apocalypse* (4Q521), which was written or copied in the first century B.C.E., is a small but significant scroll. This fragmentary text uses *Lord* (*Adonay*) for God, and features: reproof (frg. 1); an extensive section on a messianic figure (frgs. 2+4ii); a final judgment (7+5ii); Adam (frg. 8.6); "the bl]essings of Jacob" (8:7); the Temple vessels (8.8); "the priestho]od and all its anointed ones" (8.9); something "left in the hand of the Me[ssiah" (9.3); again the priesthood (11.5); and "the ki]ngdom" (12.1). The excerpt below is on final judgment, and mentions God's creative power, blessings and curse, and the Reviver raising the dead:

> [1] [. . .] see all t[hat the Lord has made, [2] the eart]h and all that is on it, the seas [and all [3] that is in them], and every lake and stream. [4] [. . . al]l [of you] who have done good before the Lor[d] [5] [bless and no]t as those who curse. They shall b[e] destined to die, [when] [6] the Reviver [rai]ses the dead of his people. (frgs. 7+5ii.1–6) (*The Dead Sea Scrolls: A New Translation*, 531–32)

7. The *Copper Scroll*, Other Documentary Texts, and Nonsectarian Texts

For ease of use, the remaining texts among the nonbiblical scrolls are grouped together.

7.1 The Copper Scroll

Several Qumran texts are documentary in character, such as contracts, receipts, and records. The *Copper Scroll* (3Q15), found in two rolled sheets, is now housed at the Jordan Archaeological Museum in Amman. It is the only text from the Qumran caves not written on leather parchment or papyrus, but on metal: copper mixed with about 1 percent tin. The metal was so oxidized that it proved impossible to unroll and so had to be cut into vertical strips.

The scroll presents a list of 65 locations at which various gold and silver treasures are hidden; scholars disagree as to whether these are real or not. The list is similar to Greek temple inventories from Delos (190–180 B.C.E.); moreover, archival public records and Temple archives were written on copper and bronze in the Roman period. Some scholars view the *Copper Scroll* as an inventory from Herod's Temple in Jerusalem, listing treasures hidden during the war against Rome in 66–70 C.E. (It was inscribed somewhere between 50 and 100.) The amount and value of all these treasures, which include tons of precious metals, are amazing. Not surprisingly, more than one explorer (such as John Allegro in 1962) has tried to locate them, but without success.

The twenty-third and twenty-fourth treasure troves are located in the Secacah Valley. Some scholars believe that *Secacah* (Josh 15:16) is an ancient name for the Qumran site:

[13] In the dam of the Secacah Valley, dig down [14] three (?) cubits: twelve talents of silver coins.

[5:1] At the head of the aqueduct [of the] [2] Secacah [Valley], on the north, under the[3] big [stone], dig down [4] [thr]ee cub[its]: seven talents of silver coins. (3Q15 4:13–5:4) (*The Dead Sea Scrolls: A New Translation,* 215)

7.2 Other Documentary Texts

Several more documentary texts, most in Aramaic, were found in Cave 4 at Qumran. They are most likely sectarian documents, although a few may not be. These scrolls shed light on daily life among the Yahad Essenes, as well as the community's economic practices and organization.

They include *Letters* (4Q242–43), *Deeds* (345–47, 348, 359), an *Acknowledgement of Debt* (344), *Accounts* (352a, 354–58), *Accounts of Cereals* (351–53), and *A Scribal Exercise* (360). One *Account* is in Greek (350), which underscores the importance of this language for everyday business, and for maintaining economic contact with outside communities.

In 1996, at the edge of the Qumran cemetery, an ostracon was found containing a deed of gift by a man named Honi to Eleazar. Line 8 may contain the word *Yahad,* which also features in the sectarian scrolls, and so would connect them to the Qumran settlement. However, the text is broken at this point, and several scholars read another word instead (such as *ea*[*rth*]).

7.3 Nonsectarian Texts

Among the nonbiblical scrolls, it is not always easy to identify nonsectarian writings. Nonsectarian writings include approximately 150 scrolls in Aramaic, which were composed in the third to second centuries B.C.E., before the Essene movement and its earliest texts came into being. These include most of the New *Pseudepigrapha.*

One such text is *Pseudo-Daniel A* (4Q243–44), in which Daniel presents to King Belshazzar an overview of history, from Noah and the flood to the Hellenistic period (323–31 B.C.E.), after which a holy kingdom will be established. Several names are given, such as *Balakros* (used for several figures in the early Hellenistic period). *Pseudo-Daniel B* (4Q245) focuses on Israel's internal history, but could be the ending of *Pseudo-Daniel A.* It gives list of high priests from the patriarchal period (Qahath) to the Hellenistic age (Onias, Simon), and continues with a list of kings (including David, Solomon, and Ahaziah). Finally, the extermination of wickedness and a return will take place:

Col. i [1] [ ]*iah* [2]] and what [3] [. . .] Daniel [4] [. . .] a book that was given [5] [. . . Lev]i, Qahat [6] [. . .] Bukki, Uzzi, [7] [. . . Zado]k, Abiathar [8] Hi[l]kiah, [9] [. . .] and Onias [10] [. . . Jona]than, Simon, [11] [. . .] and David, Solomon, [12] [. . .] Ahazi[ah, Joa]sh, [13]]. (Author Translation)

10

The Movement Associated with Qumran: Not Pharisees or Sadducees, but Essenes

Introduction

This chapter deals with an important question: Who wrote many of the sectarian scrolls found at Qumran, and placed these and the others in the nearby caves? At least half of the 600 or so nonbiblical scrolls, probably more, represent texts containing distinctive ideology or language and are thus called the *sectarian scrolls*.

Throughout this book, I identify the group or movement associated with the sectarian scrolls as the Essene (*Yahad*) movement. But is this identification secure or could another early Jewish group have written the sectarian scrolls and collected the others? One approach to this complex issue is to begin with early Jewish groups with which scholars and readers are most familiar. Several possibilities may be considered, most notably:

- The scrolls found at Qumran were associated with the Pharisees.

- They were associated with the Sadducees.

- They were associated with the Essenes.

Almost from the time of their discovery, most scholars have agreed that the sectarian scrolls contain the views and outlook of a group of Jews otherwise referred to as *Essenes*, who deposited them and the other scrolls in the caves. However, the boundaries between early Jewish groups are often blurred (see John Collins, *Beyond the Qumran Community*,

124–25). There is considerable flexibility between the labels Pharisee, Sadducee, Essene, and even Christian, so on several points the sectarian scrolls represent beliefs from each. Thus it is only fair that groups other than the Essees be considered, which may also throw welcome light on the sometimes artificial distinctions that many modern scholars have imposed between them (cf. Steve Mason, "Essenes and Lurking Spartans" [2007], 219–61).

Two important questions are: Were the scrolls found at Qumran associated with the Pharisees? and Were the Scrolls found at Qumran associated with the Sadducees?

1. Were the Scrolls Found at Qumran Associated with the Pharisees?

1.1 Who Were the Pharisees?

The Pharisees (meaning "separatists" or "the separated ones") were a Jewish religious and sometimes political movement. They were originally also known as *Hasidim* (the "Pious" or "Loyal to God"), a movement formed during the Maccabean Revolt against the Syrian ruler Antiochus Epiphanes (Antiochus IV) around 165 B.C.E.

Apart from the Qumran scrolls, the writings of Josephus and the New Testament are our two major ancient sources on the Pharisees. These do not provide a complete or always reliable description since the New Testament paints a negative picture of the Pharisees (who were opposed to Jesus), and Josephus is writing for Roman readers. Nevertheless, they provide important historical references and details of the group's ideology and social structure. These sources also help identify some characteristics of a Jewish group that plays a significant role in the Essene movement's history in the sectarian scrolls. Many of the Pharisees' ideas and traditions also survive in later compilations of Jewish law, most notably the Mishna and the Talmuds.

One clear point is that the Pharisees realized there were gaps and ambiguities in the written text and so taught that it was not always to be taken literally. The written law had to be supplemented by the oral law, a set of unwritten traditions, which (they believed) had been passed down since the days of Moses.

1.2 Pharisees in Josephus' Writings

The first direct mention of the Pharisees was by the Jewish historian Flavius Josephus (37–c. 100) in describing Judea's three established sects or "philosophical schools": Pharisees, Sadducees, and Essenes (*Jewish War* 2.119–66; *Antiquities* 18.18–22).

Mentions of the Pharisees are unevenly distributed in Josephus' writings. The *Jewish War*, written around 75 C.E., contains limited references to the Pharisees, who are contrasted against the Essenes and Sadducees. They are one of the "three forms of philosophy among Jews" (2.119), they had "the most reverential discipline" (2.119), were very careful interpreters of Jewish laws (2.162), and (in contrast to the Sadducees) "are friendly to one another, and are for the exercise of concord" (2.166).

The Pharisees play a more significant role in the *Jewish Antiquities* (completed in 93/94 C.E.). Josephus identifies points of tension with the Sadducees. Whereas the

Pharisees taught "many observances . . . from their fathers, which are not written in the law of Moses," the Sadducees recognized only "those observances . . . which are in the written word," not those "from the tradition of our forefathers" (*Antiquities* 13.297–98). In addition to this oral law, Josephus states that the Pharisees were more popular among "the masses as allies," whereas the Sadducees could persuade only the rich, so did not enjoy popular support (*Antiquities* 13.297–98).

On human will and divine sovereignty, the Pharisees held that "everything is affected by destiny," while not denying the "human will of power in these things" (*Antiquities* 18.13–14), which is the reason for their popularity (*Antiquities* 18:14). The Pharisees believed "there is an undying power in souls" and "[e]ternal punishment" for those who were unrighteous in life, but "re-creation in a new life" for those who were righteous (*Antiquities* 18.14). They also awaited a future resurrection of the righteous: "All souls are incorruptible," but "only the souls of good men are removed into other bodies, and the souls of bad men are subject to eternal punishment" (*Jewish War* 2.162). This portrait of the Pharisees' views on divine sovereignty and human fate may be only partly accurate, but seems to differentiate them from the Sadducees.

With respect to political life, the Pharisees played an active role in the Hasmonean and Herodian periods. Josephus describes the Hasmonean ruler John Hyrcanus (reigned 134–104 B.C.E.) as a disciple of the Pharisees, until a certain Eleazar made an allegation about Hyrcanus' eligibility to hold the office of high priest (*Antiquities* 13.291–92). While the Pharisees denounced Eleazar for slander, they did not advocate a punishment as severe as Hyrcanus expected. Believing that they were not very supportive, he began to support the Sadducees instead.

Another incident involves the ascent of Salome Alexandra to the Hasmonean throne after the death of her husband, Alexander Jannaeus (ruled 103–76 B.C.E.). Salome shifted her support from the Sadducees to align with the Pharisees in order to secure her reign (*Antiquities* 13.401) and consolidate her political base among a group with popular appeal.

The Herodian period did not end well for the Pharisees. At first, Herod (king 40/39–4 B.C.E.) treated them favorably (*Antiquities* 14.172–76; 15.1–4, 370), but they later opposed him and fell victim in 4 B.C.E. (*Antiquities* 17.41–45, 149–67). Some Pharisees predicted an end to Herod's rule, which was a very provocative political statement. When word reached him, Herod killed all the Pharisees accused of plotting against him, including members of his own family (*Antiquities* 17.44). References to Pharisees in Judean politics dwindle after this point, so it seems they opted for a lower political profile following the Herodian reprisals.

According to Josephus, then, the Pharisees were characterized by the transmission of the oral law alongside the written law, and their belief in divine sovereignty, destiny, human will, the immortality of the soul, an afterlife with rewards and punishments, and the resurrection of the righteous. They were more favored by the people, had tensions with the Sadducees, and played an active political role until many were killed by Herod in 4 B.C.E.

1.3 Pharisees in the New Testament

In the New Testament, the Pharisees are the foremost Jewish group, often appearing as the opponents of Jesus and his disciples and so not favorably portrayed. Accounts of the Pharisees confirm and further detail the picture of Pharisaic Judaism offered by Josephus.

New Testament authors support the view that the Pharisees preserved oral traditions for the observance of the Mosaic law. The Gospels group the Pharisees with "teachers of the law" (Matt 5:20; 12:38; 15:1; 23:2–29; Mark 2:16; 7:1, 5; Luke 5:17, 21, 30; 6:7; 11:53; 15:2; John 8:3; cf. Acts 23:9) and describe them as those who sit in the seat of Moses (Matt 23:2). According to Matthew, many Pharisees prefer to be addressed as Rabbi in public (23:7). For the New Testament authors, the identity of the Pharisees as a group is securely moored to their role as teachers of the Mosaic law.

There are also references to disputes on observing the Mosaic law. For example, the Pharisees disapproved of Jesus and his disciples' views on observing the Sabbath (Matt 12:1–8; Mark 2:23–28; Luke 6:1–5), washing before meals (Matt 15:1–9; Mark 7:1–3; Luke 11:38), and divorce (Matt 19:1–12; Mark 10:10–12; Luke 12:18).

Another theme is the Pharisees' stance on the washing of vessels. A major issue for most Jewish groups of the late Second Temple period was ritual purity. In the Synoptic Gospels, Jesus criticizes the Pharisees for ritually washing dishes as an illustration of their hypocrisy (Matt 23:26; Mark 7:4; Luke 11:39). Such passages do not offer insight into differences between the Pharisees and the Sadducees (on how Mosaic law was being observed), but affirm that one of the Pharisees' defining characteristics was their observance of Mosaic law. Early Christian communities also constructed their identity in distinction from the Pharisees.

With respect to an afterlife and the spiritual realm, the book of Acts reports that the Pharisees, in contrast to the Sadducees, believed in resurrection from death, and in angels and spirits:

> [6] When Paul noticed that some were Sadducees and others were Pharisees, he called out in the council, "Brothers, I am a Pharisee, a son of Pharisees. I am on trial concerning the hope of the resurrection of the dead." [7] When he said this, a dissension began between the Pharisees and the Sadducees, and the assembly was divided. [8] (The Sadducees say that there is no resurrection, or angel, or spirit; but the Pharisees acknowledge all three.) (Acts 23:6–8)

New Testament writers also depict the Pharisees as a socially and politically effective group. The Gospels allude to their wide range of influence, both in Palestine (Luke 5:17) and further afield (Matt 23:15; John 7:35). In their conflict with Jesus, the Gospel of Mark depicts the Pharisees as plotting with the Herodians (3:6; 12:13). This suggests they were able to sway those in power, a perception supported by the presence of the Pharisee Gamaliel as a leading member of the Sanhedrin in Acts 5:34. Gamaliel's recommendation decisively shaped Sanhedrin policy toward the early Christian movement.

Thus Josephus and the New Testament agree that the Pharisees preserved oral traditions for observing Mosaic law, believed in an afterlife and in resurrection, were a popular group, enjoyed social or political influence, and experienced tensions with the Sadducees.

1.4 Pharisees in the Dead Sea Scrolls

(a) Can the Essenes (*Yahad*) Be Identified as Pharisees?

Very few scholars identify the Essenes (*Yahad*) as Pharisees. Although the two movements shared some beliefs, they disagreed on many others. It is clear that the Pharisees were important Jewish opponents of the movement.

Similarities between the Yahad and the Pharisees include belief in resurrection and an afterlife with rewards and punishments and long sections of laws for the Sabbath and other occasions (as in the *Damascus Document*, the Mishna, and the Talmud).

Almost a century ago, rabbinics scholar Louis Ginzberg suggested (1922) that Pharisees wrote the *Damascus Document*, of which two very extensive copies had been found (1896) in the Cairo Genizah. After studying the legal section (cols. 15–16 and 9–14), he concluded that "with the exception of a single passage, . . . in our document we have a Pharisaic book of law." The fact that one ruling (on marrying one's niece) did not support Ginzberg's theory is significant. Following the finds at Qumran, a few scholars such as Saul Lieberman and Chaim Rabin suggested that the identification between the Pharisees and the *Yahad* remained possible, but this Pharisee hypothesis has few followers today.

Just too many differences exist to allow closer identification. Several of the *Yahad*'s laws did not agree with positions adopted by the Pharisees, such as on streams of liquid and on marrying one's niece. There is no evidence that the Pharisees believed in predestination, observed holidays according to a solar calendar, owed their existence to a Teacher of Righteousness, had a group of overseers, or held goods in common.

Perhaps the strongest evidence against identifying the Pharisees with the Yahad is that several key sectarian scrolls treat the Pharisees as strong opponents of the movement.

(b) Names for the Pharisees in Several Sectarian Scrolls

Numerous scrolls refer to the Pharisees by insulting names that focus on their central activity, interpreting the Law—the *Seekers of Slippery Answers*, *Ephraim*, and the *Wall-Builders*.

The Seekers of Slippery Answers. This name (literally, those who look for smooth things; compare Prov 26:28 and Dan 11:32 and 11:21, 34) appears in several sectarian scrolls. These include the *Damascus Document* (CD) 1:18; the *Thanksgiving Hymns* (1QH[a]) 10:34; 12:8; a *Commentary on Isaiah* (4Q163); the *Commentary on Nahum* (4Q169); and *Catena A* (4Q177).

These writings say that the Seekers of Slippery Answers overstepped the covenant, violated the law, and persecuted the Essene movement and its early leader, the Teacher of Righteousness. One key passage in the *Damascus Document* connects them with the New Covenanters' early history. An opponent to the new group and its leader surfaced 390 years after Nebuchadnezzar defeated the nation and 20 more years before the Teacher came on the scene:

> When the **Man of Mockery** appeared, who sprayed on Israel lying waters, he led them to wander in the trackless wasteland. He brought down the lofty heights of old, turned aside from paths of righteousness, and shifted the boundary marks that the forefathers had set up to mark their inheritance so that the curses of the covenant took hold on them. Because of this they were handed over to the sword that avenges the breach of his covenant.

> For they had **looked for slippery answers**, choosing illusions (cf. Isaiah 30:10); they looked for ways to break the law (Isaiah 30:13); they favored the fine neck. They called the guilty innocent, and the innocent guilty. They overstepped covenant, violated law; and they conspired together to kill the innocent (Psalm 94:1), for all those who lived pure lives they loathed from the bottom of their heart. So they persecuted them violently, and were happy to see the people quarrel. Because of all this God became very angry with their company. He annihilated the lot of them because all their deeds were uncleanness to him. (CD 1:14–2:1) (Adapted from *The Dead Sea Scrolls: A New Translation*, 52–53)

This hostile group is also mentioned in the *Thanksgiving Hymns*, in two hymns that many scholars believe were by the Teacher. In the first hymn (10:33–11:5), the psalmist thanks God for rescuing him "from the animosity of the mediators of lies and from the congregation of the Seekers of Slippery Answers" (10:33–34), who have tried to kill him (lines 34–35).

The Seekers of Slippery Answers appear most often in the *Commentary on Nahum* (4Q169), one of the very few scrolls to mention the names of actual people. One key passage quotes and interprets the prophet Nahum:

> **Wherever the old lion goes, there is the lion's cub** [2][***without fear***]. (Nahum 2:12b)

> [The "***old lion***" is Deme]trius, king of Greece, who sought to come to Jerusalem through the counsel of the Seekers of Slippery Answers; [3][but the city never fell into the] power of the kings of Greece from Antiochus until the appearance of the rulers of the Kittim; but afterwards it will be trampled [4][by the Gentiles . . .] (frgs. 3–4 col. i.1–4). (Adapted from *The Dead Sea Scrolls: A New Translation*, 245)

The Old Lion is most likely the Syrian king Demetrius III (ruled 96–88/87 B.C.E.), the Seekers of Slippery Answers are the Pharisees, Antiochus is Antiochus IV Epiphanes (who sacked Jerusalem in 168 B.C.E.), and the Kittim are the Romans. Josephus writes (*Jewish War* 1.92–114 and *Antiquities* 13.376–418) that Demetrius was encouraged to attack Judea by the opponents of the Hasmonean Jannaeus (who must have included Pharisees).

The Commentary then says (lines 6–8) that Nahum 2:12b ("*He has filled] his cave [with prey], his den with torn flesh*") refers to the Lion of Wrath (Jannaeus), who took vengeance against the Seekers of Slippery Answers (Pharisees) "because he used to hang men alive." This confirms Josephus' report that Jannaeus crucified 800 Pharisees, who were forced to watch from their crosses as their wives and children were then slaughtered (*Antiquities* 13.379–80). Just before Jannaeus died (after a violent reign), he advised his wife, Salome Alexandra, to reconcile with the Pharisees in order to ensure her rule (*Antiquities* 13.401).

Ephraim. The *Commentary on Nahum* (4Q169) also makes it clear that Ephraim and the Seekers of Slippery Answers are synonymous. On the prophet's words in 3:1 ("*Ah! City of bloodshed, utterly deceitful, full of booty*," Nahum 3:1), the *pesher* explains that "this is the city of Ephraim, the Seekers of Slippery Answers in the Last Days, who conduct themselves in deceit and lies" (frgs. 3–4 ii line 2).

Ephraim is most likely an allusion to Hosea 5:14, but here interpreted as referring to Alexander Jannaeus' treatment of the Pharisees. While Ephraim and Judah traditionally refer to the division of the northern and southern kingdoms after Solomon's death (Isa 7:17), our author has applied Ephraim to the Pharisees as a group. This approach is also seen in the *Damascus Document* (7:9–15), which takes the division of Ephraim from Judah to mean names of groups: Like the northern kingdom of Israel, Ephraim are those who go astray from the law and will be judged for their wickedness, while Judah are the Essenes themselves.

The Wall-Builders. This name for the Pharisees appears seven times in the *Damascus Document* (CD 4:19 [= 6Q15 frg.1.1]; CD 8:12, 18 [twice]; 19:24, 31) as those who violate the sanctuary and endorse unacceptable marriage practices. These included incorrect purity practices such as "lying with a woman during her menstrual period" (CD 5:6–9) and marriage to a niece (CD 5:9–11). The prohibition of niece marriage is drawn from Leviticus 18:12–14. These purity issues cause the Wall-Builders to be defiled in the eyes of the Yahad. The term *Wall-Builders* may refer to the rabbinic tradition of building a wall or hedge around the written law by the oral law (additional laws designed to ensure its observance; see the Mishnah, see Tractate *'Abot* 1.1). Since the Pharisees were the predecessors of the rabbis, the Wall-Builders in the *Damascus Document* are most likely the Pharisees.

2. Were the Scrolls Found at Qumran Associated with the Sadducees?

2.1 Who Were the Sadducees?

The Sadducees (meaning "upright ones") were another Jewish movement formed in the first half of the second century B.C.E. They were a priestly party that claimed lineage from Zadok, a priest descended from Aaron's son Eleazar (who aided David during Absalom's revolt and helped bring Solomon to the throne), and so were also called Zadokites. Sadducees filled various religious and political roles, above all maintaining the Temple. After its reconstruction in 516 B.C.E., the Temple became the center of worship in Judea and the center of society, which gave the priests an elite standing. This status was reinforced by their priestly duties, since priests performed sacrifices at the Temple, and supervised sacrifices on the three Festivals of Pilgrimage to Jerusalem (Passover, Weeks, and Booths). As descendants of Zadok, the Sadducees sought to preserve the priestly Zadokite line and the Temple's authority. Most priests, high priests, and aristocrats were Sadducees, but some were Pharisees, and others were not members of any group.

At various times, the Sadducees administered the state, collected taxes, resolved domestic disputes, equipped the army, and regulated relations with the Romans. They were quite liberal in their willingness to incorporate Hellenistic customs, which the Pharisees opposed. They also served with the Pharisees in the Sanhedrin, a kind of Supreme Court with the responsibility to interpret civil and religious laws, but the two groups frequently disagreed.

The Sadducees disappeared soon after the destruction of the Second Temple in 70 C.E. None of their writings survived, so the little we know about them comes from early writers such as Josephus, the New Testament, and later compilations of Jewish law (notably the Mishna and the Talmuds), which were the legacy of the Pharisees who opposed them. Some of their ideas may have also have survived among a medieval Jewish sect called the Karaites.

The Pharisees taught that the written law had to be supplemented by the oral law, a set of traditions they believed had been passed down since the days of Moses. However, Sadducees rejected the oral law, and insisted on the written law alone, which sometimes led to hostilities.

Several of the disputes between the Sadducees and the Pharisees are found in the Mishnaic tractate *Yadayim* (Hands). A major issue was ritual purity: What must I do to become clean and remain undefiled? What must I avoid because it will defile me or my community? The Sadducees had a stricter stance on avoiding impurity, and viewed the Pharisees as opponents of traditional Judaism because of their susceptibility to foreign influences. Sadducees believed that only the written law (the Scriptures) was authoritative, while the Pharisees held that other books also had some value and could be consulted:

> The Sadducees say: "We complain against you, Pharisees, for you say that the Holy Scriptures defile the hands (that is, are authoritative), but the writings of Homer (or, secular writings) do not defile the hands." (M. Yadayim 4.6) (Trans. Lawrence Schiffman, *Texts and Traditions*, 270)

Another example: Does impurity pass through a stream of liquid from an impure container to a pure one? The Pharisees taught that impurity does not pass through (the more lenient view), but the Sadducees held that it does (the stricter view); see the Mishnah, *Yadayim* 4.7.

It seems that the Sadducees did not believe in an afterlife, which is hardly mentioned, if at all, in the Torah, nor in resurrection from the dead. Instead, their main focus was on the Temple and its rituals.

2.2 Sadducees in Josephus' Writings

Josephus and the New Testament writers have less to say about the Sadducees than the Pharisees. Josephus' second Jewish philosophical school is the Sadducees (*Jewish War* 2.119), to whom he attributes three defining positions. First, they rejected the oral Torah promoted by the Pharisees (*Antiquities* 13.297–98). Second, the Sadducees did not believe in fate but in free will: "They deny destiny altogether and place God beyond doing or seeing anything bad . . . good and bad are dependent on human choice" (*Jewish War* 13.173). Finally, they did not believe in an afterlife, denying "the immortality of the soul" and "punishments in the underworld" (*Jewish War* 2.165).

Josephus also describes the behavior of the Sadducees toward one another as rather wild, and that they are quick to engage in heated debates with those outside their group. He credits a Sadducee named Jonathan for convincing John Hyrcanus (reigned 134–104 B.C.E.) that the Pharisees had slighted him by not condemning a man harshly enough who insulted him at a banquet (*Antiquities* 13.294–96). Moreover, the Sadducees were backed by the Hasmonean leadership, until Salome Alexandra shifted her support to the Pharisees to ensure her rule following the death of her husband, Alexander Jannaeus, in 76 B.C.E.

2.3 Sadducees in the New Testament

The Sadducees are mentioned only 14 times in the New Testament (nine times in the Gospels, five in Acts), which generally complements Josephus' description. As in Acts 23:6–8, the Synoptic Gospels affirm that the Sadducees denied the resurrection of the dead (Matt 22:23; Mark 12:18; Luke 20:27).

The Gospels are less clear about the relationship between the Pharisees and the Sadducees. Mark and Luke each mention the Sadducees once (with respect to resurrection). In Matthew they act in concert with the Pharisees to oppose Jesus (Matt 3:7; 16:1, 6, 11, 12). However, after Jesus has answered the Sadducees with respect to resurrection, the Pharisees do not try to refute his answer but pose a different question:

> [34] But the Pharisees, when they heard that he had put the Sadducees to silence, gathered themselves together. [35] And one of them, a lawyer, asked him a question, trying him: [34] "Teacher, which is the great commandment in the law?" (Matt 22:34–36)

The author of Acts depicts the Pharisees and the Sadducees as opposing parties in the Sanhedrin (23:6–8). Sadducees are a politically powerful group with influence among the priests and the Temple guard (4:1), and the high priest and his retinue are labeled Sadducees (5:17).

According to Josephus and several New Testament writers, the Sadducees did not believe in an afterlife, nor in resurrection (less clearly so in Josephus). Josephus also states they did not believe in fate but in free will, which is supported by passages from the Gospels and Acts in the sense of political activism. Josephus adds that they rejected the oral

Torah promoted by the Pharisees, although this is not evident in the Gospels (nor neces-sary given the context).

A few passages in the Babylonian Talmud indicate that the Sadducees did not accept the Pharisaic doctrine of the resurrection, although it is difficult to know if these sources are indeed ancient. For example, in Sanhedrin 90b the Sadducees (Hebrew *minim,* or "heretics") ask Rabban Gamaliel, "How do you prove that the Holy One, blessed be he, will resurrect the dead?" He answers, "From the Torah, from the Prophets, and from the Writings," and proceeds to interpret Deuteronomy 31:16, Isaiah 26:19, and the Song of Songs 7:9 as referring to resurrection.

2.4 Sadducees in the Dead Sea Scrolls

Some scholars believe that the Essene (*Yahad*) movement were Sadducees. The two groups shared the same basic approach to Jewish law but differed on other fundamental issues. Some sectarian scrolls (such as *Some of the Works of the Law*) suggest that the Sad-ducees were less of a threat to the movement than the Pharisees. However, the *Yahad* were opposed to the priests (mostly Sadducees) who supervised and officiated at the Temple, and believed they had corrupted true worship.

The scrolls make no mention of the name Sadducees, but this group probably appears a few times as *Manasseh*. In the Bible, Ephraim and Manasseh designate the northern kingdom, which over time departed from following the Lord, whereas Judah (the south-ern kingdom) remained faithful. So for the Essenes, Ephraim and Manasseh served as powerful names for their enemies, who opposed Judah (themselves); compare the *Damas-cus Document* (CD) 7:13.

Ephraim appears in the *Commentary on Nahum* (4Q169) in its interpretation of Nahum 3:8–10. The biblical prophecy opens (v. 3) "***Are you better than Thebes*** (Hebrew, *No-Amon*) ***that lived by the Nile*** (Hebrew, *streams*)." In fragments 3–4, the *Commentary* identifies *No-Amon* with Manasseh and her *streams* as the nobles of Manasseh (iii, line 9). The allies of *No-Amon* (Nah 3:9) are decoded as a "wicked" and "divisive group" who ally themselves to Manasseh (iv, line 1). Finally, in Nahum 3:10, No-Amon is exiled with its full population, including the nobles. The *Commentary* reveals: "This refers to Manasseh in the Last Days, for his kingdom will be brought low in Is[rael . . .] his women, his infants, and his children will go into captivity; his warriors and his nobles [will be killed] with the sword [. . .]" (iv, lines 3–4).

From the *Commentary* we learn that Manasseh was a socially prominent group (and has a "kingdom"). The Sadducees were a prominent group, and the dominant one in the days of Alexander Jannaeus. The *Commentary* also tells us that the group was wicked and divisive. "Divisive" fits with Josephus' description of the Sadducees as unruly and eager to engage in heated debates (*Jewish War* 2.166). In sum, what the *Commentary on Nahum* says about Manasseh fits well the Sadducees. However, the evidence in this text for *Manasseh* meaning "Sadducees" makes it likely, but not assured.

3. The Scrolls Found Near Qumran Were Associated with a Group of Essenes

Soon after the Dead Sea Scrolls were discovered, scholars began to suspect that they had some connection to the Essene movement. The first expert to make this connection was Eleazar Sukenik, followed soon afterward by William Albright. Most scholars agree with this position to the present day, although the "Qumran Essene Hypothesis" has undergone some refinements.

But what led Sukenik and Albright to make this early identification? The answer lies in many descriptions of the Essenes by early Greek and Roman authors, and the comparison of these with the contents of several key scrolls.

By comparing descriptions of the Essenes in the classical sources with key sectarian scrolls found at Qumran, I will deal with the two main components of the Qumran Essene Hypothesis: (a) The scrolls found near Qumran have connections to the Essene movement. (b) The community at Qumran was a branch of this movement, and deposited many or all of the scrolls in the nearby caves.

3.1 Connections to the Essene Movement (Qumran Essene Hypothesis I)

The first reason for identifying the movement as Essene is because key features of the Essenes in ancient accounts agree with ones found in the sectarian scrolls.

We are blessed with rich descriptions of the Essenes in several classical writings, whose authors were fascinated by this early Jewish "sect." The main writers are Philo of Alexandria (about 20 B.C.E.–50 C.E.), Pliny the Elder (23–79), Flavius Josephus (37–about 100), Dio Chrysostom (about 40–120), and Hippolytus of Rome (about 170–236). Some debate exists among scholars on the relationship between these early accounts of the Essenes, and whether some depend on others or on a common ancient source that no longer survives.

There are four major descriptions of the Essenes: two by Josephus (*Jewish War* 2.119–61 and *Antiquities* 13.171–73 and 18.18–22); and two by Philo (*Every Good Man Is Free* 75–91 and *Hypothetica: Apology for the Jews*).

Tiberius Philo knew a good deal about affairs in Judea, and apparently visited Jerusalem at least once. Flavius Josephus had the most to say about the Essenes, and was the only one born and raised in Judea. He also claims to have personal knowledge of the Essene community (*Life* 1.10–12), but this is disputed. No clear evidence exists that either author knew of the settlement on the western shore of the Dead Sea we call Qumran.

Among the sectarian scrolls, key texts for identifying the movement are the *Damascus Document* (CD) and the *Rule of the Community* (1QS). Comparison with the classical descriptions of the Essenes reveals a long list of parallels between. For example, Todd Beall has identified 21 parallels between the *Rule of the Community* and Josephus' writings in *Josephus' Description of the Essenes* (1988). Several themes stand out:

(a) Determinism (or Fate)

In the *Antiquities*, Josephus writes: "The doctrine of the Essenes likes to leave every-thing in the hands of God" (18.18). A longer section contrasts the views of the three main Jewish groups regarding Fate:

> [*T*]*he Pharisees* . . . say that certain events are the work of Fate, but not all; as to other events, it depends upon ourselves whether they shall take place or not. *The sect of Essenes*, however, declares that Fate is mistress of all things, and that nothing befalls men unless it be in accordance with her decree. But *the Sadducees* do away with Fate, holding that there is no such thing and that human actions are not achieved in accordance with her decree, but that all things lie within our power, so that we our-selves are responsible for our well-being, while we suffer misfortune through our own thoughtlessness. (*Antiquities* 13.171–73) (Trans. Ralph Marcus, *Josephus*, 311, 313)

Belief in fate or determinism, that God has mapped out the course of history in advance, is also prominent in many sectarian scrolls, including the *Damascus Document*, the *Rule of the Community*, the *Thanksgiving Hymns* (*Hodayot*), the *War Rule*, the *Ages of Creation* (4Q180), and several *Pesharim*. Their explanation for good and evil existing together was that God not only created everything, but determined in advance all that would happen in his creation. One striking passage in the *Rule of the Community* (1QS 3:15–16) tells us that everything that now exists and will be in the future originates with the God of knowledge (line 15). Even human actions have been foreordained by God, who established two spirits (one of truth, the other of falsehood) for two kinds of people:

> [17] He created humankind to rule over [18]the world, appointing for them two spirits in which to walk until the time ordained for his visitation. These are the spirits [19] of truth and falsehood. Upright character and fate originate with the Habitation of Light; perverse, with the Fountain of Darkness. (1QS 3:17–19) (*The Dead Sea Scrolls: A New Translation*, 120)

(b) Afterlife and Resurrection

There are differences in what is meant by an afterlife in early Hebrew and Aramaic texts on the one hand, and Greek and Latin ones on the other. Nevertheless, the ancient sources make it clear that the Essenes believed in immortality of the soul, an afterlife, and (possibly) physical resurrection. As we might expect, these writers do not agree on every detail.

Josephus tells us that the Essenes believed the souls "are immortal, and consider it necessary to struggle to obtain the reward of righteousness" (*Antiquities* 18.1). They held that the body is corruptible, but souls are immortal and become trapped in the prison of the body, awaiting liberation so they rise up to the heavenly world:

> [154] For the view is tenaciously held among them that although our bodies are perishable and their matter impermanent, our souls endure forever, deathless. They get entangled, having emanated from the most refined ether, as if drawn down by a certain

charm into the prisons that are bodies. [155] But when they are released from the restraints of the flesh, as if freed from a long period of slavery, then they rejoice and are carried upwards in suspension. (*War* 8.154–55) (Adapted from Mason, *Judean War*, 123–24)

For good souls, after death there is a home beyond the ocean, a place not oppressed by rain or snow or heat. However, after death the souls of the wicked go to a dark pit filled with endless punishments (*Jewish War* 2.155).

Hippolytus of Rome writes that the Essenes "affirm there will be both a judgment and a conflagration of the universe, and the wicked will be eternally punished" (*Refutation of All Heresies* 27). He states that the Essenes believed in a resurrection as well:

> The doctrine of the resurrection has also derived support among them, for they acknowledge both that the flesh will rise again, and that it will be immortal, in the same manner as the soul is already imperishable. They maintain that when the soul has been separated from the body, it is now borne into one place, which is well ventilated and full of light, and there it rests until judgement. This locality the Greeks were acquainted with by hearsay, calling it "Isles of the Blessed." (par. 27) (Goodman, *Classical Sources*, 73)

The *Yahad* wrote and used many eschatological texts concerning the end times. Their own texts tell us that they believed in the immortality of the soul, an afterlife, and most likely physical resurrection, which indicates they were an Essene community, or part of the Essene movement, as described by Josephus and other early writers.

(c) Entering and Joining the Community or Movement

Like many ancient authors, Josephus was fascinated by religious groups or "philosophies," which people seeking truth, righteousness, or salvation could join. He notes the requirements for becoming a member of the Essenes, a process of three years ending with full membership:

> [137] Those desiring to enter the sect do not obtain immediate admittance. The postulant waits outside for one year; the same way of life is propounded to him and he is given a hatchet, the loin-cloth which I have mentioned, and a white garment. [138] Having proved his continence during this time, he draws closer to the way of life and participates in purificatory baths at a higher degree, but he is not yet admitted into intimacy. [139] Indeed, after he has shown his constancy, his character is tested for another two years, and if he appears worthy he is received into the company permanently. But before touching the common food he makes solemn vows before his brethren. (*Jewish War* 2.137–39) (Goodman, *Classical Sources*, 73)

Among the sectarian scrolls, the *Rule of the Community* describes a similar process of admission into the Yahad, which takes two years and involves three main steps leading to full membership for each initiant. *Step 1:* Examination by the Guardian, receiving instruction, examination by the full membership. *Step 2:* One year of partial membership, further instruction, property taken over, limited rights to the meal. *Step 3:* After another year, testing, permission to touch the drink of the general membership, and—subject to members' approval—full membership, including taking part in the pure meals. Details of this step are as follows:

> [20] The initiate is not to touch the drink of the general membership prior to [21] passing a second year among the men of the *Yahad*. When that second year has passed, the general membership shall review his case. If it be ordained [22] for him to proceed to full membership in the *Yahad*, they shall enroll him at the appropriate rank among his brothers for discussion of the Law, jurisprudence, participation in pure meals, and admixture of property. Thenceforth the *Yahad* may draw upon his counsel and [23] judgment. (1QS 6:20–23) (*The Dead Sea Scrolls: A New Translation*, 126)

Some scholars claim that Josephus and the *Rule of the Community* are describing different procedures, but we may reasonably conclude they are depicting the same one. *Step 1* in the *Rule* = Josephus' one year outside the group but living by its rules. *Step 2* (+ "after another year" in *Step 3*) = Josephus' two more years of testing. *Step 3* = Josephus' final admission and permanent membership.

(d) The Pure Meal

Josephus is quite detailed on how the Essenes purify themselves by washing their bodies in cold water before eating the community meal. Also, the meal follows a formal procedure, a priest presides, and he offers a prayer before the food:

> [129] (At 11 am) they are again assembled in one area, where they belt on linen covers and *wash their bodies in frigid water*. After this purification they gather in a private hall, into which none of those who hold different views may enter: now pure themselves, they approach the dining room as if it were some [kind of] sanctuary. [130] After they have seated themselves in silence, the baker serves the loaves in order, whereas the cook serves each person one dish of one food. [131] *The priest* offers a prayer before the food, and it is forbidden to taste anything before the prayer; when he has had his breakfast he offers another concluding prayer. While starting and also while finishing, then, they honor God as the sponsor of life. (*Jewish War* 2.129–31) (Mason, *Judean War*, 106–8)

For the *Yahad* living by the *Rule of the Community*, entering the water to become purified is connected to the Pure Meal (the community meal): [13] "[The perverse man] is not to enter the water to share in the Pure Meal of the Men of Holiness, since they will not be cleansed [14] without repenting of their wickedness. For impurity adheres to who all who transgress" (1QS 5:13–14). There is also a set procedure by rank, a priest presides, and he says a blessing over the food:

> [3] Wherever ten men belonging to the party of the *Yahad* are gathered, a priest must always [4] be present. The men shall sit before the priest by rank, and in that manner their opinions will be sought on any matter. When the table has been set for eating

or the new wine readied [5] for drinking, it is the priest who shall stretch out his hand first, blessing the first portion of the bread or the new wine. (1QS 6:3–5) (*The Dead Sea Scrolls: A New Translation*, 124)

(e) Prohibition Against Spitting

A small but important point of correspondence is found in the descriptions of the Essenes in the *Jewish War* and of the Yahad in the *Rule of the Community*. Such minor details give Josephus' account the ring of authenticity with respect to the Essene movement. Compare *Jewish War* 2.147 ("In addition, they avoid spitting in the middle of the company, or to the right side") and 1QS 7:13 ("And a man who spits during the course of a meeting of the Many will be punished for thirty days").

(f) Prohibition Against Use of Oil

Josephus takes note that the Essenes avoided using oils on their bodies so as not to make themselves ritually impure (or defiled): "They regard oil as a defilement, and should any of them accidently come in contact with it, he wipes his body clean. They make a point of having their skin dry and of always being clothed in white garments" (*Jewish War* 2.123) (Adapted from Goodman, *Classical Sources*, 39).

This is consistent with the belief in some sectarian scrolls that impurity can pass through liquids (thus oil would be impure if oil in the original container was impure). Furthermore, in the *Damascus Document*, stains of oil found on pieces of wood, stones, or dust are said to communicate uncleanness (CD 12:15–17).

(g) Nondisclosure (Secretiveness)

Josephus informs us that the Essenes could not reveal to outsiders their distinctive beliefs and practices: "Moreover, he swears to conceal nothing from the members of the sect and to reveal nothing to outsiders, even if violence as far as death is used against him" (*Jewish War* 2.141).

The same rule of nondisclosure occurs in key sectarian scrolls; for example, the *Rule of the Community* ("Concealing the truth, that is, the mysteries of knowledge," 1QS 4:6; see also 9:16–19); and the *Damascus Document* ("No one is allowed to tell him the rules until he appears before the Guardian," CD 15:10–11).

(h) Strictness in Observing the Sabbath

In the *Jewish War*, Josephus writes that the Essenes were stricter than other Jewish groups with respect to observing the Sabbath day:

> They are also forbidden, more rigorously than any other Jews, to attend to their work on the seventh day. Not only do they prepare their own food on the day before to avoid lighting a fire on that day, but they dare not even move an object—or even go to relieve themselves. (*Jewish War* 2.147) (Goodman, *Classical Sources*, 45)

Sabbath observance is also enjoined in some sectarian scrolls. For example, the regulations in the *Damascus Document* (CD 10:14–11:18) make it clear that this movement was rigorous in keeping the Sabbath day.

(i) Wealth and Property

Classical writers were impressed by the Essenes' common ownership of property and avoidance of riches (for example, Pliny, *Natural History* 5.73). Philo speaks in considerable detail on this feature, in a longer section that covers their fellowship:

> [85] First of all then no one's house is his own in the sense that it is not shared by all, for besides the fact that they dwell together in communities, the door is open to visitors from elsewhere who share their convictions. [86] Secondly, they all have a single treasury and common disbursements; their clothes are held in common and also their food through their institution of public meals. In no other community can we find the custom of sharing roof, life and board more firmly established in actual practice. And that is no more than one would expect. For all the wages which they earn in the day's work they do not keep as their private property, but throw them into the common stock and allow the benefit thus accruing to be shared by those who wish to use it. [87] The sick are not neglected because they cannot provide anything, but have the cost of their treatment lying ready in the common stock, so that they can meet expenses out of the greater wealth in full security. (*Every Good Man Is Free*, 85–87) (Adapted from F. H. Coloson, *Philo IX*, 59, 61).

Josephus, too, writes with admiration on the Essenes' attitude to riches and community life:

> [122] They despise riches and their communal life is admirable. In vain would one search among them for one man with a greater fortune than another. Indeed, it is a law that those who enter the sect shall surrender their property to the order; so neither the humiliation of poverty nor the pride of wealth is to be seen anywhere among them. Since their possessions are mingled, there exists for them all, as for brothers, one single property. . . . [127] They neither buy nor sell anything among themselves; each man gives what he has to whoever needs it, and receives in return whatever he himself requires. And they can even receive freely from whomsoever they like without giving anything in exchange. (*Jewish War* 2.122, 127; cf. *Antiquities* 18.20) (Goodman, *Classical Sources*, 39)

Common ownership of property likewise features in some sectarian scrolls. As we have seen, for the closed community described in the *Rule of the Community*, there are procedures from probation to full membership of the *Yahad* (CD 6:13–23). During *Step 2*, the candidate's property is taken over, "but it shall not yet be disbursed along with that of the general membership" (lines 19–20). In *Step 3*, full membership includes "admixture of property" (line 22). The rationale for pooling personal property is given earlier in the Rule: "All who volunteer for his truth are to bring the full measure of their *knowledge, strength,* and *wealth* into the *Yahad* of God" (1QS 1:11–12). This wording deliberately recalls the biblical command: "You shall love the LORD your God with all your *heart*, and with all your *soul*, and with all your *might*" (Deut 6:5 NRSV). Thus surrendering one's wealth is to love God with all one's might.

It was (and is) not practical for most people to pool their wealth and property. For communal "camps" in the cities and towns, where members worked outside the community and had families, the *Damascus Document* lays out different rules:

> [12] **This is the Rule of the General Membership for meeting all their needs:** A wage of [13] two days every month at least will be given to the Guardian. Then the judges [14] will give some of it for their orphans, with some of it they will support the poor and needy, and the elder [15] [bent with age], the man with a skin disease, whoever is taken captive by a foreign nation, the gi[rl [16] for] whom no man cares, the boy without an advocate; and for whatever is community business, so that [17] [the community family should not be cut off]. (CD 14:12–17) (Adapted from *The Dead Sea Scrolls: A New Translation*, 76)

(j) Marriage and Celibacy

Not unexpectedly, this topic is complex with respect to the classical sources and the sectarian scrolls. The classical writers give the impression that most Essenes were celibate, but with one exception (see below). Philo writes that they "banned marriage at the same time as they ordered the practice of perfect continence. Indeed, no Essaean takes a woman because women are selfish" (*Hypothetica* 11.14; Goodman, *Classical Sources*, 29). Pliny says the Essenes near the shore of the Dead Sea were "a solitary tribe, without any women and having renounced all sexual interest" (*Natural History* 5.73). Also, Josephus explains:

> [120] [The Essenes] shun physical pleasure as a vice, but consider self-control and not succumbing to the passions as virtue. And although there is among them a disdain for marriage, they adopt the children of outsiders. . . . [121] Without doing away with marriage or the succession resulting from it, they protect themselves from the wanton ways of women, being convinced that none of them preserves her faithfulness to one man. (*Jewish War* 2.120–21) (Adapted from Mason, *Judean War*, 97–100)

The question of marriage among the Essenes could take up an entire book, but it appears that the ones at Qumran were celibate males. This is confirmed in the cemeteries, even though a very small number of women were likely buried by the sectarians to show special treatment. (Remains in later burials at the site include other women and children.)

It also seems that texts such as the *Rule of the Community* are for a group of celibate males, although it contains no legislation regarding marriage. These *Yahad* Essenes saw themselves as constantly in a holy state, in which contact with women was forbidden:

- Removed from women, whose monthly menstruations brought ritual impurity.

- Preparing for a holy war (compare 2 Sam 11:13, on Uriah not going home to sleep with his wife).

- Being always prepared for divine revelation (Exod 19:14–15, on Moses consecrating the people: "Prepare for the third day; do not go near a woman").

- Priests perpetually in a holy state (1 Sam 21:4, on David's men eating holy bread only if they have kept themselves from women).

- Constantly in the company of angels (*Songs of the Sabbath Sacrifice*).

However, there is strong evidence that the Essene movement included many groups with married members. Josephus writes of an "order" of Essenes who marry, who were most likely of great number, since he and Philo approximate the Essenes at 4,000 men living in numerous population centers (*Jewish War* 2.124; *Antiquities* 18.20; *Every Good Man Is Free* 7; *Hypothetica* 11.1).

> [160] There is also a different order of Essenes. Though agreeing with the others about regimen and customs and legal matters, it has separated in its opinion about marriage. For they hold that those who do not marry cut off the greatest part of life, the succession, and more: if all were to think the same way, the line would very quickly die out. [161] To be sure, testing the brides over a three-year interval. Once they have been purified three times as a test of their being able to bear children, they then marry them. However, they do not continue having intercourse with those who are pregnant, demonstrating that the need for marrying is not because of pleasure, but for children. Baths [are taken] by the women wrapping clothes around themselves, just as by the men in a waist-covering. (*Jewish War* 2.160–61) (Adapted from Mason, *Judean War*, 129–31)

Several of the sectarian scrolls (or texts embraced by the *Yahad*) refer to families, including the *Damascus Document* and the *Temple Scroll* (45:11–12, cf. 54:4–5). For example, the *Damascus Document* gives instructions for members living in camps who marry and have children (CD 7:6–9). Further important details are found in some Cave 4 copies of the *Damascus Document*. One mentions a member having sexual relations with his wife, and complaining against *the mothers*, who seem to have played a religious role in this community's life:

> [12] Whoever approa[ches] [13] to **have sexual relations with his wife**, which is not according to the regulation, shall depart and never return. [Whoever complains] against the fathers, [14] [he must leave] the congregation and never return; [but if] **against the mothers**, he must suffer reduced rations ten days, for the mothers have no such status within [15] [the congregation. These are the] regulations by wh[ich they judge] all who are disciplined. (4Q270 frg. 7 i lines 12–15) (Adapted from *The Dead Sea Scrolls: A New Translation*, 77)

In another Cave 4 copy (4Q271; see also 4Q270 frg. 5 lines 19–21), a man is allowed to marry a non-virgin, a widow, or a woman with a bad reputation only if she is purified under the supervision of qualified women at the Guardian's command. Here, too, women seem to have played a religious role. (Note: The text is very fragmentary, so some key words from 4Q270 are supplied in italics.)

> [13] Let no man marry such a one unless [14] *under the supervision of* dependable and knowledgeable *wom[en]*, who are selected at the command of the Guardian who is over the [15] [general membership; the]n he may marry her, . . . (4Q271 frg. 3.10–15, here 13–15) (Adapted from *Dead Sea Scrolls: A New Translation,* 67)

The *Rule of the Congregation* (1Q28a) was found as an appendix to the *Rule of the Community* (1QS), but nine more scrolls (4Q249a–i) may be independent copies. This end-times *Yahad* includes women and children (1:5):

> [1:1] This is the rule for all the congregation of Israel in the Last Days, when they are mobilized [to join the *Yahad*. They must l]ive [2] by the law of the Sons of Zadok, the priests, and the men of their Covenant, they who ce[ased to walk in the w]ay [3] of the people. [4] As they arrive, all the newcomers shall be assembled—women and children included—and read [5] [a]ll the statutes of the Covenant. . . .[6]. . . From [early ch]ildhood each boy [7] is to be instructed in the Book of Meditation. . . . [8] Then, at a[ge] twenty, [he shall be enrolled] [9] [in] the ranks and take his place among the men of his clan, thereby joining the holy congrega[tion]. He must not app[roach] [10] a woman for sexual intercourse before he is fully twenty years old, when he knows [right] [11] from wrong. With the marriage act she, for her part, is received into adult membership. (1Q28a 1:1–11) (*The Dead Sea Scrolls: A New Translation,* 137–38)

Finally, several sectarian scrolls containing purity regulations are significant for discussing women and their presence among Essene communities. Many of these regulations concern bodily secretions. For example, *Purification Rules A* (4Q274) places restrictions on a menstruating woman, and *Purification Liturgy* (4Q284) also contains a purification ritual for a woman following menstruation (frgs. 2 ii and 3) and suggests she may have been part of a sectarian community. The text mentions food and seven days; presumably she abstained from the pure food of the community during her period. Following sunset on the seventh day (the time of the ritual bath), a blessing was evidently spoken by the woman: "Blessed are you, God of Israel . . ." (frg. 2 ii line 5). A response from a male officiant (probably a priest) follows in fragment 3.

On marriage and celibacy, we may conclude that in light of the classical sources and several sectarian scrolls, the *Yahad* at Qumran was a community of Essenes who were celibate but whose beliefs about the end of times incorporated men, women, and children. There may have been similar Essene communities who were also celibate. However, most Essenes married and had children, and in these communities women may have played a religious role. The classical authors were fascinated by the non-marrying Essenes living in wilderness communities and so focused on these. The fact that Philo and Josephus agree there were 4,000 Essenes and Josephus mentions an "order" of Essenes who marry indicates that the classical texts are ultimately not in opposition to the teachings of the sectarian scrolls.

3.2 A Community of Essenes at Qumran (The Qumran Esssene Hypothesis II)

The second component of the Qumran Esssene Hypothesis is that the *Yahad* at Qumran, who deposited most or all of the scrolls in the nearby caves, were a branch of the Essene movement. To further support this view, many scholars argue that the community at Qumran is mentioned by at least one classical writer. This is a difficult issue and requires careful discussion.

(a) Pliny the Elder's *Natural History* 5.73

Pliny the Elder (23–79 C.E.) was a Roman administrator, military official, and scholar. Much of his work is lost, but the 37-volume *Natural History* has survived and is a mine of information. Pliny finished this monumental collection around 77 and says he compiled it from over 100 sources (though lists of his authorities amount to more than 400). He presented it to the Roman commander Titus, who would soon become emperor in 79.

Material relating to Judea and the Essenes is found in book 5, for which Pliny says he consulted 60 sources. In paragraph 70, he begins describing the geography of Judea and then moves on to the Jordan River and the Dead Sea (71–74). Pliny's comments on the Dead Sea area feature this famous passage:

> To the west [of the Dead Sea], the Essenes flee the shores, sufficiently far from where they cause harm. This is a unique tribe and amazing beyond all others in the world, without any women and having renounced all sexual interest, without money, with the company of palm branches only! Their assembly is born again daily from the throng of newcomers, tired of life and the fluctuations of fortune, that crowd there for their manner of living. So for thousands of ages—remarkable to say—a tribe into which no one is born lives on forever! So fruitful for them is other people's reconsideration of (or, repentance about) their lives. (*Natural History* 5.73) (Adapted from Mason, "Historical Problem of the Essenes," 219)

Pliny's description does not entail approval, but perhaps baffled fascination. He has several important agreements with the descriptions of Philo and Josephus: The Essenes are an ancient group in Judea, are without women, allow no private money, and live an isolated life. The group constantly gains new members through recruitment of newcomers that have become weary and disillusioned with their lives. The sketch of Judea in the *Natural History* concludes:

> Below these [or, *next on my list*; Latin *infra hos*] used to be the town of Ein Gedi, second only to Jerusalem in fertility and groves of palm trees, but now likewise a ruin. After that Masada, a fortress on a crag—for its part not at all far from Asphaltites. This is Judea (5.73). (Mason, "Historical Problem," 222–23)

Both sections of the quoted passage have received attention from scholars. Pliny clearly says there were Essenes along the western shore of the Dead Sea (which he later calls *Judea's Lake*, 7.65). But did he intend anything more than mentioning the amazing Essenes west of the lake? Discussion related to Essenes and the scrolls has focused on two issues: geography and verbs.

(b) Geographical Details in *Natural History* 5.73

Arguments with respect to geography in favor of Pliny's Essenes living or meeting at Qumran (and thus supporting the Qumran Essene Hypothesis) include the following:

- In the second quoted excerpt, many scholars translate or understand the first two Latin words, *infra hos*, as indicating direction (lying below these).

- Given the place-names that follow (Ein Gedi and Masada), Pliny is moving in a north-south direction, and so the Essenes were located somewhere north of Ein Gedi.

- This fits the Qumran Essene Hypothesis: Pliny has just described the Essene community at Qumran, and Ein Gedi is south of it.

- Archaeologists have found no trace of a communal center in the area other than the one at Qumran, and none in the hills above Ein Gedi.

- Pliny (or his source) is not always accurate with respect to geographical locations. For example, he locates Machaerus and Callirhoe to the south of Asphaltites (they are east), and imagines a Dead Sea about 14 times its actual size (book 5.71–72).

- There are also errors in Pliny's description in 5.73. For example, when he says Ein Gedi is "second only to Jerusalem in fertility and groves of palm trees," *Jerusalem* may be a mistake for *Jericho*.

Several arguments have also been given with respect to geography against Pliny's Essenes living or meeting at Qumran:

- Pliny was not writing about Qumran; *infra hos* here denotes elevation (at a lower altitude than).

- The closest parallel in the *Natural History* is in book 3.109: "Below the Sabines (*infra Sabinos*) is Latium," with no implication that they live at a particular site, but inland with Latium below them.

- Thus in book 5.73, Pliny is describing a different site in the mountains above Ein Gedi.

- Alternatively, the Latin may simply mean "next on my list" (as bracketed in the translation above).

- Pliny's statement that this "unique tribe" was "with the company of palm branches only" means that they lived at a more verdant site than Qumran, which was (and still is) dry and barren.

- A work that names so many places—such as Machaerus and Callirhoe (5.72) and Ein Gedi and Masada (5.73)—would also have a name for a specific Essene habitation.

- This tribe rather denotes a group not confined to one site, such as the Arabian nomads on the east or the Sabines above Latium (see Mason, "Historical Problem," 222).

- That Pliny meant Ein Gedi lay south of an Essene settlement is an innovation that was only made following the discovery of the Dead Sea Scrolls.

- This new interpretation was proposed by André Dupont-Sommer (1952), who was well aware of the standard reading of *infra hos* meaning "at a lower altitude than":

> The Essene colony described by Pliny was situated near the spring of Engedi, towards the centre of the western shore of the Dead Sea; . . . Pliny continues thus: "Below them (*infra hos*) was the town of Engada." . . . I believe this means not that the Essenes lived in the mountains just above the famous spring, but that this was a little distance from their settlement, towards the south. . . . If Pliny's text is to be understood in this way, the Essene "city" would be found towards the north of the western shore; that is to say, precisely in the region of 'Ain-Feshka [near Qumran] itself. (*The Dead Sea Scrolls: A Preliminary Study*, 106 note 3)

(c) Past and Present Verbs in *Natural History* 5.73

The Case Against Pliny's Essenes Being at Qumran. Pliny finished the *Natural History* around 77 C.E., and presented it to Titus, the Roman commander who destroyed Jerusalem. Although aware of post-70 realities, Pliny often uses the past tense to describe this area as it was before the war, when Judea was an ethnic region in the Province of Syria (5.66). He knew of the past Roman destruction of Ein Gedi and Jerusalem ("used to be the town of Ein Gedi, second only to Jerusalem" . . . "but now likewise a ruin"). However, Pliny writes of the Essenes in the present tense: "the Essenes *flee*" (Latin *fugiunt*), "their assembly *is born again*" (*renascitur*), "that *crowd there*" (*agit*), "a tribe into which no one is born *is forever*" (*aeterna est*). If the Qumran site was destroyed by the Romans in 68 (as in the Qumran Essene Hypothesis), *Natural History* 5.73 suggests that Pliny's Essenes were not at Qumran. Or if they were, this center was still in operation nearer to 77, which could mean that the Romams did not destroy it in 68.

The Case in Favor of Pliny's Essenes Being at Qumran. In describing the Essenes at Qumran, Pliny follows his usual pattern of describing people, places, and things in the present tense. Another point is that Pliny (or his source) may not have known of the destruction of the Qumran site during the Roman campaign. As mentioned above, he used at least 60 sources for book 5 of the *Natural History*. Pliny most likely drew his information on the Essenes from one of these sources, and probably never visited the area himself. Alternatively, this source about the Essene settlement at Qumran was older than the Jewish war with Rome. When he completed the *Natural History* after the war, Pliny was aware and stated that Jerusalem (or Jericho) and Ein Gedi had been destroyed, but he did not update his older information on the Essene settlement.

(d) Dio Chrysostom's Mention of an Essene City Near the Dead Sea

One later text places Essenes along the shores of the Dead Sea. Dio Chrysostom (about 40–about 120) was a Greek orator, historian, and philosopher. According to Synesius of Cyrene (about 400), Dio mentioned the Essenes: "Also somewhere he praises the Essenes, who form an entire and prosperous city near the Dead Sea, in the centre of Palestine, not far from Sodom" (Goodman, *Classical Sources*, 59). Dio does not give the location of these Essenes, but places them near the Dead Sea. In addition, his point that they "form an entire and prosperous city" will be of interest to some scholars who believe that the Qumran site was a prosperous country villa or a commercial center.

(e) Solinus' Mention of Ein Gedi Beneath the Essenes

Pliny's first surviving interpreter was the Roman historian and grammarian Julius Solinus, in his *Gallery of Remarkable Things* (early third century):

> The interior parts of Judaea toward the west are held by the Essenes. . . . The town of En Gedi used to be beneath the Essenes (*infra Essenos*), but it is now completely destroyed. . . . The boundary of Judaea is the fortress of Masada. (35.9, 12; Adapted from Mason, "Historical Problem," 227)

(f) So Is Qumran Mentioned Among the Classical Writings?

Possible: Pliny may be describing the Essenes at the Qumran site. In that case, with respect to geography, the words *below these* (Essenes) indicate direction: "Further south used to be the town of Ein Gedi." With respect to using the future tense, Pliny was then following a pattern of describing in the present tense, or Pliny/his source did not know of the destruction of the Qumran site, or Pliny knew and stated that Jerusalem (or Jericho) and Ein Gedi had been destroyed, but did not update his older source on the Essene settlement.

More Likely: Pliny is likely not describing the Essenes specifically at Qumran. First, careful examination of the key passage (*Natural History* 5.73) gives no indication that he has a particular community in mind. Pliny is describing the lifestyle of the Essenes as a unique tribe, not as a specific isolated group. Second, the use of the present tense is very telling. Pliny (or his source) says that below these Essenes used to be Ein Gedi, which, like Jerusalem, is now a ruin. When he was writing (77 or a little earlier), Pliny knew that the Romans had destroyed Jerusalem in 70, and the (quite famous) settlement at Ein Gedi a few years earlier (Josephus, *Jewish War* 4:401–4). If Pliny or his source also knew of Qumran's destruction, and his Essenes lived there, he would not have written about them in the present tense. Pliny (or his source) gives the impression that the Essenes survived long after Ein Gedi and Jerusalem were destroyed.

Thus Pliny's Essenes (or those in his source) lived along the western shore of the Dead Sea, were not confined to one site, most likely included those at Qumran, and survived in other locations after 70. There are two interesting implications: (a) Pliny's unique *tribe* (Latin *gens*) is a movement. (b) There was more than one (a few) Essene community of men who lived an isolated life, were without women, and allowed no private property. The passage by André Dupont-Sommer that was quoted above continues with remarkable insight:

> If Pliny's text is to be understood [in the way I propose], the Essene "city" would be found towards the north of the western shore; that is . . . [near Qumran] itself. Should this explanation not be acceptable, it could be supposed that the Essenes possessed monasteries other than that mentioned by Pliny and Dio in the same Wilderness of Judea. (*The Dead Sea Scrolls: A Preliminary Study*, 106 note 3)

This conclusion does not invalidate the Qumran Essene Hypothesis, but broadens it. Pliny's *unique tribe* is an Essene movement that included a few celibate communities along the western shore of the Dead Sea, and most likely the *Yahad* at Qumran.

3.3 Conclusion on the Qumran Essene Hypothesis

The Qumran Essene Hypothesis is supported by the ancient evidence, though with some refinements. I will treat the two main pillars of the hypothesis in turn.

(a) Do the Sectarian Scrolls Found Near Qumran Have Connections to the Essenes?

Comparing descriptions of the Essenes in classical writings with several key sectarian scrolls shows that the Yahad movement evident in many scrolls was part of the Essene movement described by various classical Greek and Roman authors. The Essenes in almost all the classical sources (and the *Yahad* in some sectarian scrolls) practiced celibacy, and there may have been other celibate Essene communities. However, the sectarian scrolls tell us that such groups believed the end of times would incorporate men, women, and children. Also, as Josephus hints, and some sectarian scrolls make clear, most Essenes married and had children. In these communities, women may have played a religious role.

(b) Was the Community at Qumran, Which Deposited Many or All of the Scrolls in the Nearby Caves, a Branch of This Movement?

The classical writers provide no clear answer to the above question. There is no evidence that Philo and Josephus knew of the settlement on the western shore of the Dead Sea we call Qumran. Pliny's Essenes (or those in his source) lived along the western shore of the Dead Sea, were not confined to one site, most likely included those at

Qumran, and survived in other locations after 70 C.E. Connections between the Yahad Essenes, Qumran, and the caves are more evident in key sectarian scrolls, the site itself, and the cemeteries.

4. Concluding Statement on the Pharisees, Sadducees, and Essenes

Were the Scrolls Found at Qumran Associated with the Pharisees?

Although the Essenes or *Yahad* (the group associated with the sectarian scrolls) and the Pharisees shared some beliefs (resurrection, an afterlife, future rewards and punishments, laws for festivals and community life), they disagreed on many others (predestination, interpretation of Jewish law, the calendar for observing holidays, a Teacher of Righteousness, overseers, goods in common). The Pharisees were major opponents of the Essenes, and are referred to in some sectarian scrolls by insulting names: the Seekers of Slippery Answers, Ephraim, and the Wall-Builders.

Were the Scrolls Found at Qumran Associated with the Sadducees?

Some scholars believe that the movement was led by a group of Zadokite priests (Sadducees). However, although the *Yahad* and "mainstream" Sadducees shared the same basic approach to Jewish law, they differed on other issues. For example, they were opposed to the priests (mostly Sadducees) serving at the Temple, and believed in an afterlife and resurrection, which the Sadducees most likely did not accept.

Some sectarian scrolls (*Some of the Works of the Law*) suggest that the Sadducees were less of a threat to the Essenes than the Pharisees. The name Sadducees is not found in the scrolls, but they probably appear a few times as *Manasseh* (who were a wicked and divisive group).

The Scrolls Found Near Qumran Were Associated with a Group of Essenes

The first pillar of the Qumran Essene Hypothesis (that the sectarian scrolls found near Qumran have connections to the Essenes) is supported by the ancient evidence.

The Essenes in classical writings and the *Yahad* in several key sectarian scrolls had similar or identical beliefs and practices, with respect to: determinism (fate); afterlife and resurrection; entering and joining the community or movement; the Pure Meal; prohibitions against spitting and use of oil; nondisclosure (secretiveness); strictness in observing the Sabbath; and wealth and property. On marriage and celibacy, the *Yahad* at Qumran was a community of Essenes who were celibate but whose beliefs about the end of times incorporated men, women, and children. There may have been other Essene communities who were celibate, but most Essenes married and had children, and in these communities women may have played a religious role.

On the second pillar of the Qumran Essene Hypothesis (that the community at Qumran, which deposited many or all of the scrolls in the nearby caves, was a branch of the Essene movement): The classical evidence does not reveal whether Philo and Josephus knew of the settlement at Qumran. Pliny's Essenes (or those in his source) lived along the western shore of the Dead Sea, were not confined to one site, most likely included those at Qumran, and survived in other locations after 70 C.E. This conclusion does not contradict the second part of the hypothesis, but broadens it. Pliny's unique *tribe* is an Essene movement that included a few celibate communities along the western shore of the Dead Sea, and most likely the *Yahad* at Qumran.

Were the Scrolls Found at Qumran Associated with Another Group Altogether?

Were the Scrolls Brought from Jerusalem?

Scholars such as Norman Golb propose that the scrolls were deposited in the caves near Qumran by fleeing residents of Jerusalem during the First Jewish Revolt, especially the siege of Jerusalem in 70 C.E. They add that these residents were from various Jewish groups, and the writings are from a diverse range of libraries and collections in Jerusalem.

Do Some Scrolls Have Christian Origins?

Spanish scholar José O'Callaghan has argued that fragments of several New Testament documents were in Cave 7 near Qumran (for example, Mark's Gospel, Acts, two of Paul's Epistles). More recently, Robert Eisenman (1997, 2006) has advanced a theory of *Palestinian* Christianity, according to which some scrolls describe early Christians, including James the brother of Jesus (as the Teacher of Righteousness in several Qumran texts).

Neither of these theories on the movement associated with the sectarian scrolls has found much support from other scholars.

5. History of the Essene Movement

The formation and history of the Essene or *Yahad* movement as found in the sectarian scrolls is a complex subject, not least because it was at a time of great turmoil and change in early Judaism. The sketch given in this chapter is brief and simplified, and accompanies the *Ancient Groups and Figures* that precede the Introduction to this book. There are two principal texts for identifying the writers and collectors of the Dead Sea Scrolls: the *Damascus Document* (D) and the *Rule of the Community* (S). These and several other sectarian scrolls reveal an early Jewish movement that was quite widespread and had several distinctive features.

Choosing a name for this movement is not easy. The term *Yahad* at once comes to mind, but it is rarely used (notably in col. 20:32) in the *Damascus Document*. *Qumran*

Covenanters is too restrictive because most groups in the movement were not at Qumran. Another possibility is the *Community of the New Covenant*. For the community associated with Qumran, I mostly use *Yahad*, and for the wider movement Essenes or New Covenanters.

5.1 Beginnings of the Movement

The *Damascus Document* describes the movement's origins in some detail:

> In the era of wrath—three hundred [6] and ninety years at the time (God) handed them over to the power of Nebuchadnezzar king of Babylon—[7] He took care of them and caused to grow from Israel and from Aaron a root of planting to inherit [8] his land and to grow fat on the good produce of his soil. They considered their iniquity and they knew that [9] they were guilty men, and had been like the blind and like those groping for the way [10] twenty years. But God considered their deeds, that they had sought him with a whole heart.
>
> [11] So He raised up for them a Teacher of Righteousness to guide them in the way of his heart. (CD 1:5–11) (*The Dead Sea Scrolls: A New Translation*, 52)

This passage refers to members of a small group who were repentant and acknowledged they were sinful during the time when God was punishing Israel. The number 390 is the years prophesied by Ezekiel (4:4–5) for Israel's punishment, beginning with the exile. Although scholars have debated whether this figure was meant literally, it synchronizes well with other known dates. Counting from the exile in about 586 B.C.E. (when Nebuchadnezzar destroyed Jerusalem), CD places the movement's beginnings 390 years later, at 196 B.C.E. For 20 more years, we are told, the group had difficulties establishing themselves, but then (in 176 B.C.E.) the Teacher of Righteousness assumed leadership (CD 1:11). While some scholars view 390 and 20 as approximate or symbolic, these numbers make a good case for the existence of a Jewish movement led by the Teacher in 176 B.C.E.

5.2 The Teacher of Righteousness

There are two meanings to this key early leader's name: the one who teaches right lessons, or the right (legitimate) teacher. Many striking claims were made about him. Besides being raised up by God himself (CD 1:11), according to the *Damascus Document*, the Teacher was even prophesied in Scripture (as the Interpreter of the Law): "the Star that will come out of Jacob" (Num 24:17) "means the Interpreter of the Law [19] who comes to Damascus (CD 7:18–19)."

In the *Commentary on Habakkuk*, the Teacher's God-given ability to interpret Scripture, indeed his very coming, is found in the interpretation of Habakkuk 2:1–2:

> [14] "*Then the* LORD *answered me* [15] [*and said, 'Write down the vision plainly*] *on tablets, so that with ease* [16] [*someone can read it*' " (Hab 2:1–2).

> This refers to . . .] 7:1 then God told Habakkuk to write down what is going
> to happen to [2] the generation to come; but when that period would be complete He
> did not make known to him. [3] When it says, "*so that with ease someone can read
> it*," [4] this refers to the Teacher of Righteousness to whom God made known [5] all the
> mysterious revelations of his servants the prophets. (1QpHab 6:14–7:5) (*The Dead Sea
> Scrolls: A New Translation*, 84)

As the Priest (another of his names), God gave the Teacher the power to explain
"all the words of his servants the prophets," through whom he had "foretold everything
that was to come" upon his people and the Gentiles (1QpHab 2:9–10). A *Commentary
on Psalms* (4Q171) tells us that the Priest also founded or established a community
(3:15–17).

5.3 Opposition to the Teacher Relating to Interpretation of Scripture and the Law

(a) The Man of Mockery, the Man of the Lie, the Spewer of Lies

Not surprisingly, the Teacher had opponents. There were several conflicts between
the Teacher, other Jewish groups, and individuals from those groups, and involved at least
two important issues.

One major conflict possibly arose from within the movement's own ranks. The Man
of Mockery rejected the Teacher's claims and withdrew from him and his group, taking a
number of followers with him:

> [14] When the *Man of Mockery* appeared, who sprayed on Israel [15] lying waters, he
> led them to wander in the trackless wasteland. He brought down the lofty heights of
> old, turned aside [16] from paths of righteousness, and shifted the boundary marks that
> the forefathers had set up to mark their inheritance, so that [17] the curses of his covenant
> took hold on them. (CD 1:17–17) (*The Dead Sea Scrolls: A New Translation*, 32)

A *Commentary on Psalms* (4Q171) says that the Teacher's opponent was also called
the *Man of the Lie*, was prophesied in Scripture, and appears to have enjoyed some success:

> [17] "*[Be] silent before [the Lord and] wait for him, and do not be jealous of the
> successful man* [18] *who does wicked deeds*" (Ps 37:7).
>
> [This refers] to the *Man of the Lie* who led many people astray with deceitful
> [19] statements, because they had chosen trivial matters but did not listen to the spokes-
> men for true knowledge, so that [1-2 ii.1]they will perish by sword, famine, and pestilence.
> (4Q171 frgs. 1–2.i line 17–ii line 1) (*The Dead Sea Scrolls: A New Translation*, 249)

A *Commentary on Isaiah* (4Q162) explains that the congregation of the Men of
Mockery are in Jerusalem (col. 2:6–10). The *Damascus Document* tells us that members
who have rejected the commandments of the New Covenanters "will be condemned along

with the Men of Mockery," and are "warriors who went back to the Man of the Lie" (CD 20:1, 11, 14–15).

Another passage in the *Damascus Document* describes people who do not remain faithful to the movement's laws and whose actions are contrary to them. After quoting from Deuteronomy 32:33 ("*Their wine is venom of snakes, the cruel poison of vipers*"), the interpreter explains:

> "*The snakes*" are the kings of the Gentiles and "*their wine*" is their customs and "*the poison of vipers*" is the chief of the kings of Greece, who comes to wreak vengeance on them. But the "*Wall-Builders*" and "*White-washers*" understood none of these things, for one who deals in mere wind, a *Spewer of Lies*, had spewed on them . . ." (CD 8:9–13) (Adapted from *The Dead Sea Scrolls: A New Translation*, 59–60)

Wall-Builders is a name for the Pharisees in some sectarian scrolls. The Spewer of Lies, the Man of Mockery, and the Man of the Lie seem to denote the same person, who came into conflict with the Teacher regarding interpretation of the law, and was connected to the Pharisees. Some scholars believe that he may have been the founder of the Pharisaic movement.

(b) A Possible Connection to Some of the Works of the Law (MMT)

Some of the Works of the Law (MMT) is a key text for understanding the Essene movement. One party is writing to another, giving what they believe is the correct interpretation of the calendar and many points of biblical law. Analysis of the rulings in section B (on about 24 laws mainly from the Torah and their correct interpretation) suggests that the group represented by MMT (the Essenes) had a stricter, more demanding approach to the law, and were asking the recipients to follow this approach, not the more lenient one which was incorrect and evil. Since we know from other sources that the Pharisees also had a lenient approach to interpreting biblical law (taking into account oral traditions), it is reasonable to conclude that the writer is warning the recipients not to follow the approach of the Pharisees.

The tone is firm but gentle, which leads many scholars to believe that MMT was written early in the movement's history (shortly after 150 B.C.E.). Some scholars suggest the writer is trying to persuade the high priest or the Sadducees. However, he is more likely appealing to wavering members of his own group. They must stand firm and not follow the Man of Mockery (or the Man of the Lie) who has rejected the Teacher's claims, and has allied himself with the Pharisees with their compromises on interpreting biblical law.

5.4 Opposition to the Teacher Relating to the Priesthood

(a) End of the Zadokite High Priesthood

The most severe and violent opponent of the Teacher of Righteousness was the Wicked Priest, whom we meet in three sectarian texts. All are commentaries: on Habakkuk (five mentions); Psalms (4Q171, one); and Isaiah (4Q163, one). The Wicked Priest was most likely a high priest, since in Hebrew the word *wicked* is a wordplay on *high*. If he was, only a small number of high priests served at the times reflected in these commentaries. But why would the Teacher have been opposed by the religious leader of the nation?

During most of the earlier Second Temple period, the high priesthood was held by the house of Zadok (a priest descended from Aaron's son Eleazar), from Jehoshua ben Jehozadak after the exile, down to Simon II (218–185 B.C.E.) and Onias III (185–175). When Antiochus IV Epiphanes (about 215–164) became ruler of the Seleucid Empire (which included Judea) in 175 B.C.E., Onias' brother Jason bribed Antiochus to make him high priest instead. Jason then introduced the program of hellenization that led to the Maccabean Revolt (167–164 B.C.E.). In reality, the high priesthood of the Zadokite line had come to an end, with the office now being secured by plotting and bribery.

The next high priest was Menelaus (172–162), who bribed Antiochus to appoint him in place of Jason—who later drove out Menelaus and became high priest again. Antiochus invaded the Temple, attacked Jerusalem, and pursued a destructive hellenizing policy. Finally, Alcimus (162–159), a descendant of Aaron but not in the high priestly line (1 Macc 7:14; *Antiquities* 20.235), gained the office with the help of the new Seleucid king Demetrius I (who reigned 161–150 B.C.E.).

The high priesthood was officially restored by the Hasmoneans, the descendants of the Maccabees. The Hasmonean dynasty began with Jonathan (152–143), followed by many more, including Simeon (142–134), John Hyrcanus I (134–104), Aristobulus I (104–103), and Alexander Jannaeus (103–6), down to 37 B.C.E. (some 115 years altogether).

According to Josephus (*Antiquities* 20.237), after Alcimus there was no high priest in Jerusalem from 159 to 152 B.C.E. However, there must have been one or more acting high priests, since the high priest played an essential role on the Day of Atonement that was celebrated each year at the Temple. It is possible, perhaps even likely, that the Teacher of Righteousness was a high priest (perhaps not the only one, thus co–high priest) for a while, but was driven off by Jonathan. If this was the case, it helps explain why the high priest of his day (the Wicked Priest) harbored so much resentment and violence against the Teacher.

(b) A Priestly Party, the Zadokites, the Teacher Also Called the Priest

The Essene movement's leaders claimed lineage from Zadok, and were thus also Zadokites. There are numerous references to the sons of Zadok in key sectarian texts: the *Damascus Document* (CD 4:1, 3; 5:5); the *Rule of the Community* (1QS 5:2, 9); the *Rule of the Congregation* (1Q28a 1:2; 2:3); and the *Rule of the Blessings* (1Q28b 3:22). These, as well as the distinction made between priests, Levites, and general members, confirm that the movement had a significant priestly component. As already mentioned, the Teacher of Righteousness is also called *the Priest*, according to the *Commentary on Habakkuk* (1QpHab) 11:8 and the *Commentary on Psalms* (4Q171) 3:15.

The Essenes believed themselves to be the true Zadokites and that the high priest-hood and Temple rituals had been corrupted; thus they could not participate in them. Several sectarian scrolls recognize the importance of the Temple, but also show strong opposition to its priests. Together with the *Temple Scroll,* the New Covenanters awaited a new or restored Temple in Jerusalem that God revealed to Moses and would establish "for everlasting in fulfillment of the covenant [he] made with Jacob at Bethel" (11QT[a] col. 29:10). Thus the Essenes were committed to pure Temple religion, and to Israel's future that would be realized only in a restoration of the Jerusalem Temple.

(c) Persecution by the Wicked Priest

The book with the most references to the Wicked Priest is the *Commentary on Habakkuk.* For the interpretation of Habukkuk 2:5–6 (on an arrogant man who acquires wealth that is not his, but is eventually brought down), we are told:

> [8] This refers to *the Wicked Priest* who [9] had a reputation for reliability at the beginning of his term of service; but when he became ruler [10] over Israel, he became proud and forsook God and betrayed the commandments for the sake of [11] riches. He amassed by force the riches of the lawless who had rebelled against God, [12] seizing the riches of the peoples, thus adding to the guilt of his crimes, [13] and he committed abhorrent deeds in every defiling impurity. (Col. 8:8–13) (*The Dead Sea Scrolls: A New Translation,* 85–86)

The Wicked Priest was opposed to the Teacher and pursued him even on the Teach-er's Day of Atonement, which was on a different day from his own. This shows that the Wicked Priest and the Teacher (together with their movements) calculated their fes-tivals using different calendars. For the Essenes, having the correct calendar was vital, since humans must live and celebrate their festivals according to God's own time. They regarded the Temple rituals in Jerusalem as invalid, since the festivals there took place on the wrong days. The *Commentary on Habakkuk* interprets:

> [2] *"Woe to the one who gets his friend drunk, pouring out* [3] *his anger, making him drink, just to get a look at their holy days"* (Hab 2:15).

> [4] This refers to the Wicked Priest, who pursued the Teacher of Righteousness to destroy him in [5] the heat of his anger at his place of exile. At the time set aside for the repose of [7] the Day of Atonement he appeared to them to destroy them [8] and to bring them to ruin on the fast day, the Sabbath intended for their repose. (1QpHab 11:2–8). (*The Dead Sea Scrolls: A New Translation,* 87)

According to a *Commentary on the Psalms* (4Q171), the Teacher of Righteousness sent a "law" to the Wicked Priest, who responded by seeking to kill him. Some scholars suggest that this document was the important text *Some of the Works of the Law* (MMT), but this is not at all clear.

[7] *"The wicked man observes the righteous man and seeks [to kill him. But the Lo]rd [will not leave him in his power and will not co]ndemn him when he comes to trial"* (Ps 37:32–33).

[8] This refers to the Wicked [Pri]est who ob[serv]es the [Teach]er of Righteous[ness and seeks] to kill him [. . .] and the Law [9] that he sent to him, . . . (4Q171 frgs. 3–10 iv, lines 7–9) (*The Dead Sea Scrolls: A New Translation*, 251–52)

(d) Who Was the Wicked Priest?

Most scholars agree that the Wicked Priest was one of the Hasmonean high priests. Several names have been suggested, including Jonathan and Alexander Jannaeus. According to the "Groningen hypothesis," the Wicked Priest was not a person but an office, and the *Habakkuk Commentary* applies to six high priests: Judas the Maccabee (col. 8:8–13), Alcimus (8:16–9:2), Jonathan (9:9–12), Simon (9:16–10:5), John Hyrcanus I (11:4–8), and Alexander Jannaeus (11:12–12:10).

The most likely candidate is Jonathan, who served as high priest from 152 to 143 B.C.E. After becoming very wealthy through military campaigns, he lent his support to Alexander Balas, who later (150 B.C.E.) became king of the Seleucid Empire.

Jonathan enjoyed military triumphs and successful dealings with other countries, but was eventually imprisoned by the Seleucid ruler and general Diodotus Tryphon. After holding him captive for some time (1 Macc 13:23), and despite promising to liberate him, Diodotus executed Jonathan at Baskama (somewhere east of the Jordan) in 142 B.C.E. His death at enemy hands sits well with the comments in the *Habakkuk Commentary* on the terrible end met by the Wicked Priest:

[16] [Habakkuk 2:7–8 refers to] the Priest who rebelled [17] [and violated] the commandments of [God . . . they mis]treated him [. . .] [9:1] his aflictions upon him the punishments due to such horrible wickedness, perpetrating upon him painful [2] diseases, acts of retaliation against his mortal body. (8:16–9:2) (*The Dead Sea Scrolls: A New Translation*, 86)

5.5 Can We Give a Date for the Teacher of Righteousness?

If Jonathan was the Wicked Priest described in the *Habakkuk Commentary*, the Teacher of Righteousness was most likely active in the years 176–142 B.C.E.

As mentioned above, the Wicked Priest pursued the Teacher of Righteousness to destroy him at his place of exile (1QpHab 11:4–5). This may have been Damascus, which features in the *Damascus Document* (although it could be a symbolic location), and is where a new covenant was made. At such an early date, this was not Qumran, which was settled by the Essene sectarians only late in the reign of John Hyrcanus (about 104 B.C.E.) or Alexander Jannaeus (103–76).

The opposition he encountered, especially from the Wicked Priest, must have caused the Teacher great suffering. Many scholars believe he was the author of one or more texts found at Qumran, most notably the Teacher Hymns among the *Hodayot*. The speaker tells of his suffering and trials, the plots against him, God's grace in saving him, and the knowledge that has been revealed to him.

The *Damascus Document* seems to mention the Teacher's death: "Now from the day [14] the Beloved Teacher passes away to the destruction of all the warriors who went back to [15] the Man of the Lie will be about forty years" (CD 20:13–15). His passing (literally, "gathering in") was mentioned a little earlier in the text (CD 19:35–20:1).

5.6 The Damascus Document and the New Covenant

For the *Damascus Document*, ten copies were found at Qumran, the full text only in the Cairo Genizah (CD). It falls into two main sections: the Admonition (cols. 1–8, 19–20) and a list of rules or statutes (cols. 15–16, 9–14) drawn from biblical law. The *Document* was addressed to a movement whose members lived in camps (CD 7:6; 10:23), which were communal groups at various places in Israel. Members had families, earned wages, and owned property. They were also a remnant, for whom God raised the Teacher of Righteousness to lead them in the proper way (1:10–11) and to enter the new covenant (2:2, cf. 6:12):

> [3] For when Israel abandoned him by being faithless, he turned away from Israel and from his sanctuary [4] and gave them up to the sword. But when he called to mind the covenant he made with their forefathers, he left a [5] remnant for Israel and did not allow them to be exterminated. (CD 1:3–5) (*The Dead Sea Scrolls: A New Translation*, 52)

The remnant is distinguished from their opponents, who repeatedly fail to correctly observe the law of Moses (CD 1:18–21; 7:9–8:1; 8:14–21; 20:8–13). The new covenant demands a commitment "to return to the Law of Moses with a whole heart, and to return with a whole spirit to that which is found therein to do during the era of [wickedness]" (CD 15:9–10). This shows a concern for Scripture as a source of reconciliation with God, apart from the sacrifices and offerings that took place in the Jerusalem Temple (cf. CD 6:11–14).

Joining the new covenant involved communal living for some members, who dwelt "in camps according to the rule of the land" (7:6). John Collins (*Beyond the Qumran Community*, 25) points out that these camps functioned in accordance with an ancient model for community organization prescribed in the book of Numbers.

The qualifications of those desiring membership were assessed by the Guardian (Hebrew *Mebaqqer* or *Paquid*), possibly another name for the Instructor, who also taught members about the works of God. For members of the New Covenant, strict and correct observance of the Law provided purity as a replacement for the Temple services. The laws that brought purity are laid out in columns 15–16 and 9–14 of the *Document*, and fall into two categories. Laws for "the cities of Israel" (CD 12:19) were for the nation, and more precise laws "for those living in camps" (CD 12:22–23) were for the community of the new covenant. The laws for this group were "hidden," discernible only through special insight into Scripture. The *Damascus Document* explains:

[12] But when those of them who were left held firm to the commandments of God, [13] he instituted his Covenant with Israel for ever, revealing [14] to them things hidden, in which all Israel had gone wrong: his holy Sabbaths, his glorious festivals, [15] his righteous laws, his reliable ways. The desires of his will, which Man should carry out [16] and so have life in them, he opened up to them. So they "dug a well" (cf. Num 21:18; CD 5:15–6:11), yielding much water. [17] Those who reject this water he will not allow to live. (CD 3:12–17) (*The Dead Sea Scrolls: A New Translation*, 54)

5.7 During the Qumran Era (About 4 B.C.E. to 68 C.E.)

While the *Damascus Document* helps us understand the identity and nature of the movement that wrote many of the sectarian scrolls, the most important source for identifying the "Qumran community" is the *Rule of the Community*.

Of the 11 scrolls found, the Cave 1 text (1QS) is an almost complete constitution for the *Yahad* community. It contains legislation for a group of men who have withdrawn from society and gives instructions on admission into the Covenant of Grace (1:7), fellowship, and how to live as a member. Led by the Maskil (Instructor), membership consists of priests, Levites, and Israelites. Observing the Torah is paramount, and everyone is to be ranked annually according to his obedience. Humanity is divided into two groups: the Sons of Light and the Sons of Darkness (1:9–10).

The *Yahad* Essenes did not recognize the Temple in Jerusalem because they believed the religious authorities running it were lax in ritual purity and used an unlawful calendar of festivals; see also the *Damascus Document* (CD) 20:22–23. They did not reject Temple religion, but awaited its end-times renewal. Until then, their community was an eschatological temple, with Israel (the laymen) as the holy place and Aaron (the priests) as the holy of holies:

> [3] When, united by all these precepts, such men as these come to be a community in Israel, they shall establish eternal truth [4] guided by the instruction of his holy spirit. They shall *atone* for the guilt of transgression and the rebellion of sin, becoming *an acceptable sacrifice* for the land through the flesh of *burnt offerings*, the fat of *sacrificial portions*, and [5] *prayer*, becoming—as it were—justice itself, a sweet savor of righteousness and blameless behavior, a pleasing *freewill offering*. At that time the men [6] of the *Yahad* shall withdraw, the *holy house of Aaron* uniting as a *Holy of Holies*, and the synagogue of Israel as those who walk blamelessly. (9:3–6; see also 5:4–7; 8:4–9) (*The Dead Sea Scrolls: A New Translation*, 130)

This group differs from the movement in the *Damascus Document*, especially in their communal existence and appraisal of Scripture. Unlike the *Damascus Document* (CD 7:6–7), the *Rule of the Community* does not mention or make provision for women and families. Commitment to the community is more demanding, and new initiates must surrender their property and possessions (6:19–20). The process of initiation is longer—at least two years—and requires fulfillment of oaths and repeated examination (6:13–23). For the *Rule of the Community* writers, Scripture was to be constantly recited and studied by the community:

> [6] In any place where is gathered the ten-man quorum, someone must always be engaged in the study of the Law, day and night, [7] continually, each taking his turn. The general membership will be diligent together for the first third of every night of the year, reading aloud from the Book, interpreting Scripture, and [8] praying together. (1QS 6:6–8) (*The Dead Sea Scrolls: A New Translation*, 124–25)

The change in perception is demonstrated in the group's name for itself, the *Yahad*. This term is found 74 times in the *Rule of the Community* and 254 times among Dead Sea Scrolls, almost always as a name for the group behind the texts. *Yahad* also occurs three times in the *Damascus Document*. Two are in a fragmentary Cave 4 copy (4Q270 frgs. 3iii, line 19 and 7i, line 8), but the main passage is in CD:

> [27] But all who hold fast to these rules, going out [28] and coming in according to the Law, always obeying the Teacher and confessing to God as follows: . . . [31] . . . and who discipline themselves by the ancient laws [32] by which the members of the *Yahad* were governed and listen attentively to the Teacher of Righteousness, not abandoning [33] the correct laws when they hear them: they will rejoice and be happy and exultant. (CD 20:27–28, 31–33) (*The Dead Sea Scrolls: A New Translation*, 61–62)

Like the *Damascus Document*, the *Rule of the Community* is an Essene text. Strong connections include the prominence given to the Law of Moses, procedures of initiation, community organization, rules, and disciplinary procedures. In each of these, the *Rule of the Community* appears to have a more developed system of community structure.

Most scholars attribute the similarities and differences in the *Damascus Document* and the *Rule of the Community* to different stages in the Essene movement's history. The *Rule of the Community* represents a later stage, or a different branch of the same movement. A term like *communities* of the Dead Sea Scrolls recognizes that the new covenant movement was dynamic, and existed in different sects and across several generations. Within Second Temple Judaism, these were closely related groups of Essenes.

5.8 Is the Qumran Site Mentioned in the Sectarian Scrolls?

The sectarian scrolls do not prove that the *Yahad* Essenes lived or met at Qumran. However, in the *Rule of the Community* (1QS), they explain their presence in the wilderness:

> [12] And when these have become a community in Israel [13] according to these rules, they will be separated from the dwelling-place of perverse men to go to the wilderness, in order to prepare there the way of him, [14] just as it is written: "***In the wilderness prepare the way of the LORD, make straight in the desert a highway for our God***" (Isaiah 40:3). [15] This is the expounding of the Law wh[i]ch (God) commanded by the hand of Moses, in order to act according to all that has been revealed in every each age, [16] and according to what the prophets have revealed by his holy spirit. (1QS 8:12–16) (Flint, "Jesus and the Scrolls," 117)

In light of the archaeological evidence and the absence of any other suitable site, this passage makes it likely that the *Yahad* Essenes lived or met at Qumran.

5.9 Historical References in the Qumran Period (About 4 B.C.E. to 68 C.E.)

There are very few references to historical persons or events in the later Dead Sea Scrolls. The *Pesher (Commentary) on Nahum* (4Q169) is an important text for reconstructing the history behind the *Yahad* Essenes. One section (frgs. 3–4.i, lines 2–7) mentions Seleucid king Demetrius III (the Old Lion), the Pharisees (the Seekers of Slippery Answers), Seleucid king Antiochus Epiphanes (Antiochus), the Romans (Kittim), and Alexander Jannaeus (the Lion of Wrath), who took vengeance against the Pharisees "because he used to hang men alive." Jannaeus ruled over Israel as king and high priest from 103 to 76 B.C.E. (*Antiquities* 13.375–76; *Jewish War* 1.90–92), and was affiliated with the Sadducees and priestly groups. He suppressed dissent by executing or banishing rebels, and crucified 800 Pharisees. In about 88 B.C.E., Demetrius III invaded Israel and put him to flight. However, many allies of the Pharisees switched sides to assist Jannaeus, and Demetrius withdrew his armies.

Jannaeus is most likely the king in the *Prayer for King Jonathan* (4Q448). The excerpt below seems to be in favor of the king ("Rise up, O Holy One, *for* Jonathan"), but can also be translated as opposing him ("Rise up, O Holy One, *against* Jonathan"):

> [1]Rise up, O Holy One, [2]for Jonathan, the king, [3]and all the congregation of your people [4] Israel [5]that is (dispersed) to the four [6]winds of the heavens, [7]let peace be on all of them [8]and your kingdom. [9]May your name be blessed. (4Q448 2:1–9) (*The Dead Sea Scrolls: A New Translation*, 507)

Other historical persons who are possibly mentioned in various scrolls are Queen Salome Alexandra (Shelamsion), Syrian king Hyrcanus II (Hyrcanus), Marcus Aemilius Scaurus, a Roman governor in Syria (Aemilius), and Peitholaus (a Jewish officer who was executed in 53 B.C.E.).

5.10 Concluding Comments on the New Covenanters (Essenes)

The formation and history of the Essene or *Yahad* movement as found in the sectarian scrolls is a complex topic. The two principal texts for identifying the writers and collectors of the scrolls are the *Damascus Document* and the *Rule of the Community*. The movement's origins, the Teacher of Righteousness, the opposition he endured, the years he was active (at least 152–142 B.C.E.), and details of the new covenant community are mostly found in the *Damascus Document* and the *Habakkuk Commentary*.

For the Qumran era (about 4 B.C.E. to 68 C.E.), the most important source for identifying the group involved is the *Rule of the Community*, which developed in stages. Written for a group of men who withdrew from society, it deals with admission into the Covenant of Grace, fellowship, and how to live as a member. Members were priests, Levites, and Israelites, led by the *Maskil* (Instructor). Observing the Torah was paramount, and everyone was ranked annually according to his obedience. Humanity was divided into two groups, the Sons of Light and the Sons of Darkness. The Yahad differs from the movement in the *Damascus Document* as regards commitment to the community, appraisal of Scripture, and provision for women and families. The group's name, Yahad (*Community*), is found 74 times in the *Rule of the Community*, but only three times in the *Damascus Document*.

While the sectarian scrolls do not prove that the *Yahad* Essenes lived or met at Qumran, in the *Rule of the Community* (1QS 8:12–16) they do tie their presence in the wilderness to Scripture. There are few references to historical persons or events in the later Dead Sea Scrolls. The *Pesher (Commentary) on Nahum* is an important text for reconstructing the history behind the *Yahad* Essenes, and mentions Syrian king Demetrius III, the Pharisees, Syrian king Antiochus Epiphanes, the Romans, and Alexander Jannaeus (Israel's king and high priest from 103 to 76 B.C.E.).

The *Damascus Document*, the *Rule of the Community*, and several other sectarian scrolls reveal an early Jewish movement that was quite widespread and had several distinctive features. A term like *communities* of the Dead Sea Scrolls recognizes that the new covenant movement was dynamic, and existed in different sects and across several generations. Within Second Temple Judaism, these were closely related groups of *Essenes*.

11

Religious Thought and Practice Reflected in the Qumran Scrolls

This chapter presents the main religious beliefs and practices of the Essene (*Yahad*) movement in six sections: (1) Their concept of God. (2) Explaining the reality of good and evil via predeterminism and supernatural forces. (3) Identifying one overall principle and two types of law by which the created order and humanity function (law for nature and law for humanity, including covenant). (4) The interpretation of Scripture. (5) Experiencing God and the Divine. (6) The end of days and the Messiahs.

1. Concept of God

A natural starting place for discussing a movement's religious beliefs is its concept of God. Direct statements about who God is, or how the *Yahad* Essenes imagined God, are rare in their writings, the main focus of which is satisfying God's will and ensuring conformity to God's plan. Nevertheless, the sectarian scrolls reveal much about the movement's understanding of God.

In the *Hodayot* or *Thanksgiving Hymns*, the poet emphasizes God's transcendence as Creator and Sustainer of the cosmos. For example, **Hymn 5** (col. 5:15–6:10) describes him as *powerful and strong* (col. 5:15), *unsearchable* (5:16), and mysterious (5:19–20). In **Hymn 25**, he is praised for his wonder, strength and insight:

> You are Chief of the gods and King of the glorious, Lord of every spirit and Ruler over every creature. Apart from you nothing is done, nor is there any knowing without your will. There is no one beside you and no one approaches you in strength. No one can compare to your glory and as to your strength, there is no price. (18:8–11) (*The Dead Sea Scrolls: A New Translation*, 195)

Hymn 9 also praises God as Creator of the heavens, all their hosts, the powerful spirits "according to their laws, before they became [your holy] angels, . . . luminaries," stars, storm winds, meteors, lightning bolts, and storehouses (9:11–15).

The Hymn to the Creator, found in the *Great Psalms Scroll* (11QPs^a, chapter 7.3), was most likely not composed by the Yahad, but was part of their foremost Psalter. Here the psalmist extols the Creator's majesty and holiness:

> [1]Great and holy is the LORD, the holiest of holy ones for every generation. [2]Majesty precedes him and following him is the rush of many waters. [3]Grace and truth surround his presence; truth and justice and righteousness are the foundation of his throne. [4]Separating light from deep darkness, he established the dawn by the knowledge of his mind. [5]When all his angels had witnessed it they sang aloud; for he showed them what they had not known: [6]Crowning the hills with fruit, good food for every living being. [7]Blessed be he who makes the earth by his power, establishing the world in his wisdom. (11QPs^a col. 26:9–14) (*The Dead Sea Scrolls Bible*, 582–83)

God is also praised for his role as Creator in the *War Rule*—for example, in the Prayer of the Chief Priest: "[O God, you have created] the expanse of the skies, the host of luminaries; [12]the task of spirits and the dominion of holy ones; the treasures of [your] gl[ory . . .] clouds. He who created the earth and the limits of her divisions" (1QM 10:11–12).

Some compositions focus entirely on creation, such as *Meditation on Creation A* (4Q303), a wisdom text on God's wonders starting with creation, including "the knowledge of good and evil" before the creation of Eve. Another is the *Works of God* (4Q392), which features the creation and dominion over darkness.

2. Predeterminism (or Fate), the Two Ways, and the Supernatural Origins of Evil

One issue that faces all religious movements is how to explain the presence of good and evil. All deal with this problem in some way (if only by denying they exist). For the *Yahad* Essenes, good and evil were very real, not imagined, and fell within God's control and overall plan.

2.1 Predeterminism

Their explanation for good and evil existing together was that did God not only created everything, but determined in advance all that would happen in his creation. The Essenes were distinguished from other Jewish groups by their doctrine of fate or predeterminism: "The sect of the Essenes, however, declares that Fate is the mistress of all things, and that nothing befalls men unless it be in accordance with her decree" (*Antiquities* 13.171–73).

Belief in fate or predeterminism is prominent in several key sectarian scrolls, including the *Hodayot* and the *War Rule*. Another striking passage that accords with Josephus' description is in the *Rule of the Community*:

> All that is now and ever shall be originates with the God of knowledge. Before things come to be, he has ordered all their designs, [16]so that when they do come to exist—at their appointed times as ordained by his glorious plan—they fulfill their destiny, a destiny impossible to change. (1QS 3:15–16) (*The Dead Sea Scrolls: A New Translation*, 120)

Among the *Hodayot*, one creation piece (**Hymn 8**, cols. 7:21–8:25) extols God for his all-knowing predisposition of the wicked to destruction and the righteous to life, and another (**Hymn 9**, cols. 8:26–9:41) blesses and praises him for the wonders of his creation:

> You have apportioned it to all their offspring according to the number of ever-lasting generations [19]and for all the years of eternity [. . .] and in the wisdom of your knowledge you determined their destiny before [20]they came into existence and according [to your will] everything come[s to pass], and nothing happens apart from you. (9:18–20) (*The Dead Sea Scrolls: A New Translation*, 178–79)

2.2 The Two Ways

The entire universe is involved in God's predetermined plan that two ways exist: the path of good or light and the path of evil or darkness. Angels as well as humans belong on either of these sides: the Angels of Light and Sons of Light on one side, the Angel of Darkness, his angels, and the Sons of Darkness on the other. These sides are in constant warfare—a cosmic conflict that will end only when God exercises final judgment and brings victory to the Sons of Light and their angelic allies over the Sons of Darkness (and their angelic allies).

The *Rule of the Community* tells us that human lives and actions are also part of this primal struggle. Every person has some light and darkness within him, even the Sons of Light. Fortunately, the God of Israel and "the Angel of His Truth" will assist the Sons of Light, and despises the counsel of the "spirit of darkness":

> The authority of the Angel of Darkness further extends to the corruption [22]of all the righteous. All their sins, iniquities, shameful and rebellious deeds are at his prompting, [23]a situation God in his mysteries allows to continue until his era dawns. Moreover, all the afflictions of the righteous, and every trial in its season, occur because of this Angel's diabolic rule. [24]All the spirits allied with him share but a single resolve: to cause the Sons of Light to stumble.

> Yet the God of Israel (and the Angel of his Truth) assist all [25]the Sons of Light. It is he who created the spirits of light and darkness, making them the cornerstone of every deed, [26]their impulses the premise of every action. God's love for one spirit **Col. 4** [1]lasts forever. He will be pleased with its actions for always. The counsel of the other, however, he abhors, hating its every impulse for all time (1QS 3:21–4:1). (*The Dead Sea Scrolls: A New Translation*, 120)

The *Rule* later describes (4:15–23) the struggle between good and evil, and good's ultimate triumph. The character and fate of all humankind reside with these two spirits, and all are heirs to their divisions (4:15); God has appointed them as equals and has set enmity between their divisions until the final age (lines 16–17). He has allowed an era in which perversity triumphs, but at the time appointed for judgment he will destroy it forever (18–19). God will then purify all human deeds and refine some of humanity (20), whom he has chosen for an eternal covenant (22). Then "all the glory of Adam will be theirs alone. Perversity will be extinct, every fraudulent deed put to shame" (23).

2.3 The Supernatural Origins of Evil in the World

The book (or booklets) of *1 Enoch* had enormous influence on the Essenes (*Yahad*), who viewed it as Scripture, at least in the earlier part of their history. According to *1 Enoch*, the explosion of evil in the world and human lives does not go back to Adam, Eve, and their descendants (Gen 3), but has supernatural origins. One key text is the Enochic rewriting of Genesis 6:1–4:

Table 1. The Sons of God and the Daughters of Men in Genesis and *1 Enoch*	
Genesis 6:1–2, 4 NRSV	***1 Enoch* 6:1–2; 7:1–2**
When people began to multiply on the face of the ground, and daughters were born to them, the sons of God saw that they were fair; and they took wives for themselves of all that they chose. The Nephilim were on the earth in those days—and also afterward—when the sons of God went in to the daughters of humans, who bore children to them. These were the heroes that were of old, warriors of renown.	when the sons of men had increased, that in those days there were born to them fair and beautiful daughters. And the angels, the sons of heaven, saw them and desired them. And they said to one another: "Come, let us choose for ourselves wives from the children of men, and let us beget for ourselves children. . . ." And they took wives for themselves, and everyone chose for himself one each. And they began to go in to them and were promiscuous with them. . . . And they became pregnant and bore large giants. (Trans. M. Knibb [1978] 2.67, 76–77)

The sons of God who came down from heaven are interpreted by *1 Enoch* as *angels* (Job 38:7), who married earthly women. Their offspring were large giants, who caused the great evil that made God send the flood to punish them and destroy the world. With Genesis 6:1–4 coming just before the flood story, the connection made in *1 Enoch* is powerful. This understanding of Genesis 6 is also found in books that influenced the Yahad (*Jubilees*, the *Genesis Apocryphon* [1QapGen]) and in some of their own writings: the *Damascus Document* (CD 2:17–21) and the *Ages of Creation* (4Q180).

3. One Overall Principle (Law)

For the Essene movement, the transcendent God was the divine architect of all things and placed the running of creation under the supervision of angels. God also required that everything function according to a system of divinely mandated purposes or laws, both for the natural order (the world) and for humanity. Obedience to these laws brought harmony, while disobedience brought disruption and disharmony.

3.1 Law for Nature (the World)

(a) In God's Creation, the Natural World Operates in Perfect Harmony

The fullest picture of the Essenes' understanding of nature is found in *1 Enoch* and *Jubilees*, two books they held in highest regard. There we read that the natural world operates by divinely given laws (*1 Enoch* 2–5; *Jubilees* 5).

God has appointed angels to rule over his immense universe, perhaps seven with different supervisory roles (*1 Enoch* 20). In the booklet called the Astronomical Book (*1 Enoch* 72–82), Uriel is leader of all celestial luminaries and reveals the book's contents to Enoch (cf. 72:1; 74:2; 75:3; 82:7–8). Under his command, other angels govern components of the luminaries such as the stars (75:1; 80:1; 82:10-20). *Jubilees* adds to the creation account found in Genesis; for example, on the first day God made the angels and appointed them to rule the many parts of his creation, including the natural world:

> the angels of the presence, the angels of holiness, the angels of the spirits of fire,
> . . . the angels of the spirits of cold and heat, of winter, spring, autumn, and summer,
> and of all the spirits of his creatures which are in the heavens, on earth, and in every
> (place). (*Jubilees* 2:2) (VanderKam, *The Book of Jubilees* [1989] 2.7–8)

The unchanging order of the luminaries as they go about their courses in the heavens takes place in perfect harmony. This is also evident in **Hymn 9** of the *Hodayot*:

> You have stretched out the heavens [10]for your glory, you [formed] all [their hosts]
> according to your will, and the powerful spirits according to their laws, before [11]they
> became [your holy] angels [. . .], as eternal spirits in their dominions, luminaries for
> their mysteries, [12]stars according to [their] paths, [and all the storm winds] according
> to their duty, meteors and lightning bolts according to their service, and the storehouses
> [13]designed for their needs. (9:11–13) (*The Dead Sea Scrolls: A New Translation*, 178)

(b) Measuring Time: The Calendar, Festivals, and Priestly Courses

The Astronomical Book in *1 Enoch* says that the year is measured by both the sun and the moon. The solar year lasts 364 days (72:2–32, cf. 74:10), and the lunar year 354 days. *Jubilees* also features a year of 364 days (for example, 6:38), first revealed to Enoch (4:17– 18, 21), but regards the shorter lunar year as due to "corruption" (6:23–38). The author denounces the use of the lunar year, since dating festivals by it mixes sacred and profane times (6:35–37). In retelling the fourth day of creation (Gen 1:14–19), the author omits any calendrical function for the moon (2:8–10).

The law for the natural order (or the world) is prominent in many texts authored by the Yahad, most often for establishing an accurate religious calendar. Strict calendric observance and God's transcendence reflect a sense of the world as entirely subject to God's control. A 364-day calendar that never changes pattern, presupposing the unchanging order of luminaries in the heavens, was adopted from *1 Enoch* and *Jubilees* by the *Yahad* Essenes. This calendar is found in many Dead Sea Scrolls and serves to bind these works together.

While *1 Enoch* and several calendrical texts do not connect the solar calendar with the festivals, *Jubilees* does. The calendrical texts follow a pattern of two years (a solar one of 364 days and a lunar one of 354 days), but align with *Jubilees* in dating festivals by the 364-day year. That the *Yahad*'s festivals were dated by this calendar (of 52 weeks) is confirmed by *David's Compositions*, the prose epilogue to the Psalter in the *Great Psalms Scroll* (11QPs^a):

> And the Lord gave ^{4}[David] a discerning and enlightened spirit. And he wrote ^{5}3,600 psalms; and songs to sing before the altar over the whole-burnt ^{6}perpetual offering every day, for all the days of the year, 364; ^{7}and for the offering of the Sabbaths, 52 songs . . . (*The Dead Sea Scrolls Bible*, 588–89)

The 364-Day Calendar. This calendar combines symmetry with mathematical predictability. The number 364 is an exact multiple of 7, so the calendar has exactly 52 weeks, each date falling on the same day of the week every year. Each quarter year follows this arrangement, and the year begins on Wednesday. For the authors of the Astronomical Book Jubilees, and many Essene texts found at Qumran, this made perfect sense because God created the luminaries on the fourth day (Gen 1:14–19):

Table 1.														
Day	**Months 1, 4, 7, 10**					**Months 2, 5, 8, 11**				**Months 3, 6, 9, 12**				
Wed	1	8	15	22	29	6	13	20	27	4	11	18	25	
Thurs	2	9	16	23	30	7	14	21	28	5	12	19	26	
Fri	3	10	17	24		1	8	15	22	29	6	13	20	27
Sat	4	11	18	25		2	9	16	23	30	7	14	21	28
Sun	5	12	19	26		3	10	17	24	1	8	15	22	29
Mon	6	13	20	27		4	11	18	25	2	9	16	23	30
Tues	7	14	21	28		5	12	19	26	3	10	17	24	31
Adapted from VanderKam and Flint, *The Meaning of the Dead Sea Scrolls* (2002), 258.														

In the many scrolls dealing with the calendar, the sun is central in formulating time. Knowing the correct calendar was of primary importance for the Essene (*Yahad*) movement. It ensured correct observance of the Jewish festivals, which were bound to the divinely mandated created order, and thus the accurate unfolding of God's plan. According to the *Damascus Document*:

> [God] instituted his Covenant with Israel forever, revealing to them things hidden, in which all Israel had gone wrong: His holy Sabbaths, his glorious festivals, his righteous laws, his reliable ways. The desires of his will, which Man should carry out and so have life in them, he opened up to them. (CD 3:13–16) (*The Dead Sea Scrolls: A New Translation*, 54)

The sectarian composition *Some of the Works of the Law* (4QMMT) most likely includes the calendrical text 4Q327 as section A. This gives dates on which Sabbaths and festivals fall, for example: "On the twenty-third of the month is a Sabbath. [On the] thir[tie]th [of the month is a Sabbath]" (1:4–8). For example, if the twenty-third of a month is a Sabbath (Saturday), it can only be month 2, 5, 8, or 11.

For the *Yahad* Essenes, this calendar was ideal since it was constructed and revealed by God. Yet it presented certain problems: Using the solar calendar to account for festivals that were traditionally celebrated by the lunar year would drift and not synchronize with it. To address this discrepancy, the authors of some texts developed a variety of intercalations.

Intercalations and *Mishmarot* (Priestly Courses). Calendrical texts used by the *Yahad* include the *Mishmarot* (loosely 4Q322–29), which means "Watches" or "Priestly Courses." These texts intercalate (insert the starting point) of 48 priestly cycles, based on 1 Chronicles 24:7–18. Following the traditional lunar calendar of 48 weeks, the 24 priestly divisions would each perform Temple service twice a year. This caused a surplus of four additional weeks in a solar year of 52 weeks—which was solved with an additional, rotating cycle for four of the 12 divisions each year. Some texts synchronize dates in the two calendars, and some add which priestly group would be on duty for those dates.

Mishmarot A (4Q320) gives a sequence of festivals and the priestly group in whose course each fell (frg. 4 iii.1–9). Since the Hebrew Bible also tells us when festivals were dated, and provides the list of priestly groups, the 364-day calendrical system in the *Mishmarot* becomes clear. This material is difficult to understand, and requires knowledge of the Jewish festivals. For example: *Mishmarot* A reads, "On the third day from the Sabbath (Tuesday) of the course of the sons of Maaziah is the Passover" (line 2). Maaziah is the 24th priestly group (1 Chron 24:18), and Passover falls on **1/14** (the fourteenth day of the first month, Exodus 12:6) and on the third day of this group's weekly course, which ran from **1/12 to 1/18**.

Using texts such as this and information found in the *Temple Scroll*, the full list of festivals in the *Yahad*'s calendar at Qumran is as follows (see VanderKam and Flint [2002], 259–60):

Passover	1/14
Unleavened Bread	1/15–21
Firstfruits (or Waving of the *Omer*)	1/26
Second Passover	2/14
Festival of Weeks	3/15 (50 days after the waving of the *omer*, as in *Jubilees*)
Festival of Wine	5/3 (50 days after the Festival of Weeks)
Festival of Oil	6/22 (50 days after the Festival of Wine)
Festival of Wood	6/23–30 (probably)
Day of Remembrance (or Trumpets)	7/1
Day of Atonement	7/10
Booths (or Tabernacles)	7/15–21

Two festivals celebrated by Jews today are not on the list. The first is Purim, which would fall on a Sabbath in the 364-day calendar (12/14, cf. Esth 9:21), something the *Yahad* would avoid, and is based on the book of Esther, which they did not accept. The second is Hanukkah, which celebrates the triumph of the Maccabees who were enemies of the *Yahad* Essenes. Three of their festivals not celebrated today are the Festivals of Wine and Oil—holidays of firstfruits whose dates were calculated like that of the Festival of Weeks (Lev 23:15–16)—and apparently the Festival of Wood. This festival may have been known to some early rabbis; see *Megillat Ta'anit* (a chronicle enumerating 35 eventful days), section V.

For the Essenes, God had revealed himself in creation, in which the heavenly luminaries operate in perfect harmony according to a system of divine mandated laws for the natural order. Moreover, a true understanding of these laws brought about the correct calculation of the calendar, seasons, and festivals.

3.2 Law for Humanity

The transcendent God also required that humanity operate according to a system of purposes or law, which occupied many of the *Yahad*'s writings. This was the law of Moses, which God revealed in ancient times and which people continued to study and interpret. Unlike the natural world that conforms to ordained laws, human beings often disobey the ones made for them (*1 Enoch* 2–5).

The *Yahad* Essenes followed the explanation found in *1 Enoch* that the abundance of evil in the world and human lives has supernatural origins. Sin does not go back to Adam, Eve, and their descendants, but to disobedient angels and their gigantic offspring who caused the great evil that made God send the flood. A few texts, however, echo the account about Adam, Eve, and human transgression in Genesis 3. One example is fr (4Q422) frg. 1 i.9–12.

Since the whole universe is involved in God's predetermined plan, there is a place for both good and evil. So two ways exist and are in constant warfare—a cosmic struggle of which human lives and actions are also part. God has also created two spirits or angels, under whose influence people live. This doctrine is found in several texts, but most fully in the *Rule of the Community* (3:13–4:26). One passage is directed to the *Maskil* (Instructor), so he can "teach all the Sons of Light about the character and fate of humankind" (3:13), and continues:

> All that is now and ever shall be originates with the God of knowledge. Before things come to be, he has ordered all their designs, [16]so that when they do come to exist . . . they fulfill their destiny, a destiny impossible to change. He controls [17]the laws governing all things, and he provides for all their pursuits.

> He created humankind to rule over [18]the world, appointing for them two spirits in which to walk until the time ordained for His visitation. These are the spirits [19]of truth and falsehood. Upright character and fate originate with the Habitation of Light; perverse ones with the Fountain of Darkness. [20]The authority of the Prince of Light extends to the governance of all righteous people; therefore, they walk in the paths of light. Correspondingly, the authority of the Angel [21]of Darkness embraces the governance of all wicked people, so they walk in paths of darkness. (1QS 3:15–21) (*The Dead Sea Scrolls: A New Translation*, 120)

So for the *Yahad*, all mankind is fatally predisposed to good or evil and subject to the influence of divine control in their day-to-day behavior. In line with God's transcendence and creative force, good and evil exist together as part of his plan for humanity according to his purposes. God has appointed angels to rule over humans, just as they govern the natural world. Although some Scriptures associate angels with nations (Deut 32:8–9; Dan 10:10–14), the notion of one spirit ruling the Sons of Light and another ruling the Sons of Darkness is not found in the Hebrew Bible.

3.3 The Community of the New (or Renewed) Covenant

The transcendent God entered into covenant with his people: with Abraham and his descendants, with Israel at Mount Sinai, and a renewed covenant with the remnant who returned from Babylon after the exile. The Essenes believed they were part of the remnant, the new Israel, with whom God made a new covenant.

Hymn 8 of the *Hodayot* affirms that the righteous are part of God's creation, but also "the wicked whom you created for the time of your wrath, and from the womb you set them apart for the day of slaughter" (1QH[a] 7:30). Because humans cannot sidestep God's transcendent power, it was critical for the Yahad to carry out the provisions of the covenant. As the ones who accurately understood the covenant, they enforced its laws, which were revealed in Scripture and in the inspired interpretation of Scripture. In the *Damascus Document*, the purpose of the covenant is explained historically, and revealed in a passage from Scripture (Num 21:18):

> But God called to mind the Covenant of the forefathers; and he raised up from Aaron insightful men and from Israel wise men and he taught them and they *dug the well*: "the well the princes *dug*, the *nobility of the people dug* it with *a Rod*" (CD 6:2–4). (*The Dead Sea Scrolls: A New Translation*, 56–57)

The divinely revealed interpretation follows. The *well* is the Law; its *diggers* are the repentant of Israel who went out from Judah and dwelt in the land of Damascus; the *Rod* is the Interpreter of the Law; and the *nobility of the people* are those who *dig the well* by living according to the rules made by the *Rod* during the era of wickedness, until the Teacher of Righteousness appears in the last days (CD 6:4–11). This explanation shows the importance of conformity to the Law for the *Yahad* Essenes: "without *these rules* they will obtain nothing" (6:10).

Every year, a ceremony of covenant renewal was enacted, and new members were welcomed at the Festival of Weeks (4Q266 frg. 11.17–18). According to the *Rule of the Community*, the Instructor was to induct all who volunteered to live by God's laws into the Covenant of Grace (1QS1:7–9). The ceremony was extensive (1:16–2:25), and opens:

> All who enter the *Yahad's* Rule shall be initiated into the Covenant before God, agreeing to act [17]according to all he has commanded and not to backslide because of any fear, terror, or persecution [18]that may occur during the time of Belial's dominion. While the initiates are being inducted, . . . the priests [19]and Levites shall continuously bless the God of deliverance and all his veritable deeds. All [20]the initiates into the Covenant shall continuously respond "Amen, amen." (1:16–20) (*The Dead Sea Scrolls: A New Translation*, 117)

Berakhot or Blessings (4Q286–90) apparently contains the liturgy for the annual covenant renewal ceremony.

An ideal community would thus be formed: "So together all will comprise a *Yahad* whose essence is truth, genuine humility, love of charity, and righteous intent, caring for one another after this fashion within the holy society, comrades in an eternal fellowship" (2:24–25). The *Rule* calls them "the Congregation" or "the Many," living in community, eating the pure meal together, praying and studying the Scriptures, with the Instructor as overseer, teacher, presider over meetings, assessor of new candidates, and zealous example of doing God's will.

4. Interpretation of Scripture

In order to meet the terms of the new (or renewed) covenant, the movement enforced its laws, which were revealed in Scripture and in the inspired interpretation of Scripture. For the authors and collectors of the sectarian scrolls, the meaning of Scripture (often called the law of Moses) was paramount, since the law derived from it was a critical component of their religion. However, God is transcendent and mysterious, so God's plan is not easily discerned from Scripture.

The Zadokite priests were its authoritative interpreters, and their teachings are found in many of the legal texts. The Essenes distinguished between revealed laws and laws they had learned through special interpretative techniques. The author of the *Damascus Document* writes:

> But when those of them who were left held firm to the commandments of God, he instituted his Covenant with Israel for ever, revealing to them things hidden, in which all Israel had gone wrong: His holy Sabbaths, his glorious festivals, his righteous laws, his reliable ways. The desires of his will, which Man should carry out and so have life in them, he opened up to them. So they *dug a well,* yielding much water. Those who reject this water he will not allow to live. (CD 3:12-17; cf. 6:11–7:6 and 15:7–10) (*The Dead Sea Scrolls: A New Translation,* 54)

The *Rule of the Community* (1QS) decrees that a person entering the community is to "take upon himself a binding oath to return to the Law of Moses, . . . to all that has been revealed from it to the Sons of Zadok and the majority of the men of their Covenant" (5:8–9; cf. 8:11–12). Thus it was necessary to uncover "hidden meanings" in the biblical text (5:10–12).

Thus God's laws are broken out of ignorance: God's purposes and plans are revealed in nature and in Scripture, but require special skill and insight to be understood. The community is assured this special knowledge through membership in the new covenant that was central to separation from other Jewish groups. In a later section, the *Rule* preserves a lengthy prayer that was to be uttered by the inspired Interpreter (1QS 10:5–11:22).

This Interpreter was the Teacher of Righteousness, whose teaching was urgently needed because the last days had arrived, when "those of Isra[el] will return [22]to the l[aw of Moses with all their heart] . . . But the wicked will incr[ease in wicked]ness (4QMMT C, 21–22). The Teacher's role in revealing prophetic secrets and God's hidden mysteries in Scripture is seen in the *Damascus Document:* "to guide them in the way of his heart. He taught to later generations what God did to the generation deserving wrath, a company of traitors" (CD 1:11–12). Later on, based on the success of the Teacher's divinely gifted insight, the Admonitions conclude:

> But all who hold fast to these rules, going out and coming in according to the Law, always obeying the Teacher and confessing to God . . . and who discipline themselves by the ancient laws by which the members of the *Yahad* were governed and listen attentively to the Teacher of Righteousness, not abandoning the correct laws when they hear them . . . They will prevail over all the inhabitants of the earth. Then God will make atonement for them and they will experience his deliverance because they have trusted in his holy name. (CD 20:27–34) (*The Dead Sea Scrolls: A New Translation,* 61–62)

Scripture and its interpretation were of fundamental importance for the Essene (*Yahad*) movement, as it was for all other Jewish groups. The number of biblical scrolls found at Qumran alone (about 250) shows that the community collected the Scriptures and took them very seriously. Their purpose was to discover, perform, and carry out the law of Moses, both the contents of the biblical Torah and other truths discerned by their leaders, thereby fulfilling the concealed purposes of God.

The Scriptures provided the framework or underlying source of expression for all the movement's beliefs and practices that feature in this chapter, whether about God, fate, the law for nature or humanity, the new covenant, experiencing God and the divine, or the consummation of history.

5. Experiencing God and the Divine

The *Yahad* Essenes believed they had received renewed revelations about God's will, and enjoyed a unique relationship with the heavenly realm. Did the Temple play a role in this, and how did the community worship God?

Most Jewish groups in antiquity had some sort of relationship with the Temple and its cult (rituals) in Jerusalem. A few seemed to reject it, such as the Jewish community who built the temple of Onias at Leontopolis in Egypt (Josephus, *Jewish War* 7.420–36). The *Psalms of Solomon* (composed in Palestine, mid-first century B.C.E.) also preserves a rather hostile view of the Temple (2:3–13): "The sons of Jerusalem defiled the sanctuary of the Lord, profaned the gifts of God with acts of lawlessness" (2:3) that included prostitution in its precincts. A similar perspective on the Temple is evident in Jesus' prediction in Mark 13:2 that "not one stone will be left here upon another; all will be thrown down."

The Dead Sea Scrolls include several texts that recognize the importance of the Temple, but there is also strong opposition to the Temple priests. Writers of the sectarian scrolls affirm both the Temple and the priesthood—not as they existed in the centuries just before and into the Common Era, but rather in an ideal sense. The *Temple Scroll* (most likely not compiled by the Essenes, but reflecting their ideology) presents an idealized Temple in Jerusalem that God revealed to Moses and will establish "for everlasting in fulfillment of the covenant [he] made with Jacob at Bethel" (11QT^a 29:10). The movement saw themselves as committed to pure Temple religion and to Israel's future that would be realized only in a restoration of the Jerusalem Temple.

As they awaited this restoration, the *Yahad* replaced the Temple of their day and its rituals with parallel ones. The priests at Qumran presided over meals, offered blessings, made pronouncements, and interpreted and taught the Torah. The *Rule of the Community* tells us:

> [8] [Every initiate] shall take upon himself a binding oath to return to the Law of Moses (according to all that God commanded) with all [9] his heart and with all his mind, to all that has been revealed from it to the Sons of Zadok—priests and preservers of the Covenant, seekers of his will—and the majority of the men of their Covenant. (1QS 5:8–9) (*The Dead Sea Scrolls: A New Translation*, 123)

The community also practiced an alternative form of worship in the "celestial temple" of heaven. The *Songs of the Sabbath Sacrifice* (4Q400–407, 11Q17) are Sabbath rituals for a group who believed angels were joining them in worship. Since the heavenly adoration took place according to the same calendar followed by the *Yahad*, they were worshiping God on earth in tandem with his angels.

The awe that these songs evoke is compelling. Rather than using narrative, the author presents the vision directly, inviting those who are reciting the text to experience something similar. For a congregation singing them in unison, a mystical experience would ensue, indeed a sense of union with the angels and their heavenly worship. One copy of the *Songs* (4Q405) depicts in glorious detail what takes place in the heavens:

> The [Cheru]bim fall before him and bless him; as they arise, the quiet voice of God [is heard], followed by a tumult of joyous praise. As they unfold their wings, God's q[uiet] voice is heard again. The Cherubim bless the image of the chariot-throne that appears above the firmament, [then] they joyously acclaim the [splend]or of the luminous firmament that spreads beneath his glorious seat. (Frgs. 20 ii–22.7–9) (*The Dead Sea Scrolls: A New Translation*, 473)

The *Yahad* did not participate in the sacrifices carried out at the Jerusalem Temple, which they considered corrupt and invalid, but viewed their righteous leaders as a temple, a Holy of Holies, and an atonement for sin and the land, and thus as an effective replacement:

> ¹ In the party of the *Yahad* there shall be twelve laymen and three priests who are blameless in the light of all that has been revealed from the whole ² Law, so as to work truth, righteousness, justice, lovingkindness, and humility, one with another. ³ They are to preserve faith in the land with self-control and a broken spirit, ***atoning for sin*** by working justice and suffering affliction. ⁴ . . . When such men as these come to be in Israel, ⁵ then shall the party of the *Yahad* truly be established, an "eternal planting" (*Jubilees* 16:26) a temple for Israel, and—a mystery!—a Holy ⁶ of Holies for Aaron; true witnesses to justice, chosen by God's will ***to atone for the land*** and to recompense the wicked their due. (1QS 8:1–6) (*The Dead Sea Scrolls: A New Translation*, 128–29)

Organized in many ways like Israel at Mount Sinai and as recipients of renewed revelation concerning God's will, the Yahad Essenes believed they enjoyed a unique fellowship with the heavenly realm. Just as the priestly courses were in harmony with the circuits of the celestial luminaries, they perceived themselves to be unified with the angels. In **Hymn 14** of the *Thanksgiving Hymns*, the poet writes:

> ²² The perverse spirit you have cleansed from great transgression, that he might take his stand with ²³ the host of the holy ones, and enter together (or in the *Yahad*) with the congregation of the sons of heaven. And for man, you have allotted an eternal destiny with the spirits ²⁴ of knowledge, to praise your name together. . . . (1QHᵃ 11:22–24) (*The Dead Sea Scrolls: A New Translation*, 182)

In **Hymn 19** he adds: "For you have brought [your] t[ruth and g]lory ¹⁶to all the men of your council, in the lot together with the angels of the presence" (14:15–16; cf. 19:13–15). Also, as we saw in chapter 9.6.1, the *War Scroll* pictures the Sons of Light fighting together with the angels against the Sons of Darkness and Belial's hosts: "Any ⁶man who is not ritually clean with respect to his genitals on the day of battle shall not go down with them into battle, for holy angels are present with their army" (7:5–6; cf. 9:14–16; 12:1–9; and *Priestly Blessings for the Last Days* [3:25–26; 4:23–26]).

6. The End of Days and the Messiahs

6.1 The Last Days

During the Second Temple period, long and difficult times of foreign occupation fostered a growing sense among many Jews that God's plan for Israel had not been fully realized and that a time was coming in which God would finally vindicate his people. This preoccupation with the end times is highlighted in Daniel's Vision of the Four Beasts:

> ¹³ As I watched in the night visions, I saw one like the son of man coming with the clouds of heaven. And he came to the Ancient One and was presented before him. ¹⁴ To him was given dominion and glory and kingship, that all peoples, nations, and languages should serve him. His dominion is an everlasting dominion that will not pass away, and his kingship is one that will never be destroyed. (Dan 7:13–14)

The Essene movement's concept of God (the divine Architect) required that as the natural order and human history had proceeded according to God's predetermined pattern, so would the future. The *Pesher Habakkuk* reads: "All the times fixed by God will come about in due course, just as he ordained that they should by his inscrutable insight" (7:13–14).

They were living in the end of days or last days, a period right before the decisive and final visitation. The *Damascus Document* (CD:1:5–11) places the movement's beginning at 390 years after the exile began (587 B.C.E.), that is, about 197. Moreover, their leader, the Teacher of Righteousness, appeared on the scene 20 years later, that is, about 177. (It is difficult to say whether the numbers are meant to be literal or not.)

In a revised edition, the *Damascus Document* predicts the last days will begin 40 years "from the day the Beloved Teacher passed away," in the next generation (CD 20:13–15). However, *Pesher Habakkuk* tells us the last days will be longer than the prophets anticipated, since God's revelations are truly mysterious (1QpHab 7:7–8). The author then quotes Habakkuk 2:3, and interprets it as encouraging the *Yahad* to persevere:

> ⁹ "*If it tarries, be patient, it will surely come true and not* ¹⁰ *be delayed*" (Habakkuk 2:3b). This refers to those loyal ones, ³ obedient to the law, whose hands will not cease from loyal service even when the Last Days seems long to them, . . . (1QpHab 7:9–12) (*The Dead Sea Scrolls: A New Translation*, 84)

As mentioned, the *Yahad* believed their prayers, liturgy, and actions filled the vacuum created by lack of access to the Jerusalem Temple. They practiced an alternative form of worship in the "celestial temple," joined by angels as they rehearsed the *Songs of the Sabbath Sacrifice*. According to *Rule of the Community*, they did not participate in the sacrifices carried out at the Temple, but their leaders and membership were "a temple for Israel," a "Holy of Holies for Aaron," and "an acceptable sacrifice, atoning for the land" (1QS 8:5–6, 10).

By divine mandate, the world was about to experience a cataclysmic upheaval, culminating in God's final vindication of Israel and vengeance heaped on their enemies. The *War Rule* (or *War Scroll*) gives prophetic narration of the final, cosmic war to take place between God and the Sons of Light against Belial and the Sons of Darkness, resulting in victory and God's supremacy:

> [1] For it is a time of distress for Isra[el, an appoin]tment for battle against all the nations. The purpose of God is eternal redemption, [2] but annihilation for all nations of wickedness. All those pr[epared] for battle shall set out and camp opposite the king of the Kittim and all the forces [3] of Belial that are assembled with him for a day [of vengeance] by the sword of God. (1QM 15:1–3) (*The Dead Sea Scrolls: A New Translation*, 161)

6.2 The Messiahs

(a) Two (or Three) Messiahs

As scholars studied the scrolls, especially the sectarian ones, many were interested to know what the Essene (*Yahad*) movement expected concerning the Messiah. In a nutshell, they believed that in the last days, God would send the Prophet, the priestly Messiah, and the Messiah of Israel (or, of David). Together with the angels and the Sons of Light, these would triumph over Belial, his spirits, and the Sons of Darkness in the final war and be victorious.

The *Damascus Document* appears to say that the movement expected only one Messiah: "This is the rule for those who live in [23] camps, who live by these rules in the era of wickedness, until the appearance of the Messiah of Aaron [13:1] and of Israel" (CD 12:22–13:1; also 14:18–19; 19:10–11; 19:33–20:1). The singular "Messiah" is used, but some scholars believe it does double duty: Messiahs of (Aaron and Israel).

However, the *Rule of the Congregation* (1Q28a) speaks of two figures to come. At the eschatological banquet the Priest enters first, and later the Messiah of Israel (col. 2:11–15).

The *Rule of the Community* goes further still: "They will govern themselves using the original precepts by which the men of the *Yahad* began to be instructed, [11] doing so until there come *the Prophet* and *the Messiahs of Aaron and Israel*" (1QS 9:10–11). The plural "Messiahs" makes it clear that the *Yahad* expected a priestly Messiah of Aaron and a nonpriestly one of Israel. The Prophet is not easy to identify. As the "Prophet like Moses" whom the Lord will raise up (Deut 18:15), he seems to be another messianic figure, and may well be the Teacher of Righteousness.

What emerges, then, is two Messiahs (even three if the Prophet is included). The two main ones may be the two "sons of fresh oil who stand before the Lord" (Zech 4:14).

(b) The Messiah of Israel (or, of David) and the Priestly Messiah

The Messiah of Israel has several more names. Some texts denote a royal Messiah: the Shoot of David, the Branch of David, and the Booth of David. The *Florilegium* (4Q174) interprets the promise of a descendant of David who will have an eternal throne (2 Sam 7:11–14) as the Shoot of David and Branch of David, and the fallen booth of David in Amos 9:11 (NRSV) as "the fallen *Booth of* [13] *David*, [w]hom [God] will raise up to deliver Israel" (col. 3:11–13). In *A Commentary on Genesis* (4Q252), a prophecy about Judah (Genesis 49:10) is interpreted as fulfilled in the Branch of David as Messiah:

> [1] [. . .] "*a ruler shall [no]t depart from the tribe of Judah*" while Israel has dominion. [2] [And] the one who sits on the throne of David [shall never] be cut off, because the "*ruler's scepter*" is the covenant of the kingdom, [3] [and the thous]ands of Israel are "*the feet*," until the *Righteous Messiah, the Branch of David*, has come. (4Q252 5:1–3) (*The Dead Sea Scrolls: A New Translation*, 355)

Another name for this Messiah is the Prince (or Leader) of the Congregation. In the *Rule of Blessings*, the final blessing (5:20–29) is for him, and opens with "(Words of blessing) belonging to the Instructor, by which to bless the Prince of the Congregation" (5:20). Both this title and the Branch of David are used for him in the *Rule of War* (4Q285) frg. 7.3–4.

As the Son of David, the great warrior-king, this is also the conquering Messiah, who will defeat Israel's enemies and bring justice. For example, in the *Damascus Document*, part of Balaam's prophecy ("a Star will come out of Jacob, and a Scepter will rise out of Israel; he will crush . . . the territory of all the Shethites") is interpreted:

> [18] "*The Star*" is the *Interpreter of the Law* [19] who comes to Damascus, as it is written (Num 24:17), "*A Star has left Jacob, a Scepter has risen* [20] *from Israel*." The latter is the *Prince of the whole Congregation*; when he appears, "*he will shatter* [21] *all the sons of Sheth*." (CD 7:18–21) (Adapted from *The Dead Sea Scrolls: A New Translation*, 58)

This conquering Messiah is not prominent in the *War Rule*, most likely due to the holy nature of the battles and the eminence of the Chief Priest (the priestly Messiah) and other priests, yet his role may be discerned. In column 11, more of Balaam's prophecy is quoted (Num 24:17, 19, 18ac) and interpreted: "By the hand of your anointed ones [8] . . . you have told us about the ti[mes] of the wars of your hands in order that you may glorify yourself among our enemies, to bring down the hordes of Belial" (1QM 11:7–8).

The *Damascus Document* also tells us that with this Messiah's coming, the New Covenanters will escape punishment, but the wicked will be put to the sword:

> [9] "*Then I will turn my power against the little ones*" (Zech 13:7). But those who give heed to God are "*the poor of the flock*" (Zech 11:7): [10] they will escape in the time of punishment, but all the rest will be handed over to the sword *when the Messiah of* [11] *Aaron and of Israel* comes, . . . (CD 19:9–11) (*The Dead Sea Scrolls: A New Translation*, 59)

The previous quotation reminds us that in many passages the *Messiah of Israel* comes alongside the *priestly Messiah*. With their arrival, sin will be atoned for:

> [18] . . . And this is the exposition of the regulations by which [they shall be governed [19] until the appearance of the *Messi]ah of Aaron and of Israel*, so that their iniquity may be atoned for. [Cereal offering and sin offering . . .] the appearance of the *Messi]ah of Aaron and of Israel*, so that their iniquity may be atoned for. (CD 14:18–19) (*The Dead Sea Scrolls: A New Translation*, 76)

It is difficult to find details of the priestly Messiah both because some key texts are very fragmentary and because his functions are more straightforward: to carry out priestly duties. Besides helping bring atonement for sin, he will preside at the eschatological banquet, and take precedence over the Messiah of Israel. In a passage from the *Rule of the Congregation*, the Priest takes precedence at the banquet: "None [may re]ach for the first portion of the bread or [the wine] before *the Priest*," who will bless the bread and the wine, and "afterward the *Messiah of Israel* will reach for the bread" (1Q28a 17:18–21).

(c) The Interpreter

A third figure appears in some texts and also seems to be messianic. The *Rule of the Community* includes a lengthy prayer that was to be uttered by the divinely inspired Interpreter (1QS 11:5–9). This was the Teacher of Righteousness, whose teaching was urgently needed because the *last days* had arrived. His coming is linked with the royal Messiah (the Branch of David) in the *Florilegium* (4Q174): "I will be a Father to him, and he will be my Son" (2 Sam 7:11, 12–14). This passage refers to the Shoot of David, who is to arise with [12] the *Interpreter of the Law*, and who will [arise] in Zi[on in the La]st Days" (4Q174 3:11–12).

(d) A Prophetic Messiah?

The *Messianic Apocalypse* (4Q521) features one Messiah ("For the hea]vens and the earth will listen to his Messiah," col. 2:1) and "the holy ones" (2:2), and lists the wondrous activities that will take place when he comes. For example: "setting captives free, opening the eyes of the blind, lifting up those who are op[ressed]" (line 8) and "he will make the dead live, he will bring good news to the poor" (line 12).

While it seems that God (not the Messiah) here performs these mighty acts, this text nevertheless points to a prophetic Messiah or an anointed Prophet of the last days, perhaps Elijah. (To this day, during the Passover meal Jews set aside a cup for the prophet Elijah, who will herald the coming of the Messiah.)

6.3 After the End

The sectarian scrolls are not always strightforward with respect to the afterlife, and what will happen after the Messiahs come and the Sons of Light are victorious over the Sons of Darkness.

(a) Do Some Scrolls Speak of Resurrection from Death?

What of members who had died, such as those lying in the cemeteries near Qumran? Physical resurrection seems clear in a few other apocalyptic texts. One is Daniel 12:2: "Many of those who sleep in the dust of the earth will awake, some to everlasting life, and some to shame and everlasting contempt."

For some scholars, there is no firm evidence among the Qumran scrolls, since main sectarian texts such as the *Damascus Document, Rule of the Community, War Rule,* and *Pesharim* do not feature resurrection, but communion with angels and the realization of everlasting life in the context of pure worship.

However, a few texts do seem to speak of physical resurrection. The *Messianic Apocalypse* (4Q521) says when this prophetic Messiah comes (the Lord) "will make the dead live" (frgs. 7+5ii.8). Some believe that general resurrection is not meant here, but "resuscitation": miracles of the kind performed by Elijah and Elisha in bringing back to life some who had just died. Yet a general resurrection appears in another section on final judgment:

> ¹ [. . .] see all t[hat the Lord has made, ² the eart]h and all that is on it, the seas [and all ³ that is in them], and every lake and stream. ⁴ [. . . al]l [of you] who have done good before the Lor[d ⁵ bless and no]t as those who curse. They shall b[e] destined to die, [when] ⁶ ***the Reviver [rai]ses the dead*** of his people. (4Q521 frgs. 7+5ii.1–6) (*The Dead Sea Scrolls: A New Translation,* 531)

Pseudo-Ezekiel (4Q385) interprets the prophet's vision of the "valley of dry bones" (7:1–14) into a hope for resurrection. While Ezekiel's vision could denote re-creation as a symbol for national restoration, *Pseudo-Ezekiel* points to a literal physical resurrection:

> ⁵ [And he said], "Son of man, prophesy over these bones, and say, 'Come together, bone to its bone and joint ⁶ [to its joint.' "And it wa]s s[o]. And he said a second time, "Prophesy, and let sinews come upon them and let skin cover ⁷ [them." And it was so]. And he s[ai]d, "Again prophesy to the four winds of the heavens, and let them blow ⁸ [upon the slain." And it was so]. And a great many people [revi]ved (Ezek 37:4–10). And they blessed the LORD of hosts wh[o ⁹ had revived them]. (frg. 1 ii.5–9) (*The Dead Sea Scrolls: A New Translation,* 448)

Finally, the wisdom text *Instruction* (here 4Q418) may also allude to resurrection. Note lines 7–8, which indicate that those who seek the truth will awaken (or, be awakened) from the dead to judge the children of evil at the end of the age:

> ⁶ [By the power of G]od you were created; and you will return to eternal destruction, for [. . .] your sin [. . .⁷ . . .] In darkness they will wail for your judgment. But that which exists forever, those who seek truth, ***will awaken to give judgment*** [on you. And then] ⁸ they will destroy those who are foolish of heart, and the children of evil will no longer exist, and all who cling to wickedness will be bewildered. (4Q418 frg. 69 ii lines 4–8)(Adapted from *The Dead Sea Scrolls: A New Translation,* 489–90)

So did the Essene (*Yahad*) movement believe in resurrection? Most scholars agree that *Pseudo-Ezekiel* and *Instruction* are not sectarian works, and the same could be true of the *Messianic Apocalypse*. Yet, together with Daniel and the Book of Watchers (*1 Enoch* 1–36), they affirm that resurrection was known to the *Yahad* and was positively received by them. Perhaps resurrection was a hope from other Jewish groups that they were gradually assimilating into their ideology.

In the movement's understanding of the end times, the righteous would be risen from death after the Davidic and priestly Messiahs (and evidently a prophetic Messiah) arrived, the final war was won, and the cataclysmic destruction took place.

(b) Full Communion, a New Temple, a New Jerusalem

The Essene (*Yahad*) movement believed that the communion they enjoyed with God and the angels in the last days would continue and be fully realized after the end. They would return to a purified and divinely laid out new Jerusalem and to a new Temple (which God would create), where the proper sacrifices and true festivals would be carried out, and all would be in accordance with God's own 364-day calendar.

12

The New Testament and the Dead Sea Scrolls

Introduction

Exploring the relationship between the scrolls, the Gospels, and other New Testament books presents several challenges, and has had a checkered history among scholars. Most agree that the Qumran scrolls are significant for understanding Christian origins. The location where they were found (just over 20 miles from Jerusalem), their datings (before 250 B.C.E. to 68 C.E.), and the languages they were written in (Hebrew, Aramaic, Greek) make these texts a rich resource for exploring most of the New Testament writings.

Soon after the first scrolls were discovered, similarities emerged between some writings of the Essene movement and some New Testament writings. For example, both collections feature a central figure (Jesus, the Teacher of Righteousness) and a distinctive group (the followers of Jesus, the *Yahad*) who believed they were living in the end times, and that the Messiah (or Messiahs) had arrived or was about to do so. Both groups were also led and organized in a rather similar way (the early church, Essene communities).

Such common themes led a few scholars to regard the Qumran scrolls as Christian texts, or that they contain specific references and new revelations about Jesus or his followers, or even that Jesus and the early church were Essenes. These views were fueled by earlier speculations, since the Essenes and their main ideas were known from Josephus, Philo, and Pliny the Elder.

Most scholars view the scrolls as not directly related to Jesus and early Christianity, but still illuminating several aspects of his life and teaching, and other events and passages in the New Testament. Numerous key scrolls:

- Provide helpful information about Jewish society, groups, practices, and beliefs at the time.

- Show that many aspects of the gospel message are indebted to Israelite religion.

- Increase our knowledge about early Judaism.

- Affirm several differences between the message of Jesus and those of other Jewish groups.

- Contain ideas or wording similar to that found in certain New Testament passages.

While there are no New Testament writings among the Dead Sea Scrolls, the *Yahad* Essenes and the writings they hid in the caves are very significant for understanding many New Testament passages, Jesus, and the early church.

1. The Scrolls and Early Christian Writings: New Testament Writings at Qumran?

The scrolls found at Qumran were copied from before 250 B.C.E. to 68 C.E. In 1972 Spanish scholar José O'Callaghan announced he had identified several portions of New Testament documents in Cave 7, the only one containing scrolls written on papyrus and in Greek. These included fragments of Mark's Gospel, Acts, two of Paul's Epistles, James, and 2 Peter, with all but one written before 70 C.E. (For example: 7Q5 preserves text from Mark 6:52–53, and was copied about 50 C.E.)

If correct, O'Callaghan's identifications would pose major challenges for scholars of early Judaism and the New Testament. First, they would mean that early Christians had contact with the Yahad at Qumran, or at least hid their documents in Cave 7. Second, it challenges the consensus among scholars that most of the books he mentioned were written some or many decades after 70 (although Paul's letters were written before his death in about 67 and Mark's Gospel probably before the fall of Jerusalem in 70). Almost all scholars now reject O'Callaghan's identifications of New Testament texts among the Cave 7 scrolls:

- The physical evidence is too meager, the largest piece (7Q4.2), measuring only 2.7 by 1.3 inches, and several more very tiny with just a few letters.

- Scroll editors had assigned early dates to several scrolls: 7Q1, 7Q2 and 7Q4 at about 100 B.C.E.; and 7Q5 at 50 B.C.E. to 50 C.E. In order to find connections with New Testament writings, O'Callaghan had to date almost all his pieces to the mid-first century C.E.

- His claim that 7Q5 contains text from Mark 6:52–53 (following Jesus walking on the water) aligns only if "to [the] land" is omitted in verse 53: "And when they had crossed over, they came *to* [*the*] *land at* Gennesaret." This variant reading is not supported by any significant New Testament manuscript.

Identifying the Greek scrolls from Cave 7 has proved elusive. Two were matched early on: 7Q1 (papLXXExod) with text from Exodus (28:4–7), and 7Q2 (papEpJer gr) from the *Letter of Jeremiah* (vv. 43–44). Most of the others likely also preserve text from the Greek Bible.

Some scholars view a group of fragments as from the Epistle of Enoch (*1 Enoch* 91–108), in a section on the "two ways of the righteous and the sinner"—*1 Enoch* 98:11 or 105:1 (in 7Q4.2); 100:12 (7Q11); 103:3–8 (7Q4.1; 7Q8; and 7Q12); 103:12 (7Q14); and 103:15 (7Q13). However, placing certain pieces together produces text that does not agree with previously known versions of *1 Enoch*. For example, 103:3–4 in 7Q4.1 and 7Q8 requires a shorter text. So the identification of passages from *1 Enoch* among the Cave 7 scrolls is possible, but not assured. If some fragments do preserve text from this book, they show that a Greek copy existed at Qumran.

2. Jesus and the Dead Sea Scrolls (the Gospels and the Scrolls)

2.1 Introductory Comment

A great deal may be said on this topic, but I will briefly survey attempts to read the scrolls as referring to the historical Jesus, or as containing new revelations about him (2.2). I then identify (with a list of relevant texts) nine issues for studying messianism and Jesus' life and teaching (2.3). Two more are then discussed in greater detail (2.4).

2.2 On Jesus, the Essenes, and the Sectarian Scrolls: From Karl Bahrdt to Barbara Thiering

Almost two centuries before the scrolls were discovered, several alleged links were identified between the ancient Essenes and Jesus. For example, Karl Bahrdt proposed (1780s) that Jesus was a "secret agent" of the Essenes, who counterfeited his death, and Ernest Renan wrote (1863) that Jesus had been trained by the Essenes. Speculation intensified after the first scrolls were found in late 1946 or early 1947. Most scholars recognized that these ancient documents must have some bearings on our understanding of Jesus, the Gospels, and other New Testament books. Real similarities were to emerge. In 1950, French scholar André Dupont-Sommer pointed to several similarities between Jesus ("the Galilean Master") and the Teacher of Righteousness:

> Everything in the Jewish New Covenant heralds and prepares the way for the Christian New Covenant. The Galilean Master, as He is presented in the writings of the New Testament, appears in many respects as an astonishing reincarnation of the Master of Justice [*that is, the Teacher of Righteousness*]. . . . Like him, He prescribed the observance of the Law of Moses, the whole Law, but the Law finished and perfected, thanks to His own revelations. Like him He was the Elect and the Messiah of God, the Messiah redeemer of the world. Like him He was the object of the hostility of the priests, the party of the Sadducees. Like him He was condemned and put to death. Like him He pronounced judgement on Jerusalem, which was taken and destroyed by the Romans for having put Him to death. Like him, at the end of time He will be the supreme judge. Like him He founded a Church whose adherents fervently awaited is glorious return. (Dupont-Sommer, *The Dead Sea Scrolls: A Preliminary Survey*, 99)

Dupont-Sommer did not identify Jesus with the Teacher, who preceded him, but several writers were not as careful. These include journalist Edmund Wilson, who reported (1969) that Jesus had spent his childhood years among the Essenes.

In more recent times, some scholars have questioned the traditional datings of the Qumran scrolls (before 250 B.C.E. to 68 C.E.) in favor of later ones that better fit their views on Christian origins. In *James the Brother of Jesus* (1997), Robert Eisenman places key texts in the Herodian era (about 30 B.C.E. to 70 C.E.) and beyond, which means the writers were opposing the corrupt Herodian priesthood. He also sees parallels between the sectarian scrolls and New Testament figures (the Teacher of Righteousness as Jesus' brother James; the Wicked Priest as the high priest Ananus, who executed James; the Man of the Lie as Paul).

For Eisenman, the *Habakkuk Commentary* was written later in the movement's history, witnessed the fall of the Temple in the year 70, and is Jamesian as opposed to Pauline. That is, the pesher is directed to Jews (the House of Judah), and then only to Torah-doing Jews. For him, Habakkuk 2:4 ("the righteous will live by his faith") does not apply to non-Torah-doing Jews and certainly not to non-Torah-doing Gentiles. Thus Paul's claims that it denotes salvation through faith (Rom 1:17) and justification through faith in Christ (Gal 3:11) would be incorrect.

Barbara Thiering (1992) understands the Gospels as coded Essene documents, to be read on two levels: the surface level "for babes in Christ," and a deeper level to be understood by her "pesher technique." Just as the *Pesharim* explain the true meaning of biblical passages, Thiering regards this technique as essential for unlocking the meaning of the Gospels, thus revealing events that actually took place. For her, the New Testament was written in a cryptic code, deliberately concealing historical events and persons.

Thiering then uncovers the "real identity" of the main characters in the Gospels: John the Baptist as the Teacher of Righteousness; Jesus of Nazareth as his opponent the Wicked Priest (or the Man of the Lie). The Essene group split into two factions, the first led by John (the Teacher) and the second by Jesus (the Wicked Priest). This pesher technique extends to place-names in the Gospels: Jerusalem (almost always Qumran), and the Sea of Galilee (the Dead Sea). Thiering also places much of Jesus' activity near Qumran, and reconstructs his life in detail: Jesus married Mary Magdalene twice; he was crucified near the Qumran complex but did not die; his unconscious body was placed in Cave 8; and he lived out his days in Rome as an old man.

These theories have not found support among scholars of the Dead Sea Scrolls.

2.3 John Allegro, the Qumran Scrolls, and the "Jesus Myth"

John Marco Allegro of Manchester University was one of the original editors of the Dead Sea Scrolls. Several of his contributions were significant and deserve recognition:

- Bringing the *Copper Scroll* to the university, where it was successfully opened.

- Understanding the importance of a photographic record of the scrolls before they deteriorated further and making hundreds of early photographs that are still treasured by scholars.

- Believing that the scrolls matter not to just academics but also to the wider public, and so presenting many illustrated lectures on these documents and the Qumran site.

- Realizing that many key scrolls are very important for understanding Christian origins.

Yet criticisms have been leveled against Allegro for views that became ever more radical, as he claimed to find direct connections between Jesus, the Essenes, various scrolls, and the Qumran site. In 1956, he announced a new scroll (the *Commentary on Nahum*) that says the Wicked Priest had crucified the Seekers of Slippery Answers and the Teacher of Righteousness, who would rise again. For Allegro, the Qumranites worshiped a crucified Messiah, who would return in glory. In fact, this pesher says (col. 1:4–8) that the Angry Lion (the Judean king Alexander Jannaeus, 103–76 B.C.E.) crucified the Seekers of Slippery Answers (about 800 Pharisees). No mention is made of the Wicked Priest or the Teacher of Righteousness.

In *The Sacred Mushroom and the Cross* (1970), Allegro wrote that early Christianity was a fertility cult that practiced orgies and used a hallucinogenic mushroom, and that Jesus never really existed but was invented by early Christians under the influence of this drug. Fourteen prominent British scholars repudiated the book, and the publisher apologized for issuing it. Allegro's ideas on Jesus, early Christianity, and the scrolls are most fully articulated in *The Dead Sea Scrolls and the Christian Myth* (1979). Some highlights:

- The Gospel writers took symbolic narratives found in many scrolls as literal truth.

- What Allegro termed *Gnostic Christianity* arose from the Essene movement.

- There was no historical person named Jesus Christ in first-century Palestine.

- The Jesus of the Gospels is a later adaptation of the Teacher of Righteousness.

Such sensational ideas—often claiming that the church or scholars have suppressed many scrolls because their contents pose a threat to traditional beliefs about Jesus—live on in several books and even movies. For example: Michael Baigent and Richard Leigh's *Holy Blood, Holy Grail* (1982), and Dan Brown's *The Da Vinci Code* (2003). For Allegro's 1988 obituary in London's *Daily Telegraph*, editor Hugh Massingberd famously described him as the "Liberace of biblical scholarship."

2.4 Key Scrolls on Nine Issues for Studying Messianism and Jesus' Life and Teaching

(a) A Text Related to John the Baptist, Baptism, or the Forgiveness of Sins

Baptism or Ritual Washing and the Forgiveness of Sins. Gospels: Mark 1:4; 10:38, 39; 11:30; Matthew 3:7; 21:25; Luke 3:3; 7:29; 12:50; 20:4. Scrolls: *Rule of the Community* (1QS) cols. 2:25–3:9.

(b) Four Topics Related to Practice, Teaching, or the Holy Spirit

- **Rebuking a Fellow Member of the Community.** Gospels: Matthew 18:15–17; Luke 17:3–4. Scrolls: *Rule of the Community* (1QS) 5:24–6:1; *Damascus Document* (CD) 7:2–3; 9:2–8; and *Rebukes by the Overseer* (4Q77) frg. 2 i.1–10.

- **A List of Beatitudes and Their Structure.** Gospels: Matthew 5:1–12; Luke 6:20–23. Scrolls: *Beatitudes* (4Q525) frgs. 1, 2 ii and 3.

- **A Dispute Concerning the Sabbath.** Gospels: Mark 2:23–3:5; Matthew 12:1–12; Luke 6:1–11; 13:10–16; cf. John 5:16, 18. Scrolls: CD 10:15–11:18, esp. 11:12–14; also 11:10, 16; *Miscellaneous Rules* (4Q265) frgs. 6.1–7.10.

- **Holy Spirit.** Gospels: Mark 1:8; Matthew 3:11; 12:31–32; 28:19; Luke 4:1; 11:13; 12:12; John 3:34; 14:26; 20:22. Scrolls: *Damascus Document* (CD) 2:12, (4Q266) frg. 2ii.12; 1QS 3:7; 8:15–16; 9:4; *Hodayot* (1QH^a) 4:38; 6:24; 8:20, 25, 30; 15:9; 17:32; 20:14–15; 23:29, 33; *Commentary on Psalms^a* (4Q171) frgs. 3–10iv line 25; *Aramaic Levi* (4Q213a) frg. 1.14; *Berakhot* (4Q287) frg. 10.13; *A Paraphrase of Genesis and Exodus* (4Q422) 1:7; *Incantation* (4Q444) frgs. 1–4i + 5 line 1.

(c) Four Topics Related to Jesus, His Titles, and Messianism

- **"Son of God" and "Son of the Most High" as messianic titles.** Gospels: Mark 14:61; Matthew 4:3–6; 26:63; Luke 1:26–38; 4:3–9; 22:70; cf. John 1:34, 49; 11:27; 20:31. Scrolls: *Apocryphon of Daniel* (4Q246) 1:9–2:9.

- **"Hanging on a Tree" and Crucifixion.** Gospels: Mark 15:24–25; Matthew 27:22–36; Luke 23:33; John 19:18–23. Also Deuteronomy 21:23 and Galatians 3:12–13. Scrolls: *Pesher on Nahum* (4Q169) frgs. 3–4 I lines 6–9; *Temple Scroll* (11Q19) 64:7–13.

- **A Dying or Conquering Messiah?** (The consensus is on a conquering Messiah.) Gospels: Matthew 16:15–21; Luke 24:25–26, 46; cf. Acts 2:21–36; 8:26–40. Scrolls: *Book of War* (4Q285) frg. 7.1–6.

- **The Messianic Banquet.** Gospels: Mark 14:25; Matthew 26:29; Luke 22:16, 18, 30. Also Hebrews 7:2–10. Scrolls: *Rule of the Congregation* (1Q28a) 2:11–21.

2.5 Two More Issues in Greater Detail

(a) A Shared Use of Isaiah 40:3 by John the Baptist and the *Yahad* Essenes

The significance of John the Baptist's ministry through the words of Isaiah 40:3 is expressed in all four Gospels (Mark 1:3; Matt 3:3; Luke 3:4; cf. John 1:23):

As it is written in the prophet Isaiah, "See, I am sending my messenger ahead of you, who will prepare your way; the voice of one crying out in the wilderness: 'Prepare the way of the Lord, make his paths straight.'" (Mark 1:2–3 NRSV)

The *Yahad* Essenes used the same passage from Isaiah in the *Rule of the Community* (1QS) to explain their presence in the wilderness:

> [12]. . . And when these have become a community in Israel [13] according to these rules, they will be separated from the dwelling-place of perverse men to go to the wilderness, in order to prepare there the way of him, [14] just as it is written: "***In the wilderness prepare the way of the LORD, make straight in the desert a highway for our God***" (Isaiah 40:3). [15] This is the expounding of the Law wh[i]ch (God) commanded by the hand of Moses, in order to act according to all that has been revealed in every each age, [16] and according to what the prophets have revealed by his holy spirit. (1QS 8:12–16) (Flint, "Jesus and the Scrolls," 117)

In the Gospels, prophecy is fulfilled in John's role as God's messenger in the wilderness. The author of the *Rule* follows Isaiah more closely by asserting it is only in the wilderness that the Yahad can prepare for the Lord's coming through study of the Torah. Nevertheless, the shared use of Isaiah 40:3 is important with respect to Christian origins by proving that at least one other early Jewish group associated this passage with the Messiah's coming.

(b) Jesus as Royal Messiah and Prophetic Messiah

Royal Messiah: At the beginning of the Common Era, Jewish expectations concerning the end times and the Messiah were complex. According to various Gospel texts, many expected the return of Elijah (Mal 4:5–6; cf. Mark 6:15; 8:28; 9:4–5, 11–13; Matt 11:14; Luke 1:17), or a prophet like Moses (Deut 18:15–19; cf. John 1:21; 6:14; 7:40, 52; Acts 13:25). Many also expected that the Messiah would be a descendant of King David—a royal Messiah—and would even come from Bethlehem, where David lived (Mark 12:35; 15:32; Matt 1:1; 22:42; Luke 20:41; cf. 1 Sam 16:1–13; 2 Sam 7:12–16; Pss 89:3–4; 132:11–12; Micah 5:2; Matt 2:1–6). Against this background, Jesus' response to the crowd in John 7 makes good sense:

> [40] Some in the crowd said, "This is really the Prophet." [41] Others said, "This is the Messiah." But some asked, "Surely the Messiah does not come from Galilee, does he? [42] Has not Scripture said that the Messiah is descended from David and comes from Bethlehem, the village where David lived?" (vv. 40–42)

Such expectations are found in several sectarian scrolls. For example, the *Rule of the Community* (first century B.C.E.) reads: "They will govern themselves by the original precepts in which the men of the *Yahad* began to be instructed, [11] until there will come *the Prophet* and *the Messiahs of Aaron and Israel*" (1QS 9:10–11). As the "Prophet like Moses" (Deut 18:15), the first figure is an *anointed Prophet* of the last days, perhaps Elijah or a prophetic Messiah.

The plural "Messiahs" means that the *Rule* expected two more Messiahs: one of Israel and the other of Aaron. The Messiah of Israel is the royal Messiah, who has several more names in the sectarian scrolls. Three are in the *Florilegium* (4Q174): the Shoot of David, the Branch of David, and the Booth of David (col. 3:11–13). A *Commentary on Genesis* (4Q252) interprets a prophecy about Judah (Gen 49:10) as fulfilled in "the Righteous Messiah, the Branch of David" (col. 5:1–3).

Prophetic Messiah: In Luke 7:20–23 (= Matt 11:2–5), the disciples of John the Baptist—who are becoming discouraged—come to Jesus with an important question:

> [20] "Are you the one who is to come, or are we to wait for another?" [21] Jesus had just then healed many people of diseases, plagues, and evil spirits, and had given sight to many who were blind. [22] And he answered them, "Go and tell John what you have seen and heard: the ***blind receive their sight***, the lame walk, the lepers are cleansed, the deaf hear, the ***dead are raised***, the ***poor have good news brought*** to them. [23]And blessed is anyone who takes no offense at me."

Some scholars regard this passage as a later invention by the Gospel writers seeking to portray Jesus as the Messiah. A late origin is allegedly supported by the mention of making the dead live among the list of wondrous works, since raising or reviving the dead is almost nonexistent in the Hebrew Bible. However, key phrases in the Gospel passage are also found in the *Messianic Apocalypse* (4Q521). Copied in the first century B.C.E., this text includes a list of wondrous activities that would take place with the coming of a prophetic Messiah (emphases mine):

> [1] [. . . For the hea]vens and the earth will listen to ***his Messiah***

> [2] [and all t]hat is in them shall not stray from the commandments of the holy ones.

> [3] Strengthen yourselves, you seekers of the Lord, in his service!

> [4] Will you not discover the Lord in this, all you who hope in their heart?

> [5] For the Lord will bestow care on the pious, and he will call the righteous by name;

> [6] and over the poor his spirit will hover, and he will renew the faithful with his strength.

> [7] For he will honor the pious upon the throne of an eternal kingdom,

> [8] ***setting captives free***, ***opening the eyes of the blind***, ***lifting up*** those who are op[ressed].

> [11] And the Lord will perform glorious things which have not existed, just as he s[aid].

[12] For he will **heal the afflicted,** he will **make the dead live,** he will **bring good news to the poor;**

[13] and he will [. . . the . . .]. He will lead with care the uprooted ones, and he will make the hungry rich. (4Q521 frgs. 7+5 ii.1–8, 11–13) (Flint, *Jesus and the Dead Sea Scrolls,* 118–19)

In Luke 4:16–21 Jesus' proclamation at Nazareth portrays him as a prophetic Messiah (although *Messiah* is not used). The passage he is apparently reading agrees only in part with Isaiah 61:1–2, since one element harkens back to Isaiah 35:6 and another to 58:6. Verse 18 reads: "The Spirit of the Lord is upon me, because he has anointed me to *bring good news to the poor.* He has sent me to proclaim *freedom to the captives* and *recovery of sight to the blind,* to set *free the oppressed.*" Here, too, the correspondences in the *Messianic Apocalypse* are striking.

To sum up: The many correspondences between the *Messianic Apocalypse* (4Q521) and the two passages from Luke (and for the second, Matt 11:2–5) have several implications:

- In light of 4Q521, the Gospel passages present a recipe of wondrous activities that will take place with the coming of the Messiah.

- The Messiah described in the Gospel passages and 4Q521 is a prophetic Messiah.

- 4Q521 confirms that a prophetic Messiah was known to at least some Jews in the first century B.C.E.

- The idea of a prophetic Messiah was part of the early *kerygma* (proclamation) concerning Jesus.

- Raising the dead/making the dead live was among the activities associated with the Messiah for least some Jews before the Common Era, not a later idea invented by the Gospel writers.

- The many correspondences between 4Q521 and the Gospel passages support the view that the historical Jesus saw himself as the Messiah and that he claimed to be so.

3. The Scrolls and the Early Church: Acts, Paul, and the Other Letters

3.1 Introductory Comment

I will identify (with a list of relevant texts) 14 issues concerning the early church in the book of Acts and the Letters, and then discuss one more in detail.

3.2 Fourteen Issues (with Key Texts) for Studying Acts, Paul, and the Other Letters

(a) Texts Related to Communal Life and Conduct

• **The Many or the Majority (Used for the Disciples or Community).** New Testament: Mark 14:24; 2 Corinthians 2:5–6 (and possibly Acts 6:2, 5; 15:12, 30). Scrolls: *Rule of the Community* (1QS) 8:26; *Damascus Document* (4Q269) frg. 16.6.

• **The Guardian or Bishop.** New Testament: Philippians 1:1; 1 Timothy 3:1, 2, 7; Titus 1:7 (see also 1 Pet 2:25). Scrolls: CD 13:7, 13, 16–17; 14:13; 1QS 6:12, 20 (also in 4Q266–71); *Miscellaneous Rules* (4Q265) frg. 4ii line 3; *Communal Ceremony* (4Q275) frg. 3.3; *Berakhot* or *Blessings* (4Q289) frg. 1.4.

• **Sharing of Wealth and Property.** New Testament: Acts 2:44–46; 4:32–37; 5:1–11. Scrolls: *Damascus Document* (CD) 6:20–22; 9:10; 1QS 6:17–23; 7:6–8.

• **Works of the Law, Righteousness, Justification, and Faith.** New Testament: Romans 3:20, 28; Galatians 2:16; 3:2, 5, 10. Scrolls: *Some of the Works of the Law* (4QMMT) C 26–27, *Commentary on Habakkuk* (1QpHab) 8:1–3 (on Hab 2:3).

• **Works of the Flesh and the Spirit of Falsehood.** New Testament: Galatians 5:19–21. Scrolls: 1QS 4:9–11 (see also 3:17–19).

• **Fruit of the Spirit and the Spirit of Truth.** New Testament: Galatians 5:22–23. Scrolls: 1QS 4:3–6 (see also 3:17–19).

• **Cultic and Sexual Purity and Self-Definition.** New Testament: Acts 15:20; 21:25. Scrolls: 4QMMT, 1QS 6:16–21; *Purification Liturgy* (4Q284); *Rituals of Purification A* (4Q414) and *B* (4Q512).

(b) Texts Related to Scripture, the Covenant, and Biblical Characters

• **Interpretation of Scripture.** New Testament: Acts 2:14–21 and Joel 2:28–32 (Heb 3:1–5); Acts 2:25–28 and Psalm 18:8–11; Acts 2:31 and Psalm 16:10; Acts 2:34–35 and Psalm 110:1. Scrolls: *Damascus Document* (CD) B lines 1–82; 1QS 8:12–15 and Isaiah 40:3; *Tanhumim* (4Q176) frgs. 1–2i line 7; *Otot* (4Q259) 3:4–5.

• **Series of Passages from Scripture as Proof Texts.** New Testament: Romans 3:10–18 (Paul using a string of passages from the Scriptures as proof texts). Scrolls: *Florilegium* (4Q174), *Testimonia* (4Q175), *Melchizedek* (11Q13), the *Pesharim*.

- **A New or Renewed Covenant.** New Testament: 1 Corinthians 11:25; 2 Corinthians 3:6; Hebrews 8:8, 13; 9:15; 12:24 (also Jer 31:31; Luke 22:20; and Acts 1; 2:1–13). Scrolls: *Damascus Document* (CD) 6:19; 8:21; 19:33; 20:12; (4Q269) frg. 4ii line 1 (= CD 6:19); *Rule of the Community* (1QS) 1:8, 16, 18, 20, 24; 2:10–13, 16, and more; *Rule of Blessings* (1Q28b) 3:26; 5:5, 21; *Habakkuk Pesher* (1QpHab) 2:3; *Berakhot* or *Blessings* (4Q286–90).

- **Abraham as a *Friend of God* in the Letter of James and Some Qumran Texts.** New Testament: James 2:23 (also 2 Chron 20:7; Isa 41:8). Scrolls: *Damascus Document* (CD) 3:2; *Commentary on Genesis A* (4Q452) 2:8.

(c) Texts Related to the Messiah and the End Times

- **The Meal with the Messiah or Messiahs.** New Testament: Matthew 26:26–29; Mark 14:22–25; Luke 22:17–20. Scrolls: *Rule of the Congregation* 2:11–22.

- **Enoch's Prophecy of the Coming of the Lord with His Holy Ones to Bring Final Judgment.** New Testament: Jude 14–15 (cf. Genesis 5:18–24). Scrolls (or, Books important to the Essene movement): *1 Enoch* 1:9.

- **Rebellious Angels Kept in Chains of Deepest Darkness for the Day of Judgment.** New Testament: 2 Peter 2:4; Jude 6–7 (cf. Matt 25:41; Rev 20:10). Scrolls: *1 Enoch* 10:4–6, 11–13; 18:16; 69:28; 90:24; cf. 39:2 (also *Jubilees* 5:6; 10:5–9).

3.3 In Detail: Jesus as Priestly Messiah and High Priest, Melchizedek as a Heavenly Being

Several sectarian scrolls show that the Essene (*Yahad*) movement expected the Messiah of David and the Messiah of Aaron (or Priest). This confirms that in Jesus' day many Jews expected a priestly Messiah and a royal one—which presented a dilemma for writers of the New Testament. In the sectarian scrolls, these are two distinct Messiahs, whereas Christian tradition has room for only one. Yet how could Jesus be both the priestly Messiah and the royal Messiah, since priests were descended from Aaron and he was from David's line? This issue is dealt with in the book of Hebrews.

The author explains how Jesus (from the tribe of Judah) was also a priest (priests being from the tribe of Levi) by showing that his priestly status did not come through heredity, but by divine appointment. The writer appeals to the rather mysterious figure of Melchizedek, king of Salem and a priest of the Most High God, who met Abram after he defeated the kings and rescued Lot and received offerings from Abram (Gen 14:17–20). The only other mention of Melchizedek in the Hebrew Bible is in Psalm 110:4, where God says, "You are a priest forever, according to the order of Melchizedek." Hebrews understands this as addressed to Jesus (5:5–6), and so his appointment as High Priest in the Melchizedekian order was by God himself. Hebrews is the only New Testament book that calls Jesus a High Priest (2:17; 3:1; 4:14, 15; 5:5; 7:26; 8:1, 3; 9:11), and one forever, according to the order of Melchizedek (5:10; 6:20; 7:11, 17). This carefully reasoned case provides the rationale for Jesus to be a priestly Messiah.

Melchizedek is mentioned in several texts found at Qumran. For example, the *Melchizedek Text* (11Q13) is one of the three thematic *Pesharim*. As the eschatological liberator of the righteous, Melchizedek is presented as a divine being or angel (2:9–11), probably the archangel Michael (cf. the *War Scroll* 17:6-8), the Prince of Light (cf. the *Rule of the Community* 3:20), and the Angel of Truth (*Rule of the Community* 3:24). This Melchizedek will deliver the righteous from Belial and all the spirits predestined to him:

> [11] Concerning what Scripture s[ays, "*How long will y]ou judge unjustly, and sh[ow] partiality to the wick[e]d? [S]el[ah*" (Ps 82:2)]:

> [12] The interpretation applies to Belial and the spirits predestined to him, becau[se all of them have rebe]lled, turn[ing] from God's precepts [and so becoming utterly wicked]. [13] Therefore Melchizedek will thoroughly prosecute the vengeance required by Go[d's] statutes. [In that day he will de]liv[er them from the power] of Belial, and from the power of all the sp[irits predestined to him]. [14] Allied with him will be all the ["righteous] divine beings" (Isaiah 61:3). (11Q13 2:11–14) (*The Dead Sea Scrolls: A New Translation*, 592)

The *Songs of the Sabbath Sacrifice* may also have understood Melchizedek as the heavenly high priest. The Songs describe an angelic priesthood, among them Melchizedek, with one angel presiding over other ranks of angels. Although the placement of his name is uncertain (in frgs. 21.3 and 22.3 of the 4Q401 copy), Melchizedek may well have been the seventh and highest of the heavenly chief princes—the presiding priestly angel, or heavenly high priest. Here we find an important correspondence with the Letter to the Hebrews.

The presentations of Melchizedek in Hebrews and in the *Melchizedek Text* are different, but have several points in common. First, both give an eschatological identity to Melchizedek. Second, both Jesus and Melchizedek are involved in the salvation of their people. Finally, both texts feature the Day of Atonement. In Hebrews, Jesus enters behind the heavenly curtain on the Day of Atonement; by sacrificing himself, he effects atonement for his people once and for all, without having to repeat the act year after year. In the *Melchizedek Text*, the Day of Atonement will follow after the tenth jubilee period, when Melchizedek will atone for all the Sons of Light and the people who are predestined to him (col. 2:7–8).

Melchizedek is also mentioned in the *Genesis Apocryphon* (1Q20), which recounts the Genesis narrative and clarifies some points regarding Salem and the tithe (22:14–17). 4QVisions of Amram (4Q544) refers to two angels—one good and one evil—who have been empowered to rule over human beings. The evil angel is known as Belial, the Prince of Darkness, and Melchiresha. The good angel is also known by three names, which are not preserved, but Melchizedek (in frgs. 2.15 and 3.3) must have been one of them (in opposition to Melchiresha).

4. The Dead Sea Scrolls and the Book of Revelation

4.1 The Last Days, Apocalypses, and Apocalyptic Texts Found at Qumran

With visions, numbers, symbols, eschatological war, new heaven and new earth, the book of Revelation forms a fitting finale to the New Testament and the Christian Bible. It was written in the late first century, when Christians were being persecuted by the Roman authorities.

The opening sentence says this is the "Revelation [Greek, *apokalypsis*] of Jesus Christ" (1:1). *Apocalypses* are writings in which a heavenly being reveals to a human recipient a survey of history, the end of the world, and coming salvation. Writings that deal with the end times, but without these apocalyptic features, are better described as "eschatological."

The Essenes (*Yahad*) were an eschatological movement, living in the end of days or the last days, the period just before the cataclysmic end to history. These days would have a negative side (a time of testing when the forces of Belial redoubled their efforts to defeat the righteous), and a positive side (the Sons of Light would be victorious).

No full apocalypses seem to have originated among the movement itself. Fragments of several apocalypses were found at Qumran: Daniel 7–12, *1 Enoch*, *Jubilees*, the Aramaic Levi Document, and the *New Jerusalem Text*. Several other works have been labeled apocalypses: the *Four Kingdoms* (4Q552–53), the *Aramaic Apocalypse* (4Q246), *Pseudo-Jeremiah* and *Pseudo-Ezekiel* (4Q483–90), the *Vision of Amram* (4Q543–48), and the *Messianic Apocalypse* (4Q521). However, most are too fragmentary to decide how many apocalyptic features they once included. Nevertheless, such features abound in many of the sectarian scrolls, including the *War Rule*, which shows that apocalyptic themes were very much in tune with the *Yahad*'s eschatological outlook.

Three compositions introduced earlier are especially important in relation to the book of Revelation: the *War Rule* (*War Scroll*), the *New Jerusalem Text*, and the *Temple Scroll*.

4.2 The Eschatological War and the Final Battle (the War Scroll)

There are many descriptions of a final, holy war among the events that will bring the present age to a decisive end, both in the Hebrew Bible (Ezek 38:7–16; 39:2; Joel 3:2; Zech 12:1–9; 14:2) and in later Jewish writings (*1 Enoch* 56:5–7; 90:13–19; 99:4; *Jubilees* 23:23; *4 Ezra* 13:33–34; the *Sibyllene Oracles* 3.663–68).

The most detailed description is in the *War Rule*. Although it contains apocalyptic features (such as the final battles between the Sons of Light and the Sons of Darkness), this is not an apocalypse, but a rule book that resembles Greco-Roman tactical manuals on how a war should be conducted.

The theme of final war and combat is also evident in the book of Revelation. Several short narratives describe the gathering of end-times armies with a view to destroying God's people, and outline the decisive battle that eventually takes place (16:12–16; 17:14; 19:11–21; 20:8–9). The location of this battle will be Armageddon:

[11] Then I heard a loud voice from the temple telling the seven angels, "Go and pour out on the earth the seven bowls of the wrath of God." . . . [15] "See, I am coming like a thief! Blessed is the one who stays awake and is clothed, not going about naked and exposed to shame." [16] And they assembled them at the place that in Hebrew is called *Armageddon*. (Rev 16:11, 15–16)

In contrast to Revelation, in the *War Rule* the enemies do not assemble and march in one vast body to the place of battle, but are confronted in various encounters by Israel's armies. Another important difference is that in Revelation humans and angels never join forces in any eschatological battle, whereas in the *War Rule* the holy angels fight together with the Sons of Light (1QM 1:10; 7:6; 19:1):

[9] . . . On the day when the Kittim fall there will be a battle and horrible carnage before the God of [10]Israel, for it is a day appointed by him from ancient times as a battle of annihilation for the Sons of Darkness. On that day the congregation of the gods and the congregation of men will engage one another, resulting in great carnage. [11]The Sons of Light and the forces of Darkness will fight together to show the strength of God with the roar of a great multitude and the shout of gods and men; a day of disaster. (1QM 1:9–11) (*The Dead Sea Scrolls: A New Translation*, 148)

A pertinent passage is Revelation 14:1–5, featuring the Lamb on Mount Zion with the 144,000, apparently as part of a battle narrative that focuses on Jerusalem. The members of this group are celibate males (v. 4), since sexual abstinence was required of holy warriors (Deut 23:9–14; 1 Sam 21:5; 2 Sam 11:9–13), an interesting comparison with the celibacy practiced by many Essenes.

The book of Revelation may be seen as a Christian war scroll, modeled on the *War Rule* but with extensive revision of Jewish traditions about a final battle against evil, which has already been defeated by the witness and death of Christ. Several passages use the language of holy war, but transformed to a nonmilitary means of triumphing over evil. For example, in 5:5–6, John depicts the Messiah as a military victor, but reinterpreted in terms of his sacrificial death for the redemption of people from all nations (vv. 9–10).

The eschatological holy war tradition takes two forms: the passive model (the victory won by God alone or with his heavenly armies) and the active model (God's people physically participating in warfare against their enemies). Revelation confirms the tendency of apocalyptic literature to highlight the passive model: the role of God and his angels is featured, and any role of God's people is ignored. In this respect the book of Revelation contrasts with the *War Rule*, which is a striking example of the active model.

4.3 The New Jerusalem

Most readers are familiar with the book of Revelation's description of the New Jerusalem, that glorious and holy city that will come down out of heaven with God:

[9] Then one of the seven angels who had the seven bowls full of the seven last plagues came and said to me, "Come, I will show you the bride, the wife of the Lamb."

[10] And in the spirit he carried me away to a great, high mountain and showed me the holy city Jerusalem coming down out of heaven from God. [11] It has the glory of God and a radiance like a very rare jewel, like jasper, clear as crystal. [12] It has a great, high wall with twelve gates, and at the gates twelve angels, and on the gates are inscribed the names of the twelve tribes of the Israelites; . . . [14] And the wall of the city has twelve foundations, and on them are the twelve names of the twelve apostles of the Lamb. (Rev 21:9–12, 14 NRSV)

Many parallels are found in the *New Jerusalem Text*. In the form of a guided tour of heaven, this is a true apocalypse (with revelation to a human individual through a heavenly figure, details of the heavenly world, and the end of history in a final battle). It was composed in the second century B.C.E., not by the Essene (*Yahad*) movement, but was extensively used by them (seven fragmentary copies survive).

Together with the *Temple Scroll*, this text is part of a tradition linking the eschatological Temple and city in Ezekiel 40–48 with the New Jerusalem in Revelation 21–22. The description is midway between Ezekiel's future Jerusalem and the heavenly one of Revelation.

Table 1. Outline of the New Jerusalem Text
1. The 12 gates of the city (cols. 1:1–2:10)
2. The city divided into square blocks, each surrounded by a street (col. 2:11–22)
3. Structure of the outer walls, gates, towers, and stairs to the towers (col. 3:1–22)
4. The city-blocks, houses within each block, and the city towers (4Q555; 5Q15; 4Q554)
5. The priests in the Temple, offerings, bread, incense (11Q18 frgs. 21 and 28; 2Q24 frg. 4)
6. The kingdoms to come, the final battle, and the triumph of Israel over the Gentile nations (4Q554 col. 3)

When we compare the New Jerusalem in the book of Revelation and in the *New Jerusalem Text* (as well as in Ezek 40–48 and the *Temple Scroll*), several points emerge:

(1) Revelation, the *New Jerusalem Text*, and the *Temple Scroll* draw on Ezekiel 40–48, and have several features in common: architectural features of the Temple, the return of God's glory, allotment of land, festivals, offerings, and life-giving water flowing from the Temple.

(2) A guide leads and informs the visionary: the angel of Revelation, the unnamed figure of the *New Jerusalem Text*, and the mysterious man of Ezekiel 40–48. In Revelation this angel measures the architecture, offers comments, and leads the visionary from place to place. These functions are carried out by the guides in the *New Jerusalem Text* and in Ezekiel 40–48. One phrase found in two books is "then he showed me" (Rev 21:10 and 22:1; for the *New Jerusalem Text*: 2Q24 frg. 1, line 3; 4Q554 1 ii.15; iii.20; 4Q555 1.3; 5Q15 1 i.2, 15; ii.6; and 11Q18 16.6; 18.1).

(3) The dimensions of the eschatological city in Ezekiel 40–48, the *Temple Scroll*, the *New Jerusalem Text*, and Revelation 21 are enormous. (The cubit is about 17.5 inches, but Ezekiel uses the royal cubit of 20.5 inches.) The following statistics are reasonably accurate:

- Ezekiel 40–48: The Temple's outer court is surrounded by a square wall, each side 850 feet (40:5; 42:15–20; 45:2). The city walls form a huge square of 1.45 miles on each side (48:30–35).

- The *Temple Scroll*: The sanctuary complex consists of three squares, the outer court measuring 2,860 feet per side, with a total perimeter of 11,450 feet. This was the size of the city of Jerusalem in the Hasmonean period (about 150–30 B.C.E.).

- The *New Jerusalem Text*: A rectangular city plan of 20 by 14 miles (280 square miles), with the Temple inside.

- Revelation: The dimensions reach fantastic proportions: a city in the shape of a cube, with a length, width, and height of 1,500 miles each.

(4) All three texts emphasize the 12 tribes of Israel, whose names are associated with the 12 gates of the New Jerusalem (Ezek 48:30–35; 4Q554 1 i.9–ii.9; 40:11–14; Rev 21:12; also the *Temple Scroll* [11Q19] 9:12–13). This theme anticipates the restoration of all Israel, which is stressed in some later books of the Hebrew Bible and in other early Jewish literature.

(5) The *New Jerusalem Text* and Revelation 21 feature the precious stones and metals used for the city structures. The earliest references to precious stones used in rebuilding Jerusalem are in Isaiah 54:11–12 and Tobit 13:16, and Josephus reports that gold overlay was used on parts of Herod's Temple (*Jewish War* 5.201, 205, 207–8). In the *New Jerusalem Text*, the city has buildings of electrum, sapphire, chalcedony, and gold (4Q554 frg. 2ii line 15), and every street is paved with white stone, marble, and onyx (5Q15 frg. 1i lines 6–7). In Revelation, the description of the New Jerusalem is even more dazzling, with "a radiance like a very rare jewel, like jasper, clear as crystal" (21:11), or of "pure gold, clear as glass" (21:18). The city wall is built of jasper (21:18), and its 12 foundations are constructed of a variety of precious and semiprecious stones (21:19–20).

In Jewish writings, the tradition of precious stones and metals being used for holy buildings arises from the huge and costly stones used for the foundation of Solomon's temple (1 Kgs 5:17; 7:10). This theme is also found in non-Israelite traditions. For example, the Roman author Lucian (second century C.E.) refers to a city of gold surrounded by an emerald wall with seven gates. Each gate is constructed of a single plank of cinnamon, with a river of myrrh running through it (*Verae Historiae* 2.11).

4.4 The Temple, Ritual Purity, and the Temple Scroll

The *Temple Scroll* was most likely not composed by the Essene (*Yahad*) movement, but was influential among them. It is not as significant as the *New Jerusalem Text* and Ezekiel 40–48 for understanding Revelation, whose New Jerusalem has no Temple (21:22).

This is in contrast to several other Jewish writings of that time, where the expectation of a New Jerusalem included a new Temple. Yet Jerusalem clearly functions as a Temple-city in Revelation: [22] "I saw no Temple in the city, for its Temple is the Lord God the Almighty and the Lamb. [23] And the city has no need of sun or moon to shine on it, for the glory of God is its light, and its lamp is the Lamb" (21:22–23).

The Essenes did not recognize the Temple in Jerusalem because they believed the religious authorities running it were lax in ritual purity and using an unlawful calendar of festivals; see the *Damascus Document* (CD) 20:22–23 and *Some of the Works of the Law* (4QMMT). This does not mean they rejected Temple religion; they awaited its end-times renewal. Until this took place, the *Yahad* describe their community as an eschatological temple, with Israel (the laymen) as the holy place and Aaron (the priests) as the holy of holies:

> When such men as these come to be in Israel, [5]then shall the party of the *Yahad* truly be established, an *eternal planting* (*Jubilees* 16:26), a temple for Israel, and— mystery!—a Holy [6]of Holies for Aaron; true witnesses to justice, chosen by God's will to atone for the land and to recompense [7]the wicked their due. They will be *the tested wall, the precious cornerstone* (Isaiah 28:16) whose [8]foundations shall neither be shaken nor swayed, a fortress, a Holy of Holies [9]for Aaron, all of them knowing the Covenant of Justice and thereby offering a sweet savor. (1QS 8:4–9 see also 5:4–7; 9:3–6) (*The Dead Sea Scrolls: A New Translation*, 129)

In Ezekiel 40–48, the destruction of the First Temple (in 587 or 586 B.C.E.) gave rise to the prophet's vision of an eschatological Temple. When the *New Jerusalem Text* and the *Temple Scroll* were written, the Second Temple was standing, but their authors were opposed to the religious leaders who ran it and so (like Ezekiel) envisaged an ideal future Temple. For the Essene movement, the negative view of the existing city and Temple found in the *Temple Scroll* and the *New Jerusalem Text* was very welcome. In Revelation, however, the emphasis is on the city, and the author draws attention to the absence of a Temple (21:22). This contrasts with Ezekiel and the *Temple Scroll*, where the main emphasis is on the Temple complex.

With respect to ritual, nothing unclean will enter this city, "nor anyone who practices abomination or falsehood" (Rev 21:27; a longer list of those excluded is given in 22:15). Although these two lists differ in detail, both begin with a ritual category, followed by a list of moral transgressors. In the *Temple Scroll* the Temple and the Holy City form a Temple-city unit, so the purity requirements that normally apply to the Temple were extended to the entire city. A pronouncement that parallels Revelation 21:27, with its exclusion of anything impure from the eschatological Jerusalem, is found in column 47:

The city [4]that I will sanctify by establishing my name and temp[le] there must be holy and pure [5]from anything that is in any way unclean, by which one might be defiled. Everything inside it must be [6]pure, and everything that enters it must be pure: wine, oil, edibles [7]and any foodstuff upon which liquid is poured—all must be pure. (11Q19, col. 47:3–6) (*The Dead Sea Scrolls: A New Translation*, 616)

In the Hebrew Bible, the prediction that unclean persons or things will not enter the eschatological Jerusalem occurs only in two passages, both from Isaiah:

... for the uncircumcised and the unclean will enter you no more. (Isa 52:1b)

A highway will be there, and it will be called the Holy Way; the unclean will not travel on it, but it will be for God's people. (Isa 35:8)

The passage that was quoted above from Revelation (21:27) most likely alludes to Isaiah 52:1, but no such allusion is evident in the *Temple Scroll* 47:3–6. This suggests that the exclusion of unclean persons or things from the eschatological Jerusalem was a more widely held belief, and not based only on the two passages in Isaiah.

Bibliography

Editions, English Translations, and Computer Software

Abegg, Martin G., Peter W. Flint, and Eugene Ulrich. *The Dead Sea Scrolls Bible: The Oldest Known Bible Translated for the First Time into English* (San Francisco: Harper San Francisco, 1999).

Barthélemy, D., J. T. Milik, E. Tov, and Others (editors). *Official Editions of Almost all the Dead Sea Scrolls* (Discoveries in the Judaean Desert 1–40; Oxford, Clarendon Press, 1955–2011).

Brenton, Sir Lancelot. *The Septuagint Version: Greek and English* (London: Bagster, 1844).

Burrows, Millar, with John C. Trever and William H. Brownlee. *The Dead Sea Scrolls of St. Mark's Monastery*. Vol. 1: The *Isaiah Manuscript and the Habakkuk Commentary* (New Haven, Conn.: The American Schools of Oriental Research, 1950).

———. Volume 2.2: *Plates and Transcription of the Manual Of Discipline* (1951).

Charles, R. H. *The Letter of Aristeas* (Oxford: Clarendon Press, 1913).

Charlesworth, James (General Editor). *The Princeton Theological Seminary Dead Sea Scrolls*. Ten volumes and two Concordances projected (Louisville, Ky.: Westminster-John Knox, 1994–).

Colson F. H (translator). *Philo IX* (Loeb Classical Library 363; Cambridge, Mass.: Harvard University Press, 1941).

Dead Sea Scrolls: A New Translation, The. [see under Wise]

The Dead Sea Scrolls Bible. [see under Abegg]

Dead Sea Scrolls Computer Software. For Texts and Tools, see the "Dead Sea Scrolls" and "Qumran" modules from the following companies: Accordance Bible Software (www.accordancebible.com); Bible Works (www.bibleworks.com); and Logos Bible Software (www.logos.com).

García Martínez, Florentino. *The Dead Sea Scrolls Translated: The Qumran Texts in English.* 2nd Revised edition (Grand Rapids; Eerdmans, 2012).

García Martínez, Florentino, and Eibert J. C. Tigchelaar. *The Dead Sea Scrolls Study Edition* (Leiden: Brill, 1998).

Goodman, Martin. *Classical Sources.* [see under Vermes, Geza, and Martin D. Goodman]

Goshen-Gottstein, M. H. *Isaiah* (Jerusalem: Magnes Press, 1995).

Goshen-Gottstein, M. H., Shemaryahu Talmon, and Galen Marquis. *Ezekiel* (Jerusalem: Magnes Press, 2004).

Josephus VII. [see under Marcus]

Josephus I. The Life. Against Apion. [see under Thackeray]

Knibb, Michael. *The Ethiopic Book of Enoch – A New Edition in the Light of the Aramaic Dead Sea Fragments.* Volume 1: *Text and Apparatus* (Oxford: Oxford University Press, 1978).

Marcus, Ralph (translator). *Josephus VII. Josephus: Jewish Antiquities Books XII–XIV* (Loeb Classical Library 365; Cambridge, Mass.: Harvard University Press, 1933).

Mason, Steve. *Flavius Josephus: Translation and Commentary.* Vol. 1b: *Judean War* (Leiden: Brill, 2008).

New English Translation of the Septuagint. [see under Pietersma]

Pietersma, Albert, and Benjamin G. Wright (eds.). *The New English Translation of the Septuagint* (New York: Oxford University Press, 2007).

Philo IX. [see under Colson]

Qimron, Elisha, and John Strugnell. *Qumran Cave 4: V: Miqsat Ma'ase ha-Torah* (Discoveries in the Judaean Desert 10; Oxford: Clarendon Press, 1994).

Rabin, Chaim, and Emanuel Tov. *Jeremiah* (Jerusalem: Magnes Press, 1997).

Sadaqa, Avraham, and Ratson Sadaqa. *Jewish and Samaritan Versions of the Pentateuch – With Particular Stress on the Differences Between Both Texts* (Jerusalem: Reuven Mas, 1961–1965).

Schiffman, Lawrence H. *Texts and Traditions: A Source Reader for the Study of Second Temple and Rabbinic Judaism* (New York: Ktav, 1997).

Sukenik, Eleazar. *The Dead Sea Scrolls of the Hebrew University* (Jerusalem: Magnes, 1955). [Hebrew Edition, 1954.]

Thackeray H. St. John (translator). *Josephus I. The Life. Against Apion* (Loeb Classical Library 186; Cambridge, Mass.: Harvard University Press, 1926).

Tsedaka, B., and S. Sullivan. *The Israelite Samaritan Version of the Torah: First English Translation Compared with the Masoretic Version* (Grand Rapids: Eerdmans, 2013).

VanderKam, James C. *The Book of Jubilees: A Critical Text.* Aeth. 87, Bilingual Edition (Leuven: Peeters, 1989).

VanderKam, James C. *The Dead Sea Scrolls Today, Revised Edition* (Grand Rapids: Eerdmans, 2010).

VanderKam, James C., and Peter W. Flint. *The Meaning of the Dead Sea Scrolls: Their Significance for Understanding the Bible, Judaism, Jesus, and Christianity* (San Francisco: HarperOne, 2002).

Vermes, Geza. *The Complete Dead Sea Scrolls in English* (Harmonswoth, U.K.; Penguin, 2012).

Vermes, Geza, and Martin D. Goodman. *The Essenes According to the Classical Sources* (Sheffield: Sheffield Academic Press, 1989). [Translations are by Goodman.]

Wise, Michael, Martin Abegg, and Edward Cook. *The Dead Sea Scrolls: A New Translation, Revised Edition* (San Francisco: HarperSanFrancisco, 2005).

Yadin, Yigael, and Others. *Masada I: The Yigael Yadin Excavations: 1963-1965 Final Reports*. Six Volumes (Jerusalem: Israel Exploration Society, 1989 to 1999).

Books and Articles Mentioned in This Volume

Allegro, John. *The Sacred Mushroom and the Cross: A Study of the Nature and Origins of Christianity within the Fertility Cults of the Ancient Near East* (Garden City, N.Y.: Doubleday, 1970).

———. *The Dead Sea Scrolls and the Christian Myth* (Amherst, N.Y.: Prometheus, 1979).

Baigent, Michael, and Richard Leigh. *Holy Blood, Holy Grail* (New York: Delacorte, 1982).

Bar Adon, Pessah. "Another Settlement of the Judean Desert Sect at 'En el-Ghuweir on the Shores of the Dead Sea," *BASOR* 227 (1977): 1–25.

Bar-Nathan, Rachel. "Qumran and the Hasmonaean and Herodian Winter Palaces of Jericho," in *The Site of the Dead Sea Scrolls: Archaeological Interpretations and Debates* (eds. K. Galor, J.-B. Humbert, and J. Zangenberg; Leiden: Brill, 2006), 263–77.

Beall, Todd. *Josephus' Description of the Essenes* (Cambridge: Cambridge University Press, 1988).

Beckwith, Roger. *The Old Testament Canon of the New Testament Church and Its Background in Early Judaism* (Grand Rapids: Eerdmans, 1985).

Ben-Dov, Jonathan. *Head of All Years: Calendars and Astronomy at Qumran in their Ancient Context* (Leiden: Brill, 2008).

Boccaccini, Gabriele. *Beyond the Essene Hypothesis: The Parting of Ways between Qumran and Enochic Judaism* (Grand Rapids: Eerdmans, 1998).

Broshi, Magen. "The Archaeology of Qumran: A Reconsideration," in *The Dead Sea Scrolls: Forty Years of Research* (eds. D. Dimant and U. Rappaport; Leiden: Brill; Jerusalem: Magnes Press, 1992), 113–15.

———. "Qumran: Archaeology," *Encyclopedia of the Dead Sea Scrolls* (eds. L. H. Schiffman and J. C. VanderKam; Oxford: Oxford University Press (2000), 733–39.

Broshi, Magen, and Hanan Eshel. "Residential Caves at Qumran," *Dead Sea Discoveries* 6 (1999): 328–48.

Cansdale, Lena, and Alan Crown. "Qumran: Was It an Essene Settlement?" *Biblical Archaeology Review* 20/5 (1995): 24–35, 73–78.

Charlesworth, James. *Jesus and the Dead Sea Scrolls* (New Haven, Conn.: Yale University Press, 1992).

Collins, John J. *Beyond the Qumran Community: The Sectarian Movement of the Dead Sea Scrolls* (Grand Rapids: Eerdmans, 2010).

Cross, Frank Moore. "Palaeography and the Dead Sea Scrolls," in *The Dead Sea Scrolls After Fifty Years: A Comprehensive Assessment* (eds. P. W. Flint and J. C. VanderKam (2 vols., Leiden: Brill, 1999), 1.379–402 + plates ix–xiv.

De Vaux, Roland. *Archaeology and the Dead Sea Scrolls* (Oxford: Oxford University Press, 1973).

Donceel, Robert, and Pauline Donceel-Voûte. "The Archaeology of Khirbet Qumran," in *Methods of Investigation of the Dead Sea Scrolls and the Khirbet Qumran Site: Present Realities and Future Prospects* (eds. M. Wise, N. Golb, J. Collins, and D. Pardee (New York: New York Academy of Sciences, 1994), 1–38.

Donceel-Voûte, Pauline. "'Coenaculum': La salle à l'étage du locus 30 à Khirbet Qumrân sur la Mer Morte," in *Banquets d'Orient* (eds. R. Gyselen et al.; Leuven: Peeters, 1992), 61–84.

Dupont-Sommer, André. *The Dead Sea Scrolls: A Preliminary Survey* (Oxford: Blackwell, 1950).

Eisenman, Robert. *James the Brother of Jesus: The Key to Unlocking the Secrets of Early Christianity and the Dead Sea Scrolls* (New York: Viking, 1997).

———. *The New Testament Code: The Cup of the Lord, the Damascus Covenant, and the Blood of Christ* (Beacon, N.Y.: Watkins, 2006).

Eshel, Hanan, Magen Broshi, Richard Freund, and Brian Schultz. "New Data on the Cemetery East of Khirbet Qumran," *Dead Sea Discoveries* 9/2 (2002): 135–65.

Evans, Craig A. *Ancient Texts for New Testament Studies: A Guide to the Background Literature* (Grand Rapids: Baker, 2005).

Fields, Weston W. *The Dead Sea Scrolls: A Full History*. Vol. 1: *1947–60* (Leiden: Brill, 2009).

Flint, Peter W. "Jesus and the Dead Sea Scrolls," in *The Historical Jesus in Context* (eds. A.-J. Levine, D. Allison, and J. D. Crossan; Princeton: Princeton University Press, 2006), 110–31.

Flint, Peter W., and James C. VanderKam. *The Dead Sea Scrolls After Fifty Years: A Comprehensive Assessment* (2 vols., Leiden: Brill, 1999).

Golb, Norman. *Who Wrote the Dead Sea Scrolls?: The Search for the Secret of Qumran* (New York: Charles Scribner, 1995).

Hachlili, Rachel. "The Qumran Cemetery: A Reconsideration," in *The Dead Sea Scrolls: Fifty Years After Their Discovery, 1947–1997* (eds. L. Schiffman, E. Tov, and J. C. VanderKam; Jerusalem: Israel Exploration Society, 2000), 661–72.

Hirschfeld, Yizhar. *Qumran in Context: Reassessing the Archaeological Evidence* (Grand Rapids: Baker, 2004).

Humbert, Jean-Baptiste. *The Excavations of Khirbet Qumran and Ain Feshkha*, 1B (Göttingen: Vandenhoeck & Ruprecht, 2003).

Klawans, Jonathan. "Purity in the Dead Sea Scrolls," in *The Oxford Handbook of the Dead Sea Scrolls* (eds. T. H. Lim and J. J. Collins; Oxford: Oxford University Press, 2010), 377–402.

Laperrousaz, Ernerst Marie. *Qoumran: L'Etablissement essénien des bord de la Mer Morte: Histoire et archéologie du site* (Paris: Picard, 1976).

Magen, Yitzhak, and Peleg, Yuval. "Back to Qumran: Ten Years of Excavations and Research, 1993-2004," in *The Site of the Dead Sea Scrolls: Archaeological Interpretations and Debates* (eds. K. Galor, J.-B. Humbert, and J. Zangenberg; Leiden: Brill, 2006), 55–113.

Magness, Jodi. *The Archaeology of Qumran and the Dead Sea Scrolls* (Grand Rapids: Eerdmans, 2002).

Mason, Steve. "Essenes and Lurking Spartans in Josephus' *Judaean War*: From Story to History," in *Making History: Josephus and Historical Method* (ed. Z. Rodgers; Leiden: Brill, 2007), 219–61.

———. "The Historical Problem of the Essenes," in *Celebrating the Dead Sea Scrolls: A Canadian Collection* (eds. J. Duhaime, P. W. Flint, and K. S. Baek; Atlanta: SBL Press; Leiden: Brill, 2011), 201–51.

Metso, Sarianna. *The Textual Development of the Community Rule* (Leiden: Brill, 1997).

Meyers, Eric M. "Khirbet Qumran and its Environs," in *The Oxford Handbook of the Dead Sea Scrolls* (eds. T. H Lim and J. J. Collins; Oxford: Oxford University Press, 2010), 21–45.

Patrich, Joseph. "Khirbet Qumran in the Light of New Archaeological Explorations in the Qumran Caves," in *Methods of Investigation of the Dead Sea Scrolls and the Khirbet Qumran Site: Present Realities and Future Prospects* (eds. M. Wise, N. Golb, J. Collins, and D. Pardee; New York: New York Academy of Sciences, 1994), 73–95.

Röhrer-Ertl, Olav, Ferdinand Rohrhirsch, and Dietbert Hahn. "Über die Gräberfelder von Khirbet Qumran, Insbesondere die Funde der Campagne 1956, *Revue de Qumran* 19 (1999): 3-46.

Schultz, Brian. "The Qumran *Cemetery*: 150 Years of Research," *Dead Sea Discoveries* 13/2 (2006): 194–228.

Sellers, Ovid R. "Date of Cloth from the 'Ain Fashkha Cave," *Biblical Archaeologist* 14 (1951): 29.

Sheridan, Susan Guise. "Scholars, Soldiers, Craftsmen, Elites?: Analysis of French Collection of Human Remains from Qumran," *Dead Sea Discoveries* 9/2 (2002): 199–248.

Stacey, David. "Some Archaeological Observations on the Aqueducts of Qumran." *Dead Sea Discoveries* 14/2 (2007): 222–43.

Steckoll, Solomon. "Preliminary Excavation Report in the Qumran Cemetery," *Revue de Qumran* 6 (1968): 323–44.

Talmon, Shemaryahu. *Text and Canon of the Hebrew Bible: Collected Studies* (Winona Lake, Ind: Eisenbrauns, 2010).

Thiering, Barbara. *Jesus and the Riddle of the Dead Sea Scrolls: Unlocking the Secrets of His Life Story* (New York: HarperCollins, 1992).

Tov, Emanuel. *Textual Criticism of the Hebrew Bible*. Third Expanded Edition (Minneapolis: Fortress Press, 2012).

Trever, John. *The Untold Story of Qumran* (Westwood, N.J.: Revell, 1965).

———. *The Dead Sea Scrolls: A Personal Account*. Revised Edition (Grand Rapids: Eerdmans, 1977).

———. *The Dead Sea Scrolls in Perspective* (North Richland Hills, Tex.: Bibal Press, 2004).

Ulrich, Eugene. *The Dead Sea Scrolls and the Origins of the Bible* (Grand Rapids: Eerdmans, 1977).

Wilson, Edmund. *The Dead Sea Scrolls: 1947–1969* (New York: Oxford University Press, 1969).

Yadin, Yigael. *The Message of the Scrolls* (New York: Crossroad, 1991).

Zias, Joe. "'The Cemeteries of Qumran and Celibacy' Confusion Laid to Rest?" *Dead Sea Discoveries* 7/2 (2000): 220–53.

Zissu, Boaz. "Qumran Type Graves in Jerusalem: Archaeological Evidence of an Essene Community?" *Dead Sea Discoveries* 5/2 (1998): 158–71.

Index of Modern Authors

Five additional indexes can be found online at http://www.abingdonacademic.com/dsscrolls. (1) Biblical Passages. (2) Apocrypha and *Pseudepigrapha*. (3) Dead Sea Scrolls and Related Texts. (4) Other Ancient Writings. (5) Subject Index.

Comment on the Website and Online Material

This book (*The Dead Sea Scrolls*) is a complete and stand-alone volume. Guided by the Table of Contents (p. v), readers can study, and hopefully enjoy, the rich tapestry of the scrolls, their contents, and their history.

Additional material is provided in the Online Supplement to enhance the book and provide helpful material. The supplement will be of interest to any reader who can access the worldwide web, and includes the following features:

Detailed Lists. A detailed outline of the book's contents and the complete indexes take up over 50 pages, and thus could not be provided in the printed volume. They appear in full in the supplement; readers may wish to print them out for use with the book, or consult them online when reading it.

Discussion Questions. For many readers, and for teachers using this book with students, the Discussion Questions for each chapter will prove helpful.

Study Tools and Electronic Resources. Many of these are listed in the Bibliography, under "Editions, English Translations, and Computer Software." The Online Supplement provides fuller details on the main resources, lists some additional ones, and contains active links to the most recent printed and electronic versions or to their publishers.

Photographs of the Dead Sea Scrolls. In the printed book, the section "Photographs and Illustrations" features several pictures of the Dead Sea Scrolls, archaeological remains, and other items. Because of publishing limitations, all are in black and white, although several were actually taken in color. Most readers are interested in knowing more about photographs and other images of the scrolls and the archaeological remains, both published and online. In 2011, the Israel Museum made available online five Cave 1 scrolls in high-resolution format, and in late 2012 the Israel Antiquities Authority launched the Leon Levy Dead Sea Scrolls Digital Library, with about 5,000 online images. The Online

Supplement will provide fuller details of these and other projects, of course with the latest (live) links.

Current Dead Sea Scrolls Links and Websites. The problem with providing links and websites in a printed book is that over time most change or become obsolete; as a result, most printed books list very few links and websites. By presenting these online, the author will keep them constantly up to date, and will add further links as they become available.

Contents of the Online Supplement

Website:

    www.abingdonacademic.com/dsscrolls

In Depth and Further Study:

    Detailed Outline of Contents

    Discussion Questions for each Chapter

Images, Study Tools, Online Links:

    Photographs of the Dead Sea Scrolls

    Study Tools and Electronic Resources

    Links and Websites

Complete Indexes:

    Index of Biblical Passages

    Index of Apocrypha and *Pseudepigrapha*

    Index of Dead Sea Scrolls and Related Texts

    Index of Other Ancient Writings

    Index of Modern Authors (as in Printed Book)

    Subject Index

About the Author

Peter W. Flint is the Canada Research Chair in Dead Sea Scrolls Studies and Director of the Dead Sea Scrolls Institute at Trinity Western University in British Columbia. He has edited or co-edited almost thirty Dead Sea Scrolls for publication, including the Cave 1 Isaiah Scrolls and the Cave 4 Psalms Scrolls, and co-authored *The Dead Sea Scrolls Bible*. He is also author of numerous books and articles and co-editor of a major two-volume study collection (*The Dead Sea Scrolls After Fifty Years*). Dr. Flint regularly lectures on the Dead Sea Scrolls and related topics at academic conferences, and in more popular settings.

CPSIA information can be obtained at www.ICGtesting.com
Printed in the USA
BVOW05s0003130116

432700BV00002B/47/P